T0182856

Masterclass Enterprise Architecture Management

Jürgen Jung • Bardo Fraunholz

Masterclass
Enterprise
Architecture
Management

 Springer

Jürgen Jung
Frankfurt University of Applied Sciences
Frankfurt am Main, Germany

Bardo Fraunholz
Deakin University
Burwood, VIC, Australia

ISBN 978-3-030-78494-2   ISBN 978-3-030-78495-9   (eBook)
https://doi.org/10.1007/978-3-030-78495-9

© The Editor(s) (if applicable) and The Author(s), under exclusive license to Springer Nature Switzerland
AG 2021
This work is subject to copyright. All rights are solely and exclusively licensed by the Publisher, whether
the whole or part of the material is concerned, specifically the rights of translation, reprinting, reuse
of illustrations, recitation, broadcasting, reproduction on microfilms or in any other physical way, and
transmission or information storage and retrieval, electronic adaptation, computer software, or by similar
or dissimilar methodology now known or hereafter developed.
The use of general descriptive names, registered names, trademarks, service marks, etc. in this publication
does not imply, even in the absence of a specific statement, that such names are exempt from the relevant
protective laws and regulations and therefore free for general use.
The publisher, the authors, and the editors are safe to assume that the advice and information in this book
are believed to be true and accurate at the date of publication. Neither the publisher nor the authors or
the editors give a warranty, expressed or implied, with respect to the material contained herein or for any
errors or omissions that may have been made. The publisher remains neutral with regard to jurisdictional
claims in published maps and institutional affiliations.

This Springer imprint is published by the registered company Springer Nature Switzerland AG.
The registered company address is: Gewerbestrasse 11, 6330 Cham, Switzerland

Preface

Enterprise Architecture (EA) originated as a discipline to provide a view of an organisation in order to improve business-IT alignment. Enterprise Architecture evolved beyond business-IT alignment to a more holistic perspective to support organisations in meeting their current and future objectives. Enterprise Architecture is widely understood as visualising inherent structures of an organisation. Enterprise Architecture Management is a management approach that deals with planning and driving the corporate (digital) transformation.

Our personal Enterprise Architecture journey began in the year 2000 when we started to conduct university research in the field of Enterprise Modeling. While Bardo pursued an academic career as a professor at Deakin University (Melbourne, AU), Jürgen was following a career in industry as Enterprise Architect with Deutsche Post DHL in Germany. We maintained contact and continued our joint academic interest in Information Systems. Jürgen returned to academia in 2017 as Professor for Enterprise Architecture Management at the Frankfurt University of Applied Sciences. This academic reunion led to the joint introduction of Enterprise Architecture in both universities as part of the postgraduate Information Systems curriculum.

The textbook at hand originated from lecture notes from both courses. Based on these experiences, lecture recordings and transcripts as well as a script for Enterprise Architecture management, Bardo and Jürgen identified the need for a hands-on introduction to the topic. It is our teaching philosophy that Enterprise Architecture Management is best learned by sharing experiences and guiding students through the applications of methods and tools to typical business problems. The book is intended as a guide to conduct a Masterclass for Enterprise Architecture Management.

The structure of the book represents the typical stages of the journey of an Enterprise Architect. First, we address the central question for an Enterprise Architecture initiative in Chap. 1: *What do we want to achieve with the introduction of Enterprise Architecture?* Enterprise Architecture Management is about providing value to an organisation instead of simply applying a method or tool.

Chapter 2 introduces concepts and visualisations for Business Architecture that help with understanding the business. Proven concepts like *business capabilities* and *business objects* are used as simple but powerful tools. These concepts cover a functional perspective on the business (business capabilities) together with a view on static entities (business objects). These are complemented by concepts to describe business motivation and business models.

A business capability map is used as a starting point for deriving an *application landscape* (as presented in Chap. 3). Software applications are the counterpart to business capabilities as they implement desired functionality. In the same way, business objects reflect a high-level picture on data objects maintained by business software. Applications and data objects describe corporate information systems.

Business and Application Architecture are rather descriptive, providing transparency on information systems and their business context. They also provide the information required to analyse and improve the application landscape. Enterprise architects are using several visual tools to identify optimisation potential as depicted in Chap. 4. We introduce the *business support matrix* that is used to identify typical concerns in the application landscape.

A company is subject to frequent changes driven by changing business requirements and objectives. Such changes must be managed properly and require a corresponding organisational unit. Traditional organisational forms follow a top-down approach—i.e. Enterprise Architecture Management is driven by top management. Recent experiences show that a more *collaborative Enterprise Architecture Management* approach is required. This discussion is presented in Chap. 5.

We do not want to publish a textbook on *Enterprise Architecture frameworks*. However, frameworks are still relevant for any enterprise architect. Established frameworks are introduced in Chap. 6. Common frameworks provide best practice methods and tools for documenting and improving an EA. The textbook concludes with a summary and an outlook on future research potential in Chap. 7.

We hope that you enjoy the Enterprise Architecture journey with us!

Frankfurt, Germany   Jürgen Jung
Burwood, VIC, Australia   Bardo Fraunholz
April 2021

Acknowledgements

The authors acknowledge The Open Group for permission to include text/figures derived from its copyrighted source
    https://pubs.opengroup.org/architecture/togaf92-doc/arch/.
TOGAF®is a registered trademark of The Open Group in the United States and other countries.

The authors acknowledge John A. Zachman and Zachman International®, Inc. for permission to include text/figures derived from their copyrighted source. *The Zachman Framework for Enterprise Architecture*™ is a registered trademark of John A. Zachman and Zachman International®, Inc.—www.zachman.com.

Contents

Acronyms

AA	Application Architecture
AsPac	Asia/Pacific
ADM	Architecture Development Method
APM	Application Portfolio Management
BA	Business Architecture
BO	Business Object
BPMN	Business Process Modelling and Notation
BSM	Business Support Matrix
CEO	Chief Executive Officer
CIMOSA	Computer Integrated Manufacturing Open System Architecture
CIO	Chief Information Officer
CRM	Customer Relationship Management
DBMS	Database Management System
DoDAF	Department of Defense Architecture Framework
E2AF	Extended Enterprise Architecture Framework
E2E	End-to-End
EA	Enterprise Architecture
EAM	Enterprise Architecture Management
EAO	Enterprise Architecture Organisation
EM	Event Management
ERP	Enterprise Resource Planning
HQ	Head Quarter
HR	Human Resources
HTML	HyperText Markup Language
IAF	Integrated Architecture Framework
IT	Information Technology
KPI	Key Performance Indicator
O2C	Order-to-Cash
OM	Order Management
OMS	Order Management System
PCF	Process Classification Framework

PDF	Portable Document Format
PEAF	Pragmatic Enterprise Architecture Framework
PERA	Purdue Enterprise Reference Architecture
SMACIT	Social, Mobile, Cloud, Analytics, Internet-of-Things
SMART	Specific, Measurable, Achievable, Relevant, Time-bound
T&T	Track & Trace
TM	Transport Management
TMS	Transport Management System
TOGAF	The Open Group Architecture Framework
UML	Unified Modelling Language

Chapter 1
Introduction

Learning Objectives

After completing this chapter, you will be able to . . .

* . . . explain the difference between Enterprise Architecture and Software Architecture
* . . . know typical concerns addressed by Enterprise Architecture Management
* . . . define Enterprise Architecture and Enterprise Architecture Management
* . . . know basic visualisations for Enterprise Architecture

The learning objectives for this section are pretty straightforward. First of all, you should be capable of describing the difference between enterprise architecture (EA) and the architecture of software systems. For those of you who already attended software engineering classes, you might already have a good understanding of what architecture means for software. We will now learn how the term architecture is interpreted on a broader level—at a corporate level. We will also take a look at typical concerns or problems that can be addressed with enterprise architecture methods and tools. We will do this by reviewing some of the literature, but also looking at recent reviews and surveys conducted with corporate representatives. The module will further contain definitions for the terms *enterprise architecture* and also *enterprise architecture management* forming the foundation for our common understanding. Last but not least, we present a couple of examples on how to visualise enterprise architecture so that it can be discussed with business people.

© The Author(s), under exclusive license to Springer Nature Switzerland AG 2021
J. Jung, B. Fraunholz, *Masterclass Enterprise Architecture Management*,
https://doi.org/10.1007/978-3-030-78495-9_1

1.1 Motivation

The basic idea of Enterprise Architecture Management (EAM) is represented by the diagram in Fig. 1.1. It starts with a company which has a strategy and corporate objectives. These objectives usually refer to the provision of a product on a market as a result of executing business processes. The execution of business processes will require actors, resources and an organisation. In short, the objective of a company is earning money by providing the products. This is how the company works and this is what needs to drive information technology in the corporation. This might sound straightforward or trivial as all departments need to work together in order to achieve corporate objectives. Naturally the basic understanding should be that whatever information technology is there to support, should support the business with earning money and to be successful.

Nevertheless, when looking at large enterprises you can observe that IT departments developed a culture as being a department of their own. They are focusing on information technology as well as on their own aspects and concerns. IT people, consequently, get disconnected from what the business is doing. The reasons for this mismatch are manifold:

- IT departments are measured against implementing information technology instead of achieving business goals.
- IT is often recognised just as an additional department instead of being part of the value chain (*silo thinking*).
- IT people are very good in defining and implementing information systems but still lack an understanding of the value proposition of information technology for the overall company

At this stage we are looking at EAM for bridging the gap between business and IT. We do not only want to look at information technology and or processes but look at all the concepts together so that we can make sure information technology is achieving the right things—supporting all the business processes in a very high quality way.

1.1.1 Enterprise Architecture and Town Planning

Does this sound familiar to you? *Software Engineering* follows a similar approach: Understand business requirements first and develop a system based on these requirements. However, EA has a much broader view by looking at the whole company instead of a single IT system. Figure 1.2 explains EAM by differentiating it against software architecture by using the metaphor of a town planner. Each software system has an architecture that consists of modules. They are interrelating. We have several software systems that are working with each other. But what is the new aspect of EA?

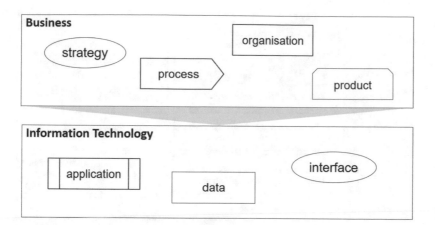

Fig. 1.1 Enterprise architecture management in a nutshell

This metaphor is very common in the literature (e.g. [1–3]). It explains the point of view of the software architect as being the one in charge of building a house or a group of houses. By contrast, Enterprise Architect is more like the town planner. The town planner is responsible for defining the infrastructure of a town, a big city (such as Burwood) or even a metropolitan area (e.g. Melbourne). He or she ensures that we have for example streets, public transport and water supplies. Town planning also includes the definition of rules for building houses—i.e. rules that the architect of an individual house needs to follow. Like in the real world, architects that build houses do not like town planners because they provide rules and restrictions. The town planner is telling them what to do and not to do. It is pretty much the same situation for an enterprise architect in a corporate environment. People developing software systems do not like the Enterprise Architect that much because they are acting in a very similar way.

The scope of the software architect is the one software system that he or she is supposed to implement. Hence, those people are busy with understanding the details of that system, how to implement it properly and managing the software development project. By contrast, the Enterprise Architect focuses on all the processes of a company and the entirety of all software systems that are working together in order to support corporate business processes. The house architect is dealing with details like the installations within a house, the colour of the walls, the placement of power outlets and switches and similar things. These are details that are not relevant for the town planner. The town planner is looking at infrastructure. The town planner is looking at making sure that we have a consistent view of our whole town. The town planner is, therefore, using maps to depict the whole town. This overview of the whole city similar to a helicopter view. He is not looking at the inside of the house but flying over the city having a view of all houses.

The town planner is sometimes supported by further organisational units that represent individual districts. A big city can consist of several districts, each of

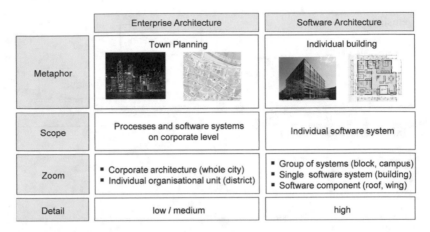

	Enterprise Architecture	Software Architecture
Metaphor	Town Planning	Individual building
Scope	Processes and software systems on corporate level	Individual software system
Zoom	▪ Corporate architecture (whole city) ▪ Individual organisational unit (district)	▪ Group of systems (block, campus) ▪ Single software system (building) ▪ Software component (roof, wing)
Detail	low / medium	high

Fig. 1.2 Enterprise architecture vs. software architecture

them managed individually by a seperate mayor. In the same way, we may have the corporate IT also divided into several parts for distinct functional domains like for example customer relationship management IT, production IT supporting our manufacturing plants and finance IT. Each of them is specialised in managing a given functional domain.

The software architect's work is driven by the rules provided by corporate architecture. Building houses is focused on an individual house or also sometimes a group of houses like the university campus. A whole campus is managed by one architect (sometimes heading a team of architects). This is a further analogy to the system architect who can be accountable for a group of interrelated IT systems.

Not surprisingly, the level of detail for building a house is very high. One needs to consider where to place doors, windows, power outlets. These details are not relevant to the town planner. In the same way, the Enterprise Architect will have a high level view with only few details compared to what the software architect is looking at when defining a software system.

This metaphor of town planner compared to the house architect is quite popular in the EA textbooks. The reason for this is because there are a couple of commonalities between the notion of construction, town planning on the one hand and then building a software system or building a corporate IT landscape on the other hand.

An overview on commonalities is provided in Fig. 1.3. One of the commonalities is that we are talking about **complex systems**. A town—imagine Burwood or even Melbourne as a huge metropolitan area—consists of a lot of houses and a lot of infrastructure elements that need to be planned and aligned. We need to make sure that we have enough housing areas and that the quality of living is as expected across the entire city. This is very similar when looking at corporate IT. We have a lot of software applications and IT systems that need to be connected with each other so that they work with each other. They might require the same infrastructure or being implemented based on the same standards. Furthermore we are not only talking

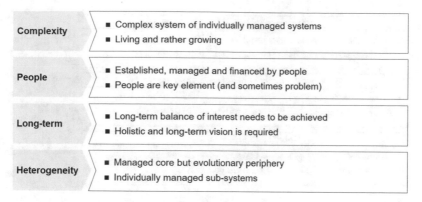

Complexity	■ Complex system of individually managed systems ■ Living and rather growing
People	■ Established, managed and financed by people ■ People are key element (and sometimes problem)
Long-term	■ Long-term balance of interest needs to be achieved ■ Holistic and long-term vision is required
Heterogeneity	■ Managed core but evolutionary periphery ■ Individually managed sub-systems

Fig. 1.3 Commonalities of town planning and EAM

about a static system. It never happens that we are planning once and then it is done forever. We are talking about a living organisation or living systems. Melbourne, for example, is expanding and—looking towards Germany—the metropolitan area of Frankfurt is growing as well. This also includes increasing demand in infrastructure. In the same way, a corporate IT landscape will never be fixed but *evolve* over time. This might be the case if the company decides to enter a new market, to develop a new product, or to add a new customer segment.

Perhaps the biggest factor to influence decisions on EA and town planning is, that we need to deal with **people**. Corporate IT is not only technology but also involves people's work. There are people using software applications and people maintaining the IT or making decisions about IT development. Looking at large organisations, it is interesting to see how people identify their role by the IT systems they own. It is similar to owning a small kingdom that defines my power. Hence, those people have an interest in making the system bigger and perhaps not shutting down a system even if it is no longer required. When planning to change EA, we have to incorporate people's attitudes, people's motivation, and people interests. We also frequently need to manage their expectations. (What will happen? Why it will happen?). Town planners need to incorporate the interest of people living in the town. Similar to the town planner, the enterprise architect is not just sitting in an ivory tower doing his or her own planning. There are many different people and many different groups of people that have various kinds of interests with respect to corporate IT.

Especially when looking at the kind of decisions that need to be taken during EAM it is rarely about short term decisions, like making decisions about an individual system change that needs to be done now. It is rather about making decisions about **long term** strategies. How do we want to establish our IT for the future? What will our IT look like in five, ten or even in fifteen years? Of course this needs to be aligned with the business strategy. We should not develop IT as a means of its own but align the development of the IT landscape together with the planned business developments. In order to do this, IT and business need a holistic

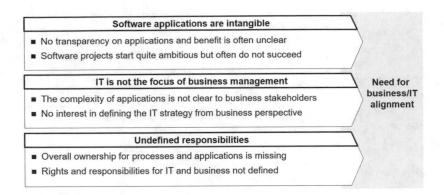

Fig. 1.4 Differences between town planning and EAM

and long term vision with a common understanding. Where do we want to be in the future? What will the company look like in the future? Which markets will we serve? Which products will we offer to the market? Answering these or similar questions will support making conscious decisions about what IT should look like in future.

Last but not least, the town planner and the enterprise architect have to deal with **heterogeneous** parts of the town and also heterogeneous groups of people. A town can consist of housing areas, industrial areas, shopping areas, infrastructure facilities like fire and police departments. We have a similar situation for the enterprise architect. IT landscapes do not only consist of the same kind of software applications but various types of systems for different purposes. This also includes systems supporting the management of IT infrastructure, allowing data flow between applications and workflow management. This situation is quite common in town planning. You can observe this in German towns very easily. There is something like a core town, the downtown, which is quite well managed. There is also the periphery consisting of suburbs around this town. There are smaller towns and villages serving as housing areas for people working in the city. They also have their own infrastructure, their own industry and commercial areas. The city and also the surrounding areas can be seen as subsystems that are managed by individual parties. A town in the Frankfurt metropolitan area has its own mayor, with its own by-laws and regulations. We have the same situation in a corporate environment. An Enterprise Architect might focus on the common core system, allowing certain functions to have their subsystems which they can manage on their own. Obviously, it is not independently managed. It needs to be aligned at the corporate level. But still we can delegate some responsibilities to suburbs or to surrounding subsystems.

Even though we have some commonalities between the town planner and the Enterprise Architect, there are a couple of differences that we need to keep in mind (cf. Fig. 1.4).

For many people, IT consists of computer hardware and infrastructure for networking. But most importantly it provides software applications that are supporting business processes. The issue with software applications is that they are **not**

tangible, hence, invisible to humans. We can see the user interface, but we cannot see the programming logic working in the background. We cannot see on the screen which other applications they are exchanging data with.

This is a common issue in plenty of software projects (software development, maintenance or shutting down applications). When building a house you can point at existing houses or parts of it. People have an elementary understanding about the physics behind it or you can explain relevant facts very easily. We can only build the first floor after finishing the ground floor, for example. Otherwise, the whole structure would collapse. Such kind of dependencies (e.g. one module requires the finalisation of another) and properties of software systems are not that visible. This is a risk for many software development projects, especially as people do not know how to express their requirements properly. The issue is even worse on a corporate level when you are talking about the systems, but cannot see what those systems are doing and how they are linked together because it is hidden behind the screen.

The second concern is a little bit subtle but still observable in many companies. The IT department is usually recognised as just another supporting department and **not considered as a focus area** for business management. Setting it up like this in the corporate organisation might have been reasonable when technology was rather simple in the past. However, we need to reconsider this as IT is getting more powerful and penetrating all functional areas of an organisation. This especially holds true when thinking of companies in which the whole business model is based on IT or innovative IT systems, even having IT services as a product to be sold on the market. IT is not only emerging in our daily life but also corporate processes. We, consequently, can observe a tighter integration between the business and the IT. But, this distinction is still part of stakeholders' perception, even though companies are already about to transform towards being a digital or an e-commerce company. In order to overcome this gap between business and IT, we need to have a discipline that is not only—like the town planner—produces nice maps, but one that changes the mindset of people involved in business decisions.

This last difference is visible in a lot of companies today. There are software systems available and used by business people, but **nobody on the business side feels responsible** for them. Responsibility would include maintenance (i.e. conducting projects to perform changes), support and funding (e.g. for licenses). It, furthermore, refers to making decisions on the future of individual software applications, like its decommissioning if it does no longer provide relevant value. Making decisions based on business relevance implies an assessment from the business perspective. In fact, many systems are just handed over to IT so that they keep them running but there is no business ownership. IT people then need to drive changes driven by business requirements. Ideally, these should be driven by business stakeholders. We still have to convince people in business and IT to understand the relevance of each IT system and then make sure the IT system has business relevance. We further need clear ownership within the business to take the responsibility for decisions on this IT system.

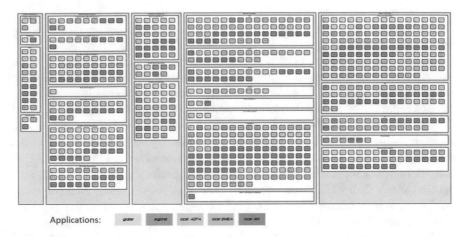

Applications: global   regional   local ASPA   local EMEA   local AM

Fig. 1.5 Real world application landscape

1.1.2   Examples

Example 1.1 (Typical Application Landscape) So far, we are only talking about business IT, the town planner and the software architect. The complexity behind those decisions to be made by an Enterprise Architect might not be that clear. Just to give you an impression of the complexity and the size of a corporate IT, we present the application landscape of a division within an international forwarding company depicted in Fig. 1.5. The application landscape contains all software applications that are used during a certain period of time. The picture is quite dated and, obviously, it is not readable because we do not intend to reveal restricted material. Just bear in mind that each of those small boxes represents one IT system or software application.

As stated, it only depicts the applications that have been recognised at this point of time. Can you guess the number of IT applications shown here? How many do you think there are? Is it 200, 300, or what number, what would you guess? There were around 850 known applications when the first iteration of this map was created. I counted the boxes in Fig. 1.5 and there are around 750 different applications. It does not look like a lot, but it still means a lot when considering the fact that each box can represent for example one of the following:

- Enterprise Resource Planning (ERP) system like SAP
- Transport Management System (TMS) for planning and monitoring all logistics operations

(continued)

Example 1.1 (continued)
• payroll management system
• finance system for generating and distributing invoices

Each of these can represent a very large IT system with a lot of complexity—and we are still not seeing the relationships between these. Those systems are not used in isolation but are working together. There is data in one application that will also be required by another. Furthermore, EA is looking at corporate business processes fulfilling an entire order for a customer. We are not only using one application but the whole workflow is distributed across various software systems. They encompass activities like accepting and validating the order, planning its execution, manufacturing the product, creating the invoice, managing dunning, collecting cash and later on completing corporate finance tasks. Each of them might be supported by a different system. Nevertheless, they need to work together so that we can fulfil a whole order for a customer.

I already emphasised the term *known applications*. The issue in many organisations today is, that IT has grown over time and people lost the overview of all software systems. You cannot simply go to the shop floor and take an inventory of all machines you recognise. You cannot see software and, therefore, rely on an existing inventory of software applications. Such an inventory can be completed by asking people in various organisational units about software systems they they are using. They will usually provide an answer, but there is no way of checking whether the information is accurate. Did they forget a system or is there a system they do not want to mention? This might happen because stakeholders do not want central IT departments to know about a particular software system.

In summary, having a picture with a lot of bubbles is only indicating the complexity with around 750 software applications. Each of them has a reasonable size, there will be connections between applications. This might only be the tip of the iceberg of the real corporate IT we currently have.

Example 1.2 (Shadow IT and Reoccurring Issues) When looking at IT in a company, we can only provide details about the systems we know. But it is a very common phenomenon that there is something called **shadow IT**. This term refers to IT which exists, but is hidden from central (IT) departments at the corporate level. This happens because individual departments decided to develop their own IT ignoring that there is a centralised corporate IT mandatory for everybody. Decision makers in subsidiaries might prefer control over their own IT instead of depending on a centralised offering.

(continued)

Example 1.2 (continued)

They implement their own infrastructure and their own software systems. And these are not communicated within the company for several reasons, like for example:

- Shadow IT is not following corporate (IT) standards.
- Hidden software applications are often redundant as there are already corporate standard applications in place.
- Redundant software systems cause additional cost to the whole organisation.
- Local software systems might violate global compliance rules.
- Unrecognised IT systems impose security risks (especially if they are not following corporate security guidelines).

Let's keep in mind that many companies are getting cost sensitive with respect to their IT. Hence, companies are aiming to switch off systems to save money. And if shadow IT is creating redundancies those systems will be decommissioned in order to reduce expenses for corporate IT.

Furthermore, there are systems in use that nobody feels responsible for. Hence, there is **no clear ownership** with respect to maintenance and support.

There will also be systems that we are aware of but **details** are unknown. Required details include the kind of data being processed in the application. This can even be quite risky for a company, especially against the background of data privacy laws that have been established in Europe recently. Companies need to know about personal data of individuals (related to customers or to human beings) and which systems are dealing with them. They need to have an overview of data and applications so that they can ensure that data of individuals is protected properly. But how can you know this if you do not know all the systems? How can you do this if for you do not know details of many systems (including the kind of data processed)? This is one of the challenges that we can address with EA methods and tools presented in Chap. 3.

There are further challenges. Sometimes, the issue is not missing details of the systems, but a missing understanding of its *purpose*. There, for example, are systems that are used to maintain data about warehouses even though the system was originally developed for a completely different purpose. But now the system is misused to maintain the locations of your warehouses.

There might also be systems with functionality that is **obscure** or not known by people. Some old software systems have been developed for a special purpose but have been found useful for another purpose. Such kind of application can confuse IT people as they are supporting a different purpose than they were intended to be used for. Example: An inventory management system that is no longer used for warehousing but is still required to create shipping labels for outgoing deliveries.

(continued)

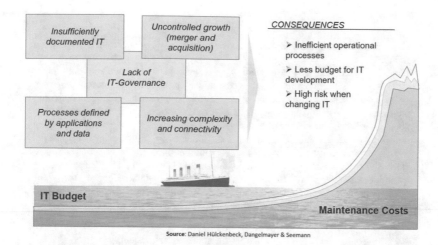

Source: Daniel Hülckenbeck, Dangelmayer & Seemann

Fig. 1.6 Situation with unmanaged IT landscape

Example 1.2 (continued)

And last but not least, maintaining a number of **legacy** applications, which are outdated without an adequate user interface. Such applications often have a monolithic architecture and are, therefore, hampering maintenance (e.g. implementing new requirements or improving the user interface).

Example 1.3 (Merger and Acquisition) Having lost control over corporate IT was a key motivator for companies to introduce EA in recent years. You can imagine a large company, which did not grow organically, but rather by merger and acquisition. Let's take a large logistics company as an example. This company did not exist 20 years ago in its current form. It started with the CEO of a postal company making the decision:

We want to transform this mail and parcel company into a global logistics group. It started with the acquisition of various logistics companies from the postal industry but also businesses from the express, freight forwarding and supply chain industry. The company is now a global player consisting of several divisions, each of them focussing on specific logistics services for different industry sectors. It is not an individual company, but several divisions within a huge corporation consisting of a lot of companies that have been acquired over the past and integrated in a more or less effective way. Also the IT of all the acquired and integrated companies needed to

(continued)

Example 1.3 (continued)

be integrated. With this scenario in mind, we can observe typical issues as mentioned in Fig. 1.6.

First of all, you don't see the software systems, perhaps you can see your data centre (sites hosting server computers) and you can see computers. But you don't see the software applications. Consequently, you rely on having **documentation** including an inventory of all software systems. But in most cases, there is no documentation about your IT system. Other if it is available its quality is rather poor. Documentation is lacking of details and all the different documents look different. You cannot get the whole picture just based on existing documentation.

Because of mergers and acquisitions we do not only have the effect that we have a complex landscape. We also have the effect that we maintain a lot of **redundant systems**. If the integration between various companies is not done properly, we end up in a situation like the logistics company, having ...

- ... around 40 systems just for managing payroll
- ... seven different customer relationship management systems
- ... more than 30 booking systems

This creates additional complexity by distributing the same kind of data over different systems, not having one single representation or one single source of truth for all data.

You can also observe in this logistics company that decisions on the business processes have not been made based on business facts, but rather based on the established software applications. Having an old large legacy system might not be very flexible with respect to changes. Even if you have new ideas for your IT system, it is usually hard to impossible to change legacy applications. People tend to adjust their behaviour (the way how they work in a corporate environment) to the IT system so that the new process also works with the legacy application. In effect, applications become the **real owners** of processes and data in a lot of organisations.

Furthermore, we had individual departments building their own IT applications, having their own standards, making their own decisions. This caused a rather **uncontrolled growth** of IT systems. Such a growth might not only be caused by merger and acquisition, but also driven by the fact that large organisations consist of many people with different interests just making decisions on their own.

Governance is a common discipline defining and monitoring measures in order to comply to given regulations. Inappropriate or missing **IT governance** will consequently lead to the symptoms mentioned above. This was the case in the past of our logistics company. It needed to learn that if you want to have a good IT to support your business, you need to have a good control on your IT to make sure that IT decisions are aligned with the business. The consequences that large organisations face are also present for any kind of company. We have a growing number of systems and even if the IT budget remains the same, the maintenance cost for all the legacy applications plus the new applications will grow over time. And it will grow significantly until we reach the point that the budget cannot cover the costs any more. This is the main driver for our logistics company to introduce EA.

In contrast to the initial motivation of this chapter, the logistics group does not only want to align business and IT. The biggest driver is cost reduction for IT. Of course not just cost reduction by switching off a lot of IT systems. It requires decisions about IT that still enable the business to continue. But at the same time it is aiming at reducing run and development costs in IT.

	Business	IT
Transparency	Overview on enterprise and processes	Overview on IT applications
Decision support	Underpin decision-making (management)	Conscious choices in solution design
Cost reduction	Eliminate redundancies	Reduce solution delivery time
Quality improvement	Business process improvement	Deliver solutions required by business
Risk / compliance	Ensure corporate compliance	Manage security and compliance
Strategy	Translate strategy into executable projects	Ensure effective IT planning

Fig. 1.7 Benefits of EAM (overview based on [4])

1.2   Purpose of Enterprise Architecture

The current section will provide an overview on the purpose of EA. There will be the text book view and also hands-on examples provided by practitioners.

1.2.1   Text Book View

Text books from the EA discipline usually provide an overview on typical purposes of EAM—also as a motivation. Their authors refer to EAM as a tool to provide transparency by showing processes and also IT applications. We can see an overview of typical purposes in Fig. 1.7. Tools provided by EAM can support decisions on the business side—including business process optimisation (left side in Fig. 1.7). They can also support decisions made in solution design, about new software systems or about changes to existing systems (right-hand side in Fig. 1.7). EA and methods promise to support cost reduction by optimising business processes, but also by eliminating redundancy in IT systems, and by supporting faster development of IT systems. If you have a global overview on your business, EA can provide visualisations that help you with improving your business. If you understand your processes and their inefficiencies, then you can improve your processes by performing business process optimisation. If you understood your processes, then you can also deliver software solutions that will perform as expected by business. Textbooks in EA also provide references so we can improve compliance and reduce risk. And last but not least, proper EAM will enable executing the strategy of the corporation.

- "Which IT applications do we own?"
- "Where can I find information about my IT application?"
- "Who is using this application?"
- "How can we save money in IT?"
- "Do we really need this new application?"
- "(When) Will adopting this standard help us with saving money?"
- "What is this application used for?"
- "How well are we supporting business?"
- "Which system directly contributes to our strategy?"
- "What happens if this application fails?"
- "Which systems are dealing with personal data?"
- "Which legal consequences may I face?"

Fig. 1.8 Typical questions for enterprise architects

Do you think that such a kind of list is really helpful in a corporate environment? Just keep in mind you are in a company and people are facing day to day issues with operations and with IT. They are doing a lot of overtime work just by solving current issues. Do you think that you can convince them by promising transparency? Imagine being a consultant and people are stuck with day-to-day routine and you tell them that introducing EA will solve issues by having the big picture. Will this be convincing? Do you think they will immediately tell you that you are hired as a consultant, provide EAM, and then we have transparency and all our problems are solved? Just think about it against the background of your own experience you may have had during internships in companies or by working in companies. Think of your peers, your colleagues or your boss. Which kind of problems do they face and which kind of questions would they expect to have answered by an enterprise architect?

1.2.2 Practictioners' Perspective

In fact, there is a lot of criticism about the way EAM is currently implemented in organisations. Practitioners and also academics are challenging the high level objectives listed in Fig. 1.7. Is this really what we can tell companies to help solve issues? What we did during a couple of months in 2019 was conducting unstructured interviews with decision makers and architects from various companies. We asked them: *What are the real questions you have to answer in your organisation?* We know methods and tools to provide transparency on business and IT. But, which kind of questions are you faced with on a daily basis? Which kind of problems are you asked to solve by your colleagues? Which of them can you solve by applying EA methods and tools?

Results of these interviews have been presented at a conference (cf. [5]) and published as a white paper in [6]. A brief overview of the topics provided by practitioners given in Fig. 1.8. In many companies, it is really a challenge, to tell which applications do we own. In fact from our experience sometimes companies cannot provide a list showing all software applications. Therefore, EAM, beside all the holistic optimisation and so on, should at least be capable of providing an IT inventory including all applications we own. Architects should also be capable of telling people from where to get more information about individual IT applications. This might sound trivial, but keeping a software inventory is still a challenge for large organisations. Let us keep in mind that large companies (also as a result of merger and acquisitions) are growing over time with plenty of systems. Sometimes people do not know about each and every system. Hence, we need to start building a repository. In fact, many EA initiatives started during the past years, started with collecting data about software applications. Also collecting data about users and stakeholders of software applications.

After starting an EA initiative, or when having an overview, one of the most important questions asked by the CIO very often is:

How can we save money? Architecture optimisation is fine. Supporting business is fine. But my objective is to save money with IT. Please tell me how can I save money with IT

Which also leads to questions like:

There is this application and I did not understand what it is used for. Do we really need it?

And again, here is another question for the Enterprise Architect to come up with an answer by telling people what this application is doing, what it is supposed to do.

The answer sometimes leads to surprising questions like having a standard in mind. Decision makers sometimes talk to people in other companies or to external consultants. They go to conferences and they get information about new technologies or new standards. They then come back to the company and say

I heard of all these fancy standards and everybody is telling you adopt this, and then you will have better business. If I adopt this standard, will this help me with saving money and by when? I don't want to wait for ages. I need to provide results within the next period—by the end of next year I need to show savings.

Another trivial question addresses the functionality implemented by an application. We do not only need to know who is using it, but also what it is doing. If we know what the application is doing we also need to understand how well it is supporting business processes. If we provided evidence that applications are required, we also need to document its degree of usefulness. In the situation of saving cost by eliminating redundant applications (i.e. implementing the same functionality), an enterprise architect needs to chose the one supporting the business in the best way. The other ones can be subject to being shut down.

There are also a few topics relating to the strategy and also to issues explained in Example 1.2 on page 9. An enterprise architect needs to know the corporate strategy and make sure that IT is contributing to it. This can only be done if the strategy and the contribution of applications to the strategy are documented in a proper way. Strategy, corporate objectives, Key Performance Indicators (KPI) need to be described and applications need to be linked to them. We will elaborate on this one in Chaps. 2 and 3.

There are also some questions concerning what-if-scenarios (Example: "What happens, if a certain application fails?"). It is a horror scenario in many companies if the central business operations system fails or crashes. Critical business processes cannot be supported any more. Imagine in a parcel logistics company a failure in the central sorting system and parcels cannot be sorted and delivered any more. Customers will not be very happy. The relevance of each application is determined by the business processes that are supported by it. If one has to make a decision which application is more important, an impact analysis is necessary.

According to data protection laws, companies have to protect data of individuals (i.e. protecting personal information). Before doing this, you need to know which systems are dealing with such kind of data. This seems to be a trivial question, especially in a small company with only a few systems. But let us keep in mind that we have a couple of hundred even more than 1000 systems and then answering this question is not that easy. Executives and stakeholders are usually driven by their own interests. People also need to consider legal consequences of violating compliance rules.

The list in Fig. 1.7 is only a fraction of the topics that have been provided by executives and enterprise architects as typical questions. The entire list is provided in [6] which is still a living document. It will be extended over time and we will also provide a survey getting more information about which of those questions are more relevant compared to others.

1.2.3 Relevance of purpose

Why is the notion of the benefit and the problems to be solved so important? Whenever we introduce a new methodology, it needs to provide benefits to the organisation and the same holds true for EA. If we introduce EA, we need people doing it (i.e. an EAM organisation). They would start collecting data and, therefore, involving further resources (e.g. other staff members).

The working mode of an enterprise architect[1] is depicted in Fig. 1.9. Work starts with collecting information about information technology (e.g. infrastructure and software applications) and business-related artefacts (e.g. processes and products). They store it in a dedicated database called a *repository* with EA data. Any kind of information will be collected here and updated over time. Enterprise architects will create visualisations for decision makers based on this repository—called *viewpoints*. You can think of a manager in a company, who might not be interested in doing queries in a database and then seeing a lot of cryptic data. They rather prefer to have (graphical) visualisations that help them addressing their concerns.

---

[1]The diagram has been created based on a similar discussion in [4, pp. 35] and [7, pp. 5].

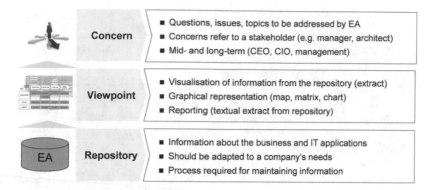

Fig. 1.9 Visualising business and IT in order to address concerns

	Example concerns
Cost	■ Which are the most expensive IT applications? ■ Where are we using redundant applications?
Quality	■ Which business processes are not (adequately) supported by IT applications? ■ In which extent are we using out-dated technology?
Risk / Compliance	■ Which business is affected if application X fails? ■ Which systems share sensitive data with others?
Strategy	■ Which systems are affected if we want to go for e-commerce? ■ Should we buy standard software or develop our own system?

Fig. 1.10 Example concerns in EAM

Stakeholder concerns are the driving factor for all work done by an enterprise architect. We already discussed those concerns in the context of the purpose of EA in the previous Sect. 1.2. Whatever question we had in Fig. 1.7 on page 13 also represents a stakeholder concern. The visualisation of the architecture of the IT and the processes of the organisation can be used to address those concerns. And this visualisation is usually created out of the repository all the data collected by the Enterprise Architect.Throughout the course we will get more details about which kind of data will be collected, which visualisations will have to be generated and how can it help a company or a stakeholder to make the company better.

A general overview on typical concerns from corporate stakeholders is shown in Fig. 1.10. They address effectiveness (quality of results), efficiency (cost reduction) and compliance at an operational level. They are complemented by strategic concerns from an IT perspective. These concerns will be discussed in a more detailed way in Sect. 4.1. The next section will introduce some common visualisations so that you get an impression of how architecture can be documented.

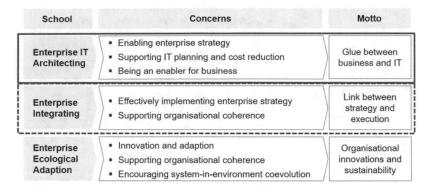

School	Concerns	Motto
Enterprise IT Architecting	• Enabling enterprise strategy • Supporting IT planning and cost reduction • Being an enabler for business	Glue between business and IT
Enterprise Integrating	• Effectively implementing enterprise strategy • Supporting organisational coherence	Link between strategy and execution
Enterprise Ecological Adaption	• Innovation and adaption • Supporting organisational coherence • Encouraging system-in-environment coevolution	Organisational innovations and sustainability

Fig. 1.11 Enterprise architecture—Three schools

1.3   Enterprise Architecture and Visualisation

Previous sections are presenting the motivation for EA from a rather practical point of view. We were discussing aspects like typical problems to be solved with EA and issues to be addressed. This section will now shift our attention to the academic perspective by providing a definition and references to research. There will also be some example diagrams for showing how (enterprise) architecture can be visualised.

1.3.1   Three Schools

James LaPalme and co-authors performed a literature review to check how people interpret the notion of the EA discipline and EAM [8]. They identified three different directions which they call *school of enterprise architecture* as depicted in Fig. 1.11.

The first one, *enterprise IT architecting*, addresses aspects such as supporting IT planning and cost reduction. We already discussed these topics in previous sections. It includes enabling the enterprise strategy and business processes. They describe it by a metaphor that *enterprise IT architecting* provides the glue between the business and IT. This correlates very much with the notion of *business-IT alignment*.

A further interpretation is called *enterprise integrating* by LaPalme et al. It does not only have a focus on how IT can support business, but also, how EA methods can effectively implement the enterprise strategy and IT strategy. Enterprise integration supports setting up the organisation and implementing business processes. It aims to ensure that the whole organisation is achieving common objectives and a consistent implementation of measures on an operational level in order to follow the corporate strategy. This interpretation refers to being the link between strategy and execution. Please note that it is not only about IT operations. It is about any kind of execution, including workflows, business processes, and activities. Hence, this notion is quite broader than enterprise IT architecting.

The third school of EA is some kind of visionary interpretation. It refers to driving innovations within a company by EA methods and tools. Instead of just performing changes or adopting a given strategy, *Enterprise Ecological Adaption* represents the driver for evolving into a new company or business model in the future. This idea is quite appealing as the environment and markets will change over time. Adopting to a new situation and reacting to changing requirements should be one of the core competences of an organisation.

These three schools provide a summary of how the authors perceive EA based on existing publications during that time. It does not provide any methods or tools but just an overview on how the term can be interpreted. In the course of this book, we will remain with the first interpretation, enterprise IT architecting. We will focus on dedicated methods that can help us to describe the relationship between business and IT and also help us with the analysis of the quality of IT support for the business (i.e. business-IT alignment).

The other two schools, enterprise integrating and enterprise ecological adaptation, are not wrong, but they are more high-level, sometimes even visionary. They are looking at the organisation from a very high level and it will be hard to provide concrete methods and tools. Having a holistic scope will make them quite abstract. They also overlap with existing disciplines like business process management, enterprise modelling, and others that promise similar benefits. Nevertheless, we will sometimes also look at benefits provided by EA beyond business-IT alignment. IT does not only have the potential for being an enabler or providing a translation between business and IT. EA can also drive a coherent business (including IT) or even create new business models. When thinking of digital firms or company providing digital services, we will not even see the distinction between business and IT (at least in the organisation. Therefore, we will also partially address aspects from the enterprise integration meaning deriving a proper execution of the corporate strategy.

1.3.2   Definition of Enterprise Architecture

Let's start with the definition of EA that will be relevant for this book (Definition 1.1). As we saw on the paper published by James LaPalme and others, there are different interpretations. When reading various books or papers about EAM, you might see different ones.[2] Definition 1.1 distils the essence of other definitions.

Definition 1.1 (Enterprise Architecture)   Enterprise Architecture (EA) is the representation of an organisation's IT landscape (structure and behaviour) together with its business environment. EA incorporates the current use of IT in the

---

[2] A systematic literature review on definitions for EAM can be found in [9]. Further definitions are given for example in [10, p. 24] and [2, p. 3].

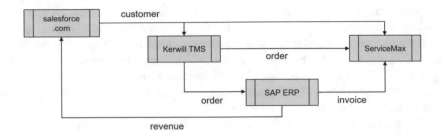

Fig. 1.12 Example: Applications and data flows

organisation (as-is), a vision for future IT support (to-be) as well as a roadmap describing the transition from as-is to to-be.

An EA is the representation of an organisation's IT landscape, together with a business environment. We will not only consider IT, but always incorporate IT in the context of its corporate environment. The notion of IT will encompass structure (e.g. systems and their relationships) and behaviour (functionality implemented by software applications). How do the various systems interact? How are they integrated? And how will all of this provide benefit for the business?

Established methods and initiatives aim at understanding, how does the IT landscape look today. They also support analysis and decision making concerning the future architecture. Where can we reduce costs? Where can we save money? Where do we need new systems for having a new product we want to serve? If, for example, a logistics company delivering letters and parcels also wants to deliver bulk freight, they might need a new system managing the transportation of bulk freight. This needs to be done differently from mail and parcels deliveries and will also require a new software application. In general, business strategy, new products and to-be processes will influence decision about the future IT landscape. When having the as-is picture as well as the to be architecture, we also need a plan for transforming from the as-is to the to-be. This plan will be further called *road map*. The road map is supposed to be a plan containing of certain steps, initiatives and activities that need to be conducted in order to achieve the to-be architecture in the future.

1.3.3   Example Visualisations for Enterprise Architecture

Leaving the abstract definition behind for a moment, let us now look at driving decisions for IT against the business background. We already discussed one of the most important tools of the architects for visualisations: *maps*. Let us get a grip on the notion of map by just looking at a few examples. Which kinds of maps are used in today's EA initiatives?

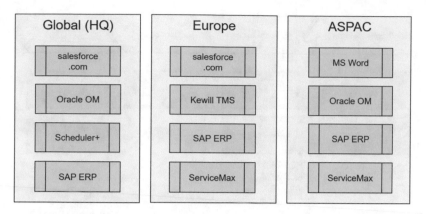

Fig. 1.13 Example: Applications in their business context

There is an example showing four software systems in Fig. 1.12. The arrows between those systems indicate data flowing from one system to the other. salesforce.com, for example is a Customer Relationship Management (CRM) software, maintaining customer data and providing it to Kewill TMS (a Transport Management System) and to our customer service system, called Service Max. Order data is transferred from the transport management system to the financial system—in this case, SAP ERP—and to the customer service system. SAP ERP will then generate and manage invoices based on order and transmit them to the customer service application. Customer service employees will then have all the information required for handling customer requests (e.g. invoice dispute). It is a very simple example. Obviously, it consists of only four systems, which is much less than the 750 or even more than 1000 systems that are common in large enterprises. However, the example should just provide an impression of which kind of information can be represented on an EA map.

Another popular visualisation in EA is assigning systems to organisational units as given in Fig. 1.13. It describes which organisational unit is using which system. In this case, we have, various software applications: salesforce.com again, Oracle Order Management (OM), Scheduler+ (a scheduling system) and others. The example is also showing three different organisational units of our companies, represented by grey columns. We have the global head quarter using four applications. It also shows applications used by a subsidiary in Europe using. And we have an organisation in the Asia-Pacific regions (short *AsPac*) also using several systems. We cannot see what those systems are used for. We can only describe which organisational unit is using which software system by just placing the application within the organisational unit.

Another frequently used visualisation is a map showing individual process steps together with software applications required for their execution (Fig. 1.14). In this

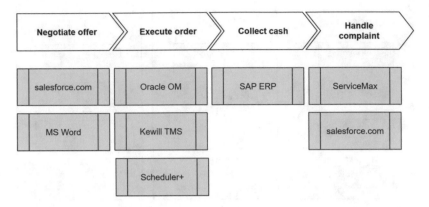

Fig. 1.14 Example: Applications supporting processes

case, we have a complete order management process, which starts with negotiating an offer with the customer. Such an offer can, for example, refer to a car having a certain configuration (e.g. engine, car, extras). This is some sales activity leading to executing the order after the customer made the final decision on accepting the offer. Data can then be provided to the manufacturing department, which will produce the car and deliver it to the customer (as part of *Execute order*). After delivering the car to the customer, he/she will have to pay for it (an amount agreed upon during negotiating the offer). This will be performed in the *Collect cash* process step. And in case there is any issue with the car, he might come to our office and complain about it. It might, for example, not work or it is too noisy or it is not as fast as expected. In essence, there might be complaints by the customer that need to be handled in the last process step..

A similar kind of process may exist in any kind of industry. Another example would be the logistics industry: It starts with having a customer asking for the transportation of a huge amount of cars, or transportation of live horses that need to be delivered to a competition somewhere in another country. The logistics company can provide an offer for this transportation by using data from the CRM system and creating the offer using Microsoft Word (cf. Fig. 1.14). When the customer decides yes, I want you to move my horses from Germany to Australia for the race, then we can execute the order using the Oracle Order Management system. The company also uses the Kerwill transport management system for planning the transportation, for booking flights with airlines, which will then transport the horses. Additional timing and scheduling will be performed with Scheduler+ as shown in Fig. 1.14. Furthermore, the company can use other systems like SAP ERP system for all the financial aspects and as we can see here two different systems for customer service (e.g. handling complaints). Let us also keep in mind here that it is just a small example for illustration purposes—showing concepts and typical representation. Of course, a real map in a corporate environment is much larger. We should always keep in mind a typical corporation has a couple of hundred or even more than 1000

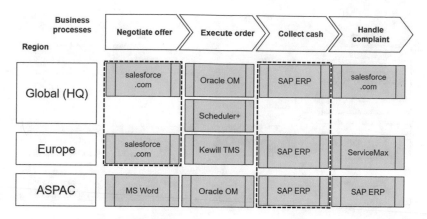

Fig. 1.15   Example: Combined viewpoint

applications (as shown in Fig. 1.5 on page 8), business processes are larger and have more detailed steps. We will usually have much more information. Drawing it in PowerPoint is good for showing the concept as we are doing here. But we will need a dedicated tool for analysing real world EA.

The examples presented so far are each focusing on a single aspect. We can also combine different views as shown in Fig. 1.15. Figure 1.14 is showing process steps for the corresponding IT applications. Figure 1.13 shows IT applications used by different organisations. Figure 1.7 combines the two viewpoints into a new visualisation: Showing systems per organisational unit, which represent regions here. And then showing which system is supporting which step in each organisational unit.

The examples provided in the section at hand are just meant to give an impression on simple visualisations used in EA. We will discuss further viewpoints in subsequent sections. There are also more examples in available publications like for example [11]. After now having some idea of what EA means, we will now have a look at what managing an EA is about.

1.4   Enterprise Architecture Management (EAM)

The previous sections provide a brief overview on EA and its visualisation. They addressed questions like: *How can we describe business and IT?* The examples are just meant to provide a short introduction and there will be more visualisations in subsequent chapters.

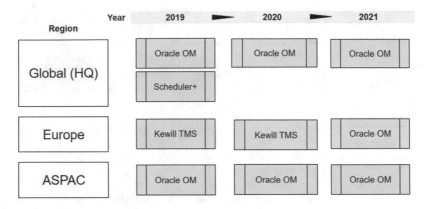

Fig. 1.16 Example: Roadmap

1.4.1 Definition of EAM

Before going into detail with method and tools, we also need to define the notion of EAM (cf. Definition 1.2). We characterised EA as a representation of the IT landscape and its business context, including time. We also need to consider changes in EA as we have an as-is state and want to develop it into an optimised architecture (to-be). This is exactly provided by EAM, which is a structured approach for establishing EA and maintaining the maps showing the business and applications landscapes. EAM is further aligning IT with corporate objectives defined by the business. EAM also provides methods and organisational structures and best practises that help us with introducing and performing EA activities in a corporate environment.

Definition 1.2 (Enterprise Architecture Management) Enterprise Architecture Management (EAM) is a structured approach for establishing, maintaining and using EA in order to align IT with corporate objectives. EAM defines methods and an organisational structure for enabling EA activities.

1.4.2 Roadmaps for Visualising Transformations

What does it mean, performing a change in the context of EAM? Again, we have a small example showing how we can describe the evolution of our application landscape over time in Fig. 1.16. Please note, we are using the same organisational units on the left-hand side as we did in previous examples in Sect. 1.3 (corporate headquarters, the European subsidiary, and also the Asia-Pacific organisation). Each of them is using its own set of software applications.

We can see a lot of different applications used perhaps for the same purpose in Fig. 1.16. Global HQ is using Oracle Order Management and Scheduler Plus. The Europe organisation is using a completely different system, called Kewill TMS, and the Asia-Pacific region is using Oracle Order Management (same as Global HQ). Let us now consider the fact that, IT people at EAM will focus on eliminating redundancies (i.e. saving money).

One might have made the decision that we need to reduce the amount of systems. And those two systems, Oracle Scheduler and Kewill TMS, are providing the same functionality. In addition to that, we want to get rid of Scheduler+ by end of next year. As the ASPAC organisation can only work with Oracle Order Management, it should also be possible to use only Oracle in the global headquarters. Consequently, Scheduler+ will be phased out (i.e. shut off). People might recognise during further analysis that Kewill TMS and Oracle are doing pretty much the same. We should, consequently, decommission Kewill TMS and replace it by Oracle Order Management in Europe. By the end of the year 2021, we will have only one system supporting order management globally. Oracle OMS will be the standard system within the organisation.

Why this example in Fig. 1.16? First of all, this is a typical representation showing how those kinds of changes are documented. It is providing a time frame for changes (years 2019 until 2021) and the changes that are planned to be conducted during that time. The example is also showing typical changes like

- eliminating a software application (Scheduler)
- replacing one application (Kewill TMS) by another (Oracle OMS)

There are more kinds of changes that may be triggered as a result of EA analysis. They will be explained in the course of EA analysis in Chap. 4 and when explaning the role of an enterprise architect in Chap. 5.

Another example for documenting changes on corporate IT is provided in Figs. 1.17 and 1.18. A roadmap showing the transition from as-is to to-be does not necessarily have to be documented by one map only but can also span several maps. We can have different maps documenting a change—so starting with the map we have already seen previously for showing which process step is supported by which IT application (Fig. 1.17). Based on this view, we might consider changes in order to optimise our landscape and derive an ideal to-be state as depicted in Fig. 1.18. Starting with a dedicated as-is map helps with focusing on understanding current inefficiencies and, therefore, optimisation potential.

Changes can then be documented by shifting the lens towards a to-be view as in Fig. 1.18. We should try to get rid of certain systems by 2020, like stating we don't want to write each and every offer using Microsoft Word. We want it to be generated on Salesforce.com. We are also owning two software applications for complaint handling. Why are we providing redundant systems for customer relationship management? Salesforce.com can also be used for the same purpose. Somebody made the decision that, by 2020, we want to switch off MS Word and ServiceMax in our to-be architecture.

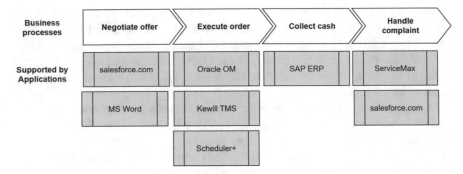

Fig. 1.17 Example: As-is as starting point for transition

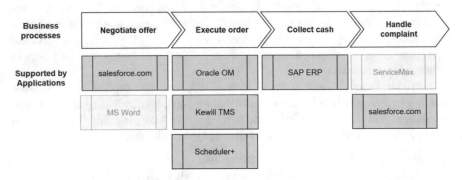

Fig. 1.18 Example: To-be as objective for transition

A roadmap can generally consist of at least two maps, showing the as-is and the to-be architecture as provided in Figs. 1.17 and 1.18. More complex roadmaps may span all changes over several maps, showing transformations over a period of time.

1.4.3   EAM and Related Disciplines

We are about to end this Chap. 1 and should have some basic understanding of EA and EAM. We should not forget about the fact that EAM is not a universal discipline for managing a company and solving all problems. We already know a couple of other management disciplines already being implemented in companies (Fig. 1.19) which are subject to academic research.

We have the discipline of **project portfolio management**. Companies are not only conducting projects, but having many projects that have interdependencies, and we need to make a decision about which projects we want to execute now, and in which order. And also, the technical discipline of **IT infrastructure management**. Even though EAM always promises to be a holistic approach, it is not meant to

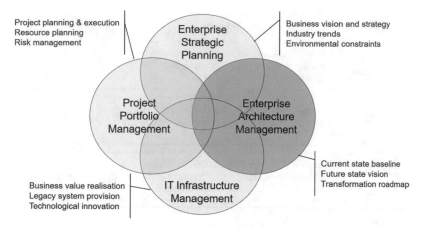

Fig. 1.19 EAM related to other disciplines (based on a figure in [12, p. 36])

replace all the other disciplines. To be more precise, for EAM, we need input from the **strategic planning**. Strategic planning still provides methods and tools for analysing the company, the context, markets, and so on, or making conscious decisions about, how do we want to act in the future, which will then be the input for EAM.

EAM is dealing with IT and software applications. This will have an impact on how to manage the IT infrastructure. IT infrastructure management is not part of EAM. It still has a couple of aspects in addition to what we will discuss in the course of EAM. Nevertheless, there is a huge overlap. And the same holds true for project portfolio management. We already mentioned potential changes that are performed on the corporate application landscape. We can introduce new software systems, switch off legacy systems that are not used anymore. We can change existing systems with respect to new requirements, or merge individual software applications into one system. Each change needs to be conducted within a project. And as EAM is rather having the holistic view, it is not only one project being triggered by EAM, but a portfolio of projects, which will use methods and tools also from project portfolio management. Therefore, it is not one toolset being used for managing a company. EAM coexists with others and will help with aligning business and IT properly as well as providing information and decisions that can help the other disciplines.

1.4.4 Architectural Layers

Defining architectural layers is a common concept that is part of each and every method, or part of each and every *EA framework*. It is driven by the principle divide

Layer	Description	Examples
Business architecture	Depicts business-relevant concepts for aligning business needs with software applications in the application architecture.	process, strategy, goal
Application architecture	Depicts software systems (i.e. applications) required for supporting business processes as well as their interaction.	application, interface
Technology architecture	Depicts IT infrastructure required for running software systems in a corporate environment so that processes are supported in any location.	hardware, network, location

Fig. 1.20 Common enterprise architecture layers

and conquer, not having the architecture as a whole. But rather cutting the entire view into several layers or into several points of views.

We will use a very simple distinction of layers in our text book and it is shown in Fig. 1.20. There is one layer called the *business architecture* (or also *business layer*). It contains all details and fragments that describe the business. We can use, for example, business processes, the strategy, KPI, objectives, goals for describing the business environment. We will cover this topic in the following Chap. 2. The term *business architecture* is often used by enterprise architects when they refer to their knowledge about the business.

Below the business architecture is the *application architecture* (or *application layer*). The application architecture consists of all software applications that are used and maintained by an organisation. It also includes data within the applications, data flows and interfaces between applications. Real world application landscapes tend to grow very large. All of this will be covered by the notion of application architecture in Chap. 3.

Separate from the top two layers is a third layer called *technology architecture* (*technology layer*). Technology architecture encapsulates all hardware and IT infrastructure (like networks, data centres, location where we need to establish and maintain IT). It is representing a very technical perspective.

Classical EA frameworks can have even more layers and a more complex way for arranging them. For our purpose such an easy layering making the distinction between business and applications and then also providing IT technology in addition is quite sufficient.

We will not elaborate on technology architecture, IT infrastructure and we will not discuss IT service management or any related topic. This book basically focuses on

- How can we describe the business architecture as the top layer of Fig. 1.20? (Chap. 2)
- How can we describe the application architecture? (Chap. 3)

- How do we link applications to business-related concepts (i.e. relationships between business and application architecture)? (Chap. 4)
- And how can we drive changes on the application architecture for the future? (Chap. 5)

1.5 Further Reading

We finish this chapter with an overview on existing publications that are worth reading. First of all, there is one textbook published by a Dutch guy with the last name Op't Land and co-authors (cf. [4]). Even though it is quite old they provide a good overview on frameworks. Also on the organisational aspect of and also the question, how can we create value by applying EA?

As we saw on the slides the value they are promising is rather high level. Like providing transparency, we can reduce risk, we would save costs. Real world enterprise architects have quite more hands on questions (cf. [5]). We collected them in documents that will be provided as supplementary material in [6]. There are further reviews like the one published by Lindström et al. in [13].

We also have to look at the theory behind EA—also looking at what researchers are publishing about this one. One prominent paper is published by James Lapalme and co-authors called *Three Schools of Thought on Enterprise Architecture* [8]. One of those schools is having a focus on *enterprise IT architecting* but there are also wider views up to how EA being the innovator or the driver for innovations within a company.

There are also a couple of publications on the definition of the term *enterprise architecture*. Saint-Louis and co-authors provide a systematic literature review in [9].

There are a couple of books available at the moment who are criticising the classical EAM approach with being on high level a lot of documentation also suggesting we need to incorporate more agile and lean techniques. One of them is published by Bente and two co-authors (cf. [12]). The three of them are consultants with Tata consultancy and developing their own methodology for the start for understanding what is EA being used for. It is a good introductory reading. We will reiterate the same book later on in the book when talking about setting up an organisation for EAM.

And last but not least, there is a book published and authored by an Australian guy with the last name Kotusev (cf. [14]). He is also located in Melbourne and provided some textbook with an overview on typical visualisations being used in EAM. This book is some kind of a recommendation for everybody who wants to see which different kinds of maps are being used. Of course, we will present and discuss further views in the following chapters of the book. We started already with some simple examples. But there is more to come ...

1.6   Summary

That's it so far for the first chapter. During the introduction to EA, we started with describing why is EA different from system or software architecture. We are not only thinking of individual software applications, but of the IT landscape as a whole. We had the metaphor of the town planner, compared to the architect creating an individual house. We then looked at how is EA beneficial for us and which kinds of problems can we solve with applying EA methods and tools by having some definitions—providing definitions on how we see the notion of EA and also having some typical maps of visualisations to be used by enterprise architects. It was not meant to be a complete overview, but just having some typical examples, just for making the theoretical part a little bit more visual.

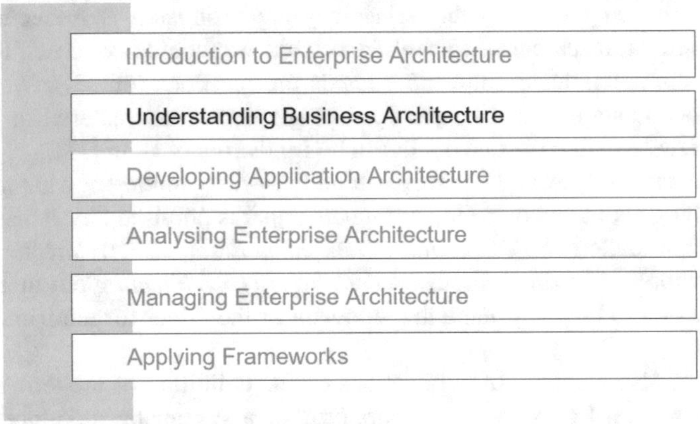

Introduction to Enterprise Architecture

Understanding Business Architecture

Developing Application Architecture

Analysing Enterprise Architecture

Managing Enterprise Architecture

Applying Frameworks

Fig. 1.21 Following next: Understanding business architecture

In the next section, we will have a closer look at *understanding business architecture* as depicted in Fig. 1.21. At the end of this section, we introduce the distinction between business architecture and application architecture. The two of them will be further looked at in the following Chaps. 2 and 3. The next one will focus on the business architecture, by covering the following topics:

• Are business processes the best way for aligning business and IT?
• What are business capabilities and how can they be used for deriving an application landscape?
• Which further concepts exist on business architecture?

1.7 Exercises

Exercise 1.1 (Legacy Systems) Please, answer the following questions using your own words:

1. What is a legacy system? You can look up the term in the literature.
2. Which are common problems associated with legacy systems? Try to find some in publications on legacy applications (i.e. software, system).
3. Why are legacy systems still in use? You can investigate for reasons in publications on the topic or also mention some from your own experience.

Exercise 1.2 (Your Experience) Consider a company or organisation you already know (like current/past employer, internship or business partner). Please, summarise your experience with respect to the following questions:

1. How well do IT people know business processes of that company?
2. How do business and IT people collaborate?
3. Is IT contributing to the business model of the company?

Exercise 1.3 (Purpose of EAM) Download the following document [5] from your library and read it carefully. Which of the topics listed there are relevant from your experience?

Exercise 1.4 (Digital Enterprise) Identify at least **three** companies who transformed their business model from classical products into a digital service offering. How does the separation between business and IT influence a company's capability with respect to a digital service offering?

Exercise 1.5 (Start-Up) Bob founded a company based on venture capital. He needs to set up IT for key corporate functions.

1. Which drivers are influencing the IT?
2. Which challenges might Bob need to be aware of?

Exercise 1.6 (Merger/Acquisition) A big company CA bought the main competitor CB. Information technology of CA and CB needs to be integrated.

1. Which challenges need to be addressed?
2. How should the IT look like ideally?

Exercise 1.7 (Business Context) How can we describe or visualize the following business concepts?

- Strategy, objectives and KPI
- Business processes
- Organisation and resources
- Software systems and data
- Cost an benefits
- Risk and mitigation actions
- Compliance rules

Choose at least three from the list above and provide examples on how to visualise or describe them.

References

1. Y. Namba, City planning approach for rebuilding enterprise information systems, Ph.D. Thesis, Tokyo Institute of Technology, Jan. 2005
2. M. Lankhorst, et al., *Enterprise Architecture at Work: Modelling, Communication and Analysis*, 3rd edn. ser. The Enterprise Engineering Series (Springer, Berlin, Heidelberg, New York, NY, 2013)
3. J. McKee, *Applying Principles from IT Architecture to Strategic Business Planning* (Business Science Reference, 2013)
4. M. Op't Land, E. Proper, M. Waage, J. Cloo, C. Steghuis, *Enterprise Architecture, Creating Value by Informed Governance*. ser. The Enterprise Engineering Series (Springer, Berlin, London, 2009)
5. J. Jung, Purpose of enterprise architecture management: Investigating tangible benefits in the german logistics industry, in *2019 IEEE 23rd International Enterprise Distributed Object Computing Workshop (EDOCW)*, Oct. 2019, pp. 25–31
6. J. Jung, E. Proper, *Why Are Practitioners Doing EAM? Tangible Benefits from Enterprise Architecture Management*, Frankfurt, 2019. [Online]. Available: http://eamlab.frankfurt-university.de/wordpress/purpose-of-eam/
7. P.A. Khosroshahi, M. Hauder, A.W. Schneider, F. Matthes, Enterprise architecture management pattern catalog, Version 2.0, Software Engineering for Business Information Systems (sebis), Technische Universität München, München, Tech. Rep., 2015
8. J. Lapalme, Three schools of thought on enterprise architecture. IT Professional **14**(6), 37–43 (2012)
9. P. Saint-Louis, M.C. Morency, J. Lapalme, Defining enterprise architecture: A systematic literature review, in *2017 IEEE 21st International Enterprise Distributed Object Computing Workshop (EDOCW)* (IEEE, 2017), pp. 41–49
10. D. Greefhorst, E. Proper, *Architecture Principles: The Cornerstones of Enterprise Architecture*, ser. The enterprise engineering series. (Springer, Heidelberg and New York, 2011
11. S. Kotusev, Enterprise architecture: What did we study? Int. J. Coop. Inf. Syst. **26**(04), 1730002:1–1730002:84 (2017)
12. S. Bente, U. Bombosch, S. Langade, *Collaborative Enterprise Architecture, Enriching EA with Lean, Agile, and Enterprise 2.0 Practices* (Elsevier/Morgan Kaufmann, Amsterdam, 2012)
13. Å. Lindström, P. Johnson, E. Johansson, M. Ekstedt, M. Simonsson, A survey on CIO concerns: Do enterprise architecture frameworks support them? Inf. Syst. Front. **8**(2), 81–90 (2006)
14. S. Kotusev, *The Practice of Enterprise Architecture: A Modern Approach to Business and IT Alignment* (SK Publishing, Carlton, VIC, 2018)

Chapter 2
Understanding Business Architecture

The previous Chap. 1 introduced the definitions for *EA* (Definition 1.1 on page 19) as well as *EAM* (Definition 1.2 on page 24). It also discussed why such a discipline like EA is required (Sect. 1.2) and how it relates to other established disciplines (an overview is provided in Fig. 1.19 on page 27).

We already had talked about that EA is usually divided into several layers (depicted in Fig. 1.20 on page 28). The top one is called *business architecture* and will be subject of the current section. Subsequent chapters will then deal with further architectural layers, like the application architecture. We will talk about analysing EA throughout the book, and how to manage an EA. But now, let's have a look at business architecture.

Learning Objectives

After completing this chapter, you will be able to ...

- ... explain the difference between business processes and capabilities
- ... create a business capability map
- ... identify relevant business objects
- ... provide an overview on business architecture concept

The learning objectives for these sections are as follows. After carefully studying this chapter, you should be capable of explaining the difference between business processes and business capabilities. The concept of **business processes** is briefly explained in Sect. 2.1 together with its limitations with respect to EAM.

The notion of **business capabilities** is explained in Sect. 2.2. You will learn about their differences to business processes based on hands-on examples. You will be capable of explaining the difference to other people like, in the future, your boss or your peers. You will also learn how to create a business capability map for a given

© The Author(s), under exclusive license to Springer Nature Switzerland AG 2021
J. Jung, B. Fraunholz, *Masterclass Enterprise Architecture Management*,
https://doi.org/10.1007/978-3-030-78495-9_2

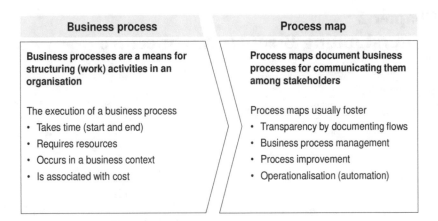

Fig. 2.1 Business process and process map

organisation. Imagine being a consultant that defines the capability map for a client. You can even imagine creating it for your current or future employer.

Next learning objective deals with identifying **business objects** for a given enterprise (cf. Sect. 2.3). Last but not least, there are many more concepts in **business architecture**, more than we will discuss in Sect. 2.4. We will provide an overview with a brief explanation of each, and you should be capable of summarising them to anybody else who will ask you in your future.

2.1 Business Process

Let us start with the concept of *business processes*. This textbook is not supposed to substitute a dedicated course on business process management, but provides a brief introduction to the notion of business processes. Later on, there will be an overview on how business processes relate to further concepts being used in business architecture.

A business process represents a series of activities that happen in an organisation or in a company (cf. Fig. 2.1). It takes time for execution, hence, it has a given start and end time. It is usually requiring resources for executing, i.e. people doing some piece of work, or machines used by people. Fully automated processes just requires machines (including computers) and no human actor. We can find processes anywhere, even outside companies in our personal environment. We will have a narrow view on business processes within this textbook: business processes are happening in a business context. Therefore, the execution of business processes is associated with costs. Whenever people are talking about business processes, and especially business process optimization, they are thinking of, how to save money.

2.1.1 Business Process Maps

We would like to have a clear distinction between a *business process* and its *description*. When using the term *business process*, we are referring to the actual work that is done in a company. Besides of this, the term *process map* stands for the (sometimes graphical) description of a process. You might have worked with process maps already or seen them in text books on business process modelling.[1] You might have seen them during an internship or any other work experience. They are also part of the definition how people should do their work in some organisations.

There is a clear distinction between the business process and the process map. The business process only refers to the actual work and is usually not visible. While looking at a shop floor in a company, you can see machines, busy people or material lying around. But you cannot see the processes themselves while they are happening there. Therefore, people are making drawings describing the process and this is what we call the process map. The purpose of the process map is its description so that other people—who don't know the process—can understand it. They can follow it like a step-by-step instruction about what to do.

Business process maps are also used for a corporate business process management, as you can only manage what you understand. And for understanding, you need some documentation which is provided on the map. One special aspect in business process management is, process improvement. Managing processes does not only mean making sure they are running, but also making sure that we are getting better with our processes over time. Process maps can also be used as a prescription for process automation. This will be supported by so called business process management systems (BPMS) or also referred to as *workflow management system*(WfMS). They require a formal description of the process and can then manage and control the execution of business processes automatically.

Business processes can be characterised by the properties provided in Fig. 2.2. First of all, the business process usually represents a **transformation**. It is not some work that is done without any reason or outcome. It always focuses on creating a result, and this result should provide a value for customers. It also requires an input. When creating a car, for example, we have the car as an output. Which also provides some value add for the customer, the person buying the car. And for producing it, the company requires materials and prefabricated parts that will then be assembled.

When dealing with business processes, and especially when keeping in mind that we want to improve processes, we are not looking at projects that only happen once but rather at activities that will be **repeated** over time very much in the same way. You can imagine drawing a business process map does not make much sense for a process that has been executed once and will never be executed again. It only makes sense if we are describing something that will also be useful in the future.

---

[1]Business process modelling is for example explained in [1]. We will use the term *business process map* and *business process model* as synonyms throughout this book.

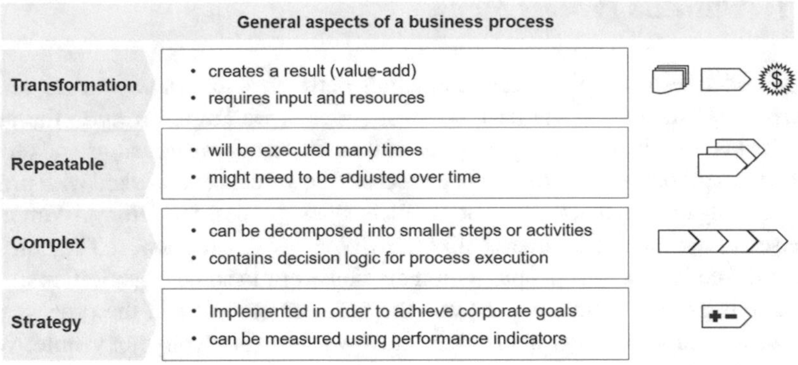

General aspects of a business process		
Transformation	• creates a result (value-add) • requires input and resources	
Repeatable	• will be executed many times • might need to be adjusted over time	
Complex	• can be decomposed into smaller steps or activities • contains decision logic for process execution	
Strategy	• Implemented in order to achieve corporate goals • can be measured using performance indicators	

Fig. 2.2 Properties of a business process

Real life business processes usually be of some **complexity**. The complexity is often not visible, because there are many decisions to be made within the process.

Example 2.1 (Decision in Process Flow) An e-commerce company receives orders from their customers. Each order needs to be validated whether it is complete and can be executed. This can result in either *accepting* or *rejecting* the order.

Many decisions within a business process might lead to a complex control flow. Depending on decisions, one step might be done or the other. We have resources being involved. We have people being involved. We have customers and other stakeholders with certain expectations, which increases the complexity of a business process.

A business process is not just a means on its own but needs to fit to the corporate *strategy*. The car manufacturing business process only makes sense if this is part of our corporate strategy. Producing cars is not that relevant for a logistic company, because their strategy deals with managing and delivering parcels to its customers (i.e. it is different from the one of a car manufacturer). They are using cars, so therefore, they will focus on business process that will support their parcel strategy.

Those, who are familiar with business processes should already know some visualisations (i.e. business process models). Around the world, there are many different ways how to describe a business process. You can describe it with a text. You can describe it with a dedicated tool. There are standardised languages for describing. But you can also use presentation slides for putting process symbols one after the other.

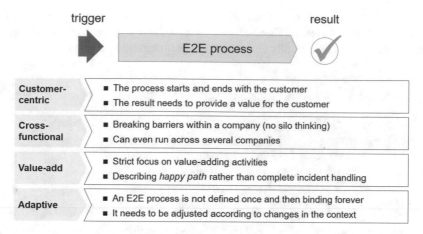

Fig. 2.3 End-to-end (E2E) process

2.1.2   End-to-End Business Process

There is a special notion of business processes and also business process maps that got quite popular, the so-called *end-to-end processes* (short: E2E process) or the end-to-end process view. Figure 2.3 shows an abstract example of an end-to-end process. An E2E process is always started by a trigger. It does not only have a time when it is started but also some event that is relevant for triggering the execution of the process. Each end-to-end process description covers any step that is required for achieving the result. In general, when creating such process maps, the basic idea is to have a **customer-centric** view. The execution is triggered by a customer—for example by placing an order. The customer is interested in getting the final result (i.e. the goods ordered). The process then covers all steps from taking the order, the order being executed, the product being delivered, and the order being paid by the customer. He does not have an interest in paying but this is part of the contract.

Whenever people are dealing with end-to-end processes, they will ask the following questions first:

1. Who is the customer?
2. What is the result expected by the customer?
3. How will the process be triggered (by the customer)?
4. What are the major steps to be executed from trigger to result?

The basic idea sounds easy, but many people still struggle with implementing processes end-to-end. Many companies have processes in place which have not been implemented by E2E principles. For sure, companies are providing products to customers. But especially large organisations have a lot of legacy processes that evolved over time following different or even no consistent principles. They appear as fragments without a clear customer perspective. There might be processes just for individual departments or functions, but not optimising the whole value-adding chain from trigger to result. The execution of an order then requires the involvement of different parties and usually also several departments working together.

> *Example 2.2 (Departments in Order Processing)* Executing a customer order might involve the following organisation units:
>
> - *Customer service* for taking and validating a new order
> - *Operations* for planning and scheduling the order execution
> - *Manufacturing* for creating the final product
> - *Logistics* for shipping the product to the customer
> - *Finance* for doing invoicing and cash collection
>
> These would be individual processes in a classical organisation (focus on division of labour). The E2E view fosters focussing on the value-add across the processes listed above.

Boundaries between departments usually hamper the execution of such a **cross-functional** business process. Individual departments just focus on their share of the work. That kind of division of labour also leads to local optimisation of individual process steps (owned by a department) instead of aiming at an overall optimisation. There is a shift in mindset with the end-to-end processes as people recognise that it is not only about your individual piece of work. It is all about the whole end-to-end process for the customer. And we need to make sure that we aim at optimising the whole process—even across departments.

As with any business process, the **value-add** is usually associated with the final result. Consequently, each steps of an E2E process needs to be value-adding by providing some value towards the final result. Non-value adding steps are not productive and, therefore, can be regarded as waste.[2] It can be observed in many process workshops during the past decades that people are not aware of the inefficiencies of their own work. We are talking about operations people who are executing the processes. Their heads are full with all the exceptions, with all the exception handling, with workarounds, what needs to be done if something goes wrong. This happens because there is no end-to-end process design and people are only focusing on their little piece of work. Many processes exist because they have been established many years ago and people are still executing them in the old-fashioned way.

---

[2]Eliminating waste is one of the key principles in Lean process management (cf. [2]). It aims at optimising processes by eliminating any non-value-adding activity.

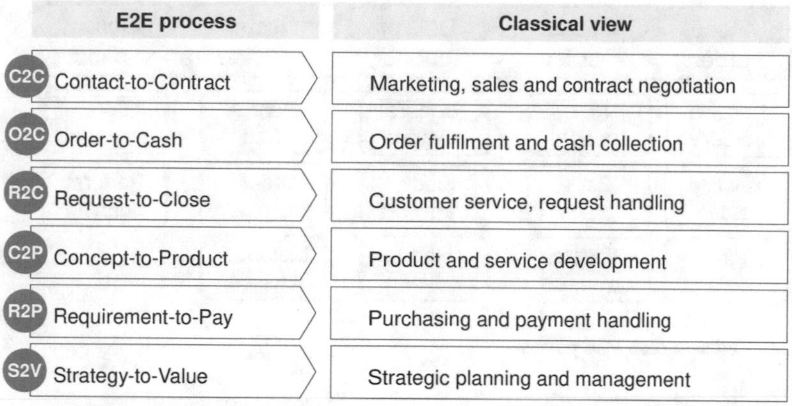

E2E process	Classical view
C2C Contact-to-Contract	Marketing, sales and contract negotiation
O2C Order-to-Cash	Order fulfilment and cash collection
R2C Request-to-Close	Customer service, request handling
C2P Concept-to-Product	Product and service development
R2P Requirement-to-Pay	Purchasing and payment handling
S2V Strategy-to-Value	Strategic planning and management

Fig. 2.4 Typical end-to-end processes

It is important to focus on the value-add during end-to-end process design. We call this the *happy path*, because it is omitting exceptions in the beginning, making sure that the whole process is stable. Examples for those exceptions are:

- missing information
- defective part
- resource unavailable

People in today's processes often spend a lot of time with handling those issues—sometimes using inefficient workarounds. Starting with a clear end-to-end process design can also help with avoiding those exceptions instead of handling them (e.g. improving data quality from the beginning). This will prevent the team for defining and executing failure handling procedures but having a process with built-in quality assurance.

Business processes and also end-to-end processes are not carved in stone. You do not just define them once, and then they will exist forever. Business processes need to be **adapted** continuously as there will be constant change. Customer expectations are changing. Competition is changing. Markets are changing. Even though we describe our business processes and business process maps for repeatable processes, we always need to keep in mind that an end-to-end process will be subject to changes over time. This will be done by business process management.

Figure 2.4 provides examples for common end-to-end processes. There are a couple of books available on the notion of end-to-end processes, including examples.[3] Hammer and Champy already presented the notion of end-to-end processes in the 1990s as part of their book on *Business Process Reenginering* [4]. Beside promoting their approach, they also describe a lot of examples from their

---

[3]Whittle and Myrick include some example E2E processes in a case study in their book *Enterprise Business Architecture* [3].

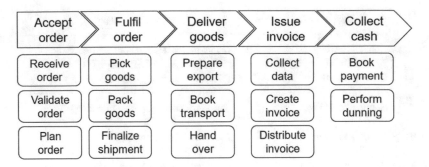

Fig. 2.5 Order-to-cash E2E process

consultancy experience. They found out-dated, complex or unproductive processes in large companies and showed their optimisation by implementing end-to-end processes. This notion has been adopted by other consultants and also researchers since then. There are some common end-to-end processes available in the literature and also in the consulting industry.

Let us have a look at Fig. 2.5, showing the **Order-to-Cash** (O2C) process (which is also listed in Fig. 2.4). It is implemented in SAP and also available in other *Enterprise Resource Planning* (ERP) systems. It is a common process that covers the execution of a customer order from the start to the end (i.e. trigger-to-result). The *Order-to-Cash* process is triggered by receiving a customer order. It then covers all the steps necessary for making sure that the order is completed. The result consists of a completed order as well as its payment by the customer. It ends with receiving the payment from the customer and then the whole end-to-end process is done. With the final result, the customer having the ordered product and also fulfilled his or her obligations with respect to paying for the product.

There are some other established end-to-end processes listed in Fig. 2.4 and also mapped to the corresponding functional view. **Contact-to-Contract** incorporates the classical marketing, sales and contract management functions. **Request-to-Close** refers to a classical customer service process which supports for example *complaint handling*, *incident management* or handling customer inquiries. The customer has a request (e.g. question or inquiry for sending information) and we need to provide the answer as a result and provide it to the customer. There are also rather long-lasting processes like **Concept-to-Product** for product development or *Concept-to-Service* in case of the service industriy. There is **Requirement-to-Pay** for covering purchasing activities and performing outgoing payments. Last but not least, **Strategy-to-Value** deals with strategies: Defining the strategy, implementing and executing it so that it can provide value for the organisation (and shareholders).

All E2E processes share the same naming convention. They start with a noun indicating the trigger (or the first object being involved), then followed by the word *to* and then the last component showing the result or the final object. The concrete naming might defer in various organisations or text books. But they all share the same naming pattern *noun to noun* (i.e. *trigger-to-result*).

Each E2E process can be cut into several steps, as shown by the *Order-to-Cash* process in Fig. 2.5. It consists of five main steps in our case. First, we are getting the order from the customer. After receiving it, we can fulfil the order. Which means either producing something or providing another service. Our example shows a typical order fulfilment process: taking goods from the warehouse, packing them into parcels, and then finalising them for being delivered to the end-customer. The next step consists of delivering the goods (as listed in the customer order) to the customer and issuing the invoice. At the end, we need to make sure that we can receive the payment from the customer. You might have recognised already that the example captures an ordering process (so-called fulfilment process in logistics) where we have goods stored in a warehouse. A customer can order these goods. We pack them into a parcel and deliver the parcel to the customer.

Each of the main steps listed on top can be decomposed into smaller steps:

- *Accept order* starts with receiving the order from the customer. It is checked with respect to feasibility. We can check if all goods are on stock or if the order itself is complete and correct. Then we can plan how to ship the order.
- *Fulfil order* consists of somebody going into the warehouse, picking the goods out of the shelves, packing them into the parcel, printing the shipment labels or the address label, and then putting it onto the parcel.
- *Deliver goods* starts with handing over the parcel to delivery department that will then deliver all the data to the logistics company, will book a truck for the shipment, and then hand over the goods to the logistics partner.
- *Issue invoice* is done by the finance department. It collects all the data for all the orders, creates invoices for individual customers, and distributes them to the customer.
- *Collect cash* will be performed after the customer received the invoice. He or she is expected to pay for the delivery. What could happen is the customer is happy and pays, so we can recognise there has been a bank transfer. And we can book the payment as being done, so the order has been paid. Or in case the customer is not paying, we need to perform some dunning activities.

The small example is aiming at showing the following

1. Activities of a typical Order-to-Cash process for a fulfillment order. It shares some similarities with order management processes in other industries (especially the financial aspects).
2. Common way of drawing an end-to-end process by showing main steps listed from left to right and then adding detailed activities below.

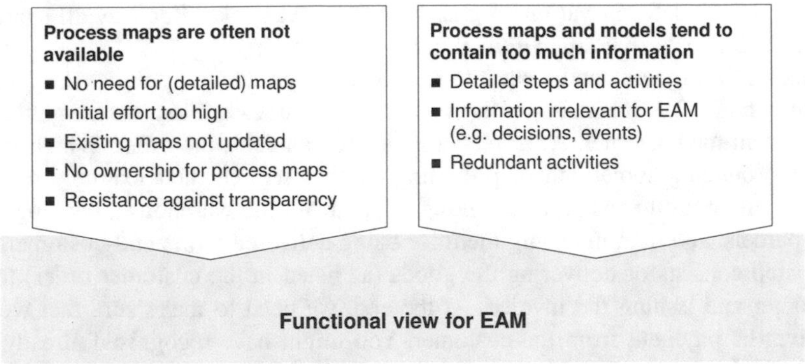

Process maps are often not available	Process maps and models tend to contain too much information
■ No need for (detailed) maps	■ Detailed steps and activities
■ Initial effort too high	■ Information irrelevant for EAM (e.g. decisions, events)
■ Existing maps not updated	■ Redundant activities
■ No ownership for process maps	
■ Resistance against transparency	

Functional view for EAM

Fig. 2.6 Challenges with business processes

2.1.3   Business Processes and EAM

Business processes are a very prominent method for describing what the company is doing. Many of companies already introduced Business Process Management (BPM) by providing business process maps as a standard for managing and improving business processes. This seems to be an excellent starting point for developing the application landscape. When I started working in logistics, I got hired for introducing and supporting business process modelling. However, when starting doing my work, I was told that I am member of the business architecture team now. The job was expected to support process modelling so that the models can be handed over to the enterprise architects. The company did not have extensive business process maps and we were expected to support business experts with describing their processes in a standardised way. We also expected business people to see any value in having process maps for communication purposes.

Nevertheless, this was quite a challenging task. There were a couple of reasons why the detailed maps have not been made already before (cf. Fig. 2.6). First of all, documenting processes is a big **effort**. It is not just going around for a week and making some drawings with business experts. It rather takes a couple of months or even years having interviews with all departments, documenting the processes, and validating them.

A big challenge is then keeping process maps up-to-date. After creating a process map, you need to make sure that changes in the process are also **updated** and incorporated in the process map. Processes can change based on external factors or due to a business process optimisation. In contrast to this, the process map is only updated if somebody actively takes care of it. If you documented your process a while ago by a process map, the process will most probably work differently as of today. But if nobody updated the process maps, then it is not relevant and you cannot use it any more. This happens, especially if people do not feel responsible for maintaining the process maps.

There is always some **resistance** to change by people and they even try to avoid transparency.[4] They are afraid of showing how they are working, because other people might think that it is easier than expected. People might be afraid of being obsolete if others can do their work as well (as described in process maps). There is still some kind of silo thinking (being trapped in the own functional area) or kingdom mentality. Managers can interpret their department as their own kingdom and do not allow others to intervene. Providing process maps would allow others to understand their work and even start telling them how to do things differently. Consequently, you might not get process maps from these departments—even no support for creating them.

Even if you have a complete set of process maps, they usually contain a lot of **details** like for example:

- textual description for each individual activity
- processes decomposed into tiny activities
- formal logic for specifying decisions (e.g. conditions for evaluating a job application)
- resources required for performing a task
- information required for processing
- exception handling

Companies who documented their processes, will hand over a big book to you. This book consists of many pages with a diagrams and text. Business process maps also tend to include a lot of **redundancies** as the same kind of activity can be performed in different business processes. This might also lead to different names for the same activity, and it can be hard to identify similarities.

A less detailed (i.e. appropriate) representation of the business is required for a holistic EAM. In fact, we need a common understanding about what the company is doing and not that much how processes are executed. This also refers back to the notion of the town planner as introduced in Sect. 1.1 starting from page 2. The town planner is not interested in how the building looks like inside. He/she does not care for the colour of the walls inside or the location of the power outlets, or the switches, or for anything else inside. He or she is only looking from a high level. It is very much the same here. Business process models are deep into details and not helpful for somebody with a high level view.

Process redundancies are mentioned in Fig. 2.6 and this might look quite abstract. We prepared a small example in Fig. 2.7 in order to show typical redundancies across different processes.

---

[4]We will discuss the topic of change management and resistance to change in Sect. 5.1.

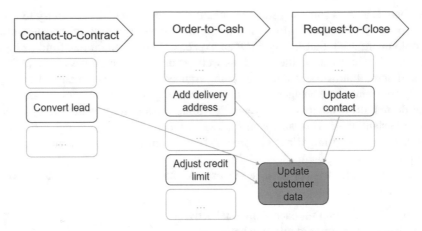

Fig. 2.7 Example: Redundancies in business processes

Example 2.3 (Redundant Activities in Processes) There is a company with various business processes. The **Contact-to-Contract** process encompasses any sales activity. One of them is a process step called **Convert lead**. Lead conversion usually refers to activities gathering and consolidating information about a prospective customer (i.e. sales lead). A company can get contact details and then enriches them with further information for future sales contacts. It also gets some idea about which kind of products to be sold to this lead. A combination of a lead and a product is called *opportunity*.

There is another process for order execution within our fictional company. We already talked about **Order-to-Cash** in more detail starting from page 41. It encompasses several process steps only two of which are shown in Fig. 2.7. There is one activity for adding the delivery address for the order (i.e. the shipping address of the parcel)–**Add delivery address**. This address might be stored in our order management system already but it sometimes needs to be updated (i.e. if the order at hand is not delivered to the standard address or the customer relocated recently).

Adjust credit limit is also done during order execution. A customer can usually place several orders, but sometimes companies put a limit for order volume or accumulated value. The company only accepts orders from one single customer until the order values sum up to 1000 Euros. If the limit is reached, then it will not accept any further order unless previous ones are paid. In other words, outstanding payments of one customer are always below 1000 Euros. Such a limit (like the 1000 Euros) is called the *credit limit*. Credit limits can be adjusted in a finance system or an order management system.

(continued)

Example 2.3 (continued)

The third process is the customer service process, called **Request-to-Close**. The process handles any inquiry made by a customer. Such an inquiry can be a complaint (because the order was not delivered completely or it was delivered to the wrong address), just a question, or a request for updating the customer account. The last example is done by the **Update contact** step shown in Fig. 2.7. The activity will update the customer account whenever the company gets aware of any changes (by phone or message). Updates can lead to a new delivery address, contact details or payment information.

Did you recognise the redundancies already? In fact, all the highlighted activities refer to the same kind of activity. Let us start on the right-hand side. Updating contact details refers to an activity with respect to updating customer data. The same holds true for **Add delivery address**. It is always an update operation on customer data. By providing a new address or an additional address, we are updating the customer data. Also, adjusting the credit limit is not done somewhere apart from the customer data. The credit limit for a customer is stored in the customer data or the data record for one specific customer. Adjusting the credit limit is updating customer data as well. Even converting leads is just an operation on a customer data record. Some CRM or ERP systems store lead data already in a customer data record. This means that adding a lead is the same as adding a new customer data record (even if it is only a prospective customer).

It is just a small example, indicating there are a couple of activities—converting leads, adding information, adjusting information, updating existing information, and then so on, which are not completely different process steps. Even though they are in different end-to-end processes, they all refer to the same kind of activity, updating customer data.

When planning a corporate application landscape for an organisation, we want to make sure that we are not buying too many software applications. Instead of having redundant applications doing the same thing we want to consolidate functionality in less systems. We, therefore, also want to avoid duplicates caused by redundant process steps. Furthermore, any kind of details provided by business processes might hamper EA as they represent unnecessary (or even misleading) input. The left hand side of Fig. 2.8 shows typical information of a business process map. It mentions detailed steps and in some companies, we even have something like work instructions or standard operating procedures. Work instructions are detailed descriptions for individuals, how to perform certain tasks in business processes. Business process maps also contain information about actors or human beings doing the work as well as their responsibilities. We have many lines showing in which order to execute process steps, how to make decisions, and how to handle loops.

However, when doing EAM, we are not the system architect and we are not implementing the system. We need to have information about systems on a high

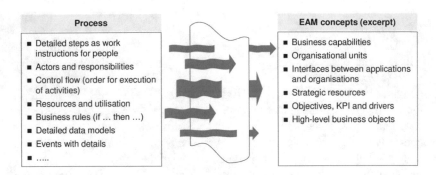

Fig. 2.8 Level of detail provided by process models compared requirements for EA

level and their mapping to business concepts. Consequently, we also need business concepts that help us with understanding the high level view on the business for then linking it to the IT landscape. An overview on those concepts is given on the right-hand side of Fig. 2.8. The list starts with the notion of **business capability** which will be further explained in the remainder of this section.

For managing software applications, we do not need individual information about users and what each user is supposed to do. We are rather thinking of organisational units or roles. We will have a look at interfaces between applications, including data exchange and service provisioning in Chap. 3. The notion of *resources* does not refer to individual resources (car, computer, machine, material) but to strategic resources. Also general business concepts are in scope for EAM. We will get an overview on *strategy*, *objective* and *key performance indicator* (KPI) for measuring if we achieved the objectives in Sect. 2.4. Section 2.3 will then introduce the concept of *business object* representing entities or concepts that are relevant for the organisation.

2.2   Business Capabilities

Let us first start with the notion of the *business capability* as defined by Definition 2.1. The definition will be key to EAM and characterises a business capability as a functional abstraction within the business architecture. It is located within the business architecture (not part of the application landscape) and it refers to **what** is the business doing. It is not an IT concept or an IT specific view on the business.

Compared to processes, it does not look that much at details describing **how** activities are performed but only look at **what** is done. A capability does not exist in isolation but has relationships to further business concepts. A capability supports the strategy and is required for achieving corporate objectives which can be measured by KPI. It always has a relation to the business model of the company and, of course, business processes.

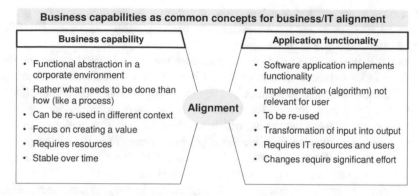

Fig. 2.9 Capabilities related to software applications

Definition 2.1 (Business Capability) A business capability (or just capability) is a functional abstraction within the business architecture and represents what the business is doing instead of providing details about how activities are performed. A capability (directly or indirectly) relates to the business model and supports achieving the business strategy.

Why are business capabilities so important when managing application landscapes for a company? Let us compare the notion of the business capability with software applications as shown in Fig. 2.9. A *business capability* is a functional abstraction in the business architecture. It presents a relevant function or some piece of work that needs to be executed in the business environment. It does not look at detail. It does not describe how activities are performed but rather represents that such an activity exists in the organisation. They are supposed to eliminate redundancies, meaning that business functions can be reused in different processes. Remember the example concerning updating customer data. This can be represented by one (small) capability and then be reused in various processes dealing with updating a customer account. Capabilities also provide a value by creating an outcome. They require resources for being executed, and they should be quite stable over time. Why stable over time? We will discuss this starting from page 50.

Comparing capabilities with software applications reveals a lot of commonalities (Fig. 2.9). Software applications are referring to some piece of **functionality** (implemented in the software). When looking at an application from an outside perspective or from a top-level perspective, it is not that important how it is implemented. We are not caring about the sorting algorithm that will sort the data to be shown in our user interface, because it is not relevant for the user and it is also not relevant for the enterprise architect as a town planner.

Applications are implemented with the objective of being **reused** in different contexts—at least in a limited way. A logistics planning software you cannot substitute an operating system (or being reused as such). Nevertheless, when creating a logistics management system, you try to implement current requirements but also try to anticipate future use cases. A software application can offer generic features that are supposed to be reused or can have a flexible architecture[5] so that it can be extended easily in the future.

Similar to the business capability, applications **transform** input into output. Both can have input data and then store data (in a database) create new information (i.e. output calculated from the input). They can also generate required documents. Software applications require **resources** for being executed:computer hardware, other software and users interacting with the system. Software is developed for reuse because we do not want to change the application frequently. Each change takes time, requires significant **effort** and can also be a risk. The change might result in new errors and can increase the complexity of the system.

Let us take a minute and compare the list again. Try to imagine how the restriction of application functionality refers to something we can find in the business—called business capability. *Business capability* will be the core concept that we are using for aligning the business with the IT.

We would like to explain the concept of *business capabilities* by an example capability map shown in Fig. 2.10. It presents a capability map for a fictional logistics company including core business capabilities for **Logistics operations** and **Network management**. The latter one is covering managing a logistics network consisting of hubs and transportation routes. The **Customer support** capability deals with handling any claim, complaint or request made by customers. **Market development** encompasses for example gaining new markets, finding new customers and getting new customers from existing markets. Any kind of marketing activity can be reflected here.

Beside of this, we have some guiding capabilities on corporate level (Fig. 2.10, top). **Strategy development** obviously is about developing the strategy and then executing it. This is one of the capabilities associated with top executives in a company. Management people also do planning activities for the corporation (long- and short-term planning), represented by the **Corporate planning** capability. There is also a capability related to managing relationships with any kind of business partner: **Partner management**. Partners might be suppliers, strategic customers and strategic alliances. This is also located on a corporate level in this example.

Some common capabilities that you can find in any corporation are listed in the lower part of Fig. 2.10. Human resources (**HR**) consists of hiring, training, and supporting existing people working with a company. The **Finance** capability represents financial transaction management, budgeting, and year's end closing activities. Last but not least, it shows a capability for **Information management** that deals with data management, information processing, reporting and general IT functions.

This map is not supposed to provide a complete overview for one specific company. It just gives you some impression on how business capabilities can look

---

[5]The term *architecture* here relates to the software architecture (i.e. the house) and not the EA (town planning).

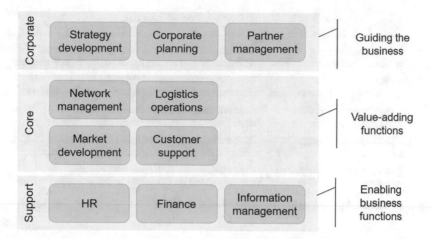

Fig. 2.10 Example capability map

like. You can see that they all have a name that refers to some kind of activity. They include a noun representing an activity like *development*, *planning* or *management*. The company is operating logistics (therefore *operations*, managing the network (*management*) and supporting the customer (*support*). Even though not all of them contain verbs, all of them have a noun that is derived by a verb for showing something is done here.[6]

The example is also using a certain kind of grouping for business capabilities.[7] This grouping is quite common for distinguishing core capabilities, from corporate and support capabilities. Core capabilities represent the core business and, therefore, are **value-adding**. They directly create value for the customers, the organisation or shareholders. They are immediately related to core processes or contribute to their value creation.

The ones on corporate level play a **guiding** role for the company. The strategy, for example, guides operations with respect to general aspects of their work. It does not provide the details, but most relevant expectations on how to execute work. Also partner management is not only about each and every business lunch or each and every event, but addressing long-term relationship also on a strategic level.

Support capabilities play an **enabling** role for the business. They do not directly create value, but are required by the value-adding functions so that they, in turn, can create value. Support capabilities enable core capabilities. The company needs personnel for doing logistics operations. It needs finance for collecting money

---

[6]The textbook at hand is following a consistent naming convention for processes and capabilities:
1. Process: *verb + noun* (example: *Check order*)
2. Capability: *noun + activity-noun* (example: *Order management*).

[7]The same grouping is also common for business processes.

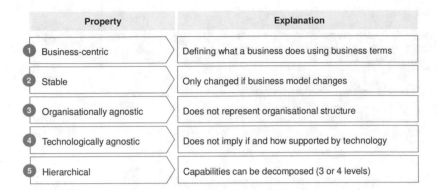

Property	Explanation
1 Business-centric	Defining what a business does using business terms
2 Stable	Only changed if business model changes
3 Organisationally agnostic	Does not represent organisational structure
4 Technologically agnostic	Does not imply if and how supported by technology
5 Hierarchical	Capabilities can be decomposed (3 or 4 levels)

Fig. 2.11 Required properties of a capability (based on [5])

customers need to pay after delivering parcels. Information management (including IT) provides information processing systems used within the corporation.

Business capabilities are commonly used and people associate a couple of mandatory properties, as depicted in Fig. 2.11. First of all, business capabilities are **business-centric**. You might ask *Why is this mentioned in the beginning?* It seems to be obvious as we are in the context of business capabilities and business architecture. Capabilities are supposed to be a central concept for planning application landscapes with respect to business needs.

Capability maps often reflect an IT view on the company instead of the business perspective because capabilities have been evolved as a tool used by IT people for EAM. EA initiatives have been initiated by IT departments because IT wants to align IT with the business. As business process maps are not available in many organisations, creating capability maps seems to be a good starting point. It takes less effort than modelling all processes. However, IT people depend on business experts explaining the business capabilities. This support is often missing. Consequently, IT people start defining business capabilities the way they perceived the business.

This kind of map is not helpful for EAM, as we want to understand the business and then align the IT. Therefore, don't create them on your own as being an IT department. Discuss them with the business. Use business terminology, and not your terminology because its common in IT or because your software system is using this terminology. Business concepts can only be accepted by business people if you speak their language. If you start pushing your own IT or technical language onto them, they will almost immediately stop listening to you.

Second one, business capabilities need to be **stable** over time. Business capabilities are a description of what the business is doing so that we can use it as an input for creating the IT landscape for the application landscape. It should not happen that they are changing frequently as they are used as a baseline for planning the application landscape. Consequently, any change in the capability map will incur a change in plans concerning the application architecture. Planning and transforming the application landscape is not a one-day task. It takes months, even years until it is completed. Imagine getting an overview on the business capabilities now and we plan our whole transformation roadmap. If the business suddenly informs us about new or removed capabilities, all our plans will be obsolete. And of course, if there are frequent changes, we will never achieve any objective. Therefore, for EAM, it is quite important to get the business capabilities from the business, but not as detailed so that we need to face changes frequently.

It also happens very often that people are not thinking about *what* are we doing, but rather about *who* is responsible for certain functions. We have, for example, an air freight department and we have an ocean freight department, each of them managing respective transportations. People tend to start with two kinds of capabilities as the bookings are handled differently. Considering the details, we can recognise several differences

- *Partner*: Airlines and ocean freight carriers are different kinds of business partners as they follow differing regulations.
- *Skill*: Planning ocean freight shipments requires slightly different skills compared to airlines.
- *Document*: Even though logistics documents share a similar structure across means of transport, there are specific differences
- *Process*: Processes are different due to industry regulations also by different paces of ocean vessels compared to air planes. This usually implies a different sequencing of steps.

However, we are getting distracted by the details! Let us consider the business processes for performing airfreight and ocean freight bookings. Do you think they are completely different? In fact, business experts from the industry will tell you a lot of differences because they have a solid knowledge. However, we need to focus on *what* people are doing instead of *who* and *how*.

Especially performing bookings is very much the same on a high level. Performing a booking means that we provide details about the shipment to the partner. We need to reserve capacity in a means of transport. We can then adjust the booking over time or cancel it. This can happen as cargo volumes are changing even after sending bookings to the carrier. These activities are the same on a high level of abstraction. Even though you have different organisational units, you should always check if the function is different. There might be different departments for a very good reason because they need different skills, different competencies, but we are looking at *what* they are doing. A business capability map should not recreate the organisational chart but be **organisationally agnostic**.

One of the most common mistakes we observed in our professional life is justifying the introduction of a capability because there is a corresponding IT application. This can also be a consequence of having an IT perspective on defining a capability map. This is not defining business capabilities because we want to derive the application landscape but the other way around. Such a reasoning will rather recreate the application landscape as a capability map.[8] We need the capabilities for getting a clear picture of the business, and then derive the technology.

The business capability map needs to be **technologically agnostic**. We should create a business capability map together with business experts. It is not about recreating something we already know, but rather describing what the business is supposed to do. This will be the baseline for defining our application landscape. We can then analyse existing applications and identify typical issues like indicated by the following examples:[9]

1. An application is not supporting any of the business capabilities. This indicates that the application does not provide any business value. This happens quite often as applications are still maintained but not or only rarely used.
2. There might be redundant applications supporting the same business capability. Companies want to reduce the number of applications in order to reduce the IT budget.
3. Business capabilities that are not supported by IT applications are an indicator for missed automation potential.

The introductory example in Fig. 2.9 just showed a flat list of business capabilities. However, real life capabilities maps follow a hierarchical structure as capabilities can be decomposed in smaller capabilities. It can result in a tree having three or four levels. This will be illustrated by the following two examples.

Example 2.4 (Capability Map: Health Industry) Figure 2.12 shows an example for a business capability map from the health industry. The overall capability of the company in the health industry is **Health service management**. This is the big box around all the other ones. And then within this capability, we have **Hospital Management**, **Client Pathology**, **Client Triage**, **Patient Treatment**, **Patient Rehabilitation**, **Citizen Education Management** and **Medical Research Management**. All of them are direct sub-capabilities within the overall capability.

Each of them can be further cut into smaller business capabilities. Special kinds of patient treatments can consist of surgery (**Patient Surgery**), radiation (**Patient Radiation**), conducting exercises (**Patient Exercise**) or additional treatments (**Supplementary Treatments**). Any of them is represented by an individual sub capability within the capability patient treatment (rectangle

(continued)

---

[8]Recreating the organisational chart or the application landscape are very similar mistakes. They are driven by something you already know instead of focussing on a clear representation of business functions.

[9]Some more use cases for capability-based application landscape planning are provided in [6, pp. 4608].

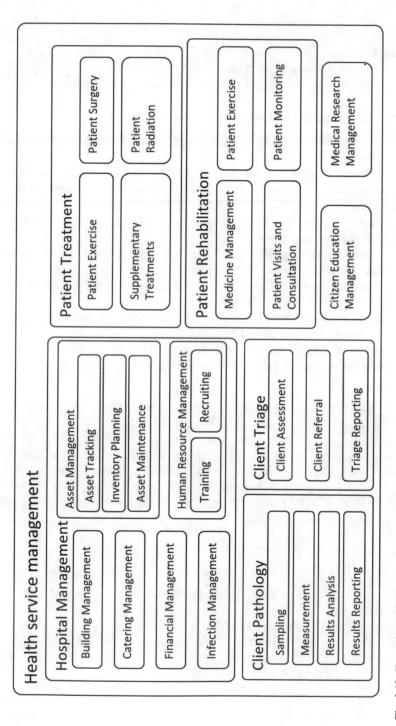

Fig. 2.12 Example capability map: health industry

Example 2.4 (continued)

within rectangle). Every capability can be decomposed into smaller capabilities, but does not necessarily has to. For example **Asset Management** consists of **Asset Tracking**, **Inventory Planning** and **Asset Maintenance**.

A few notes on creating such a capability map:

1. Each (sub-)capability needs to have a description (rule of thumb: at least two or three sentences).
2. Placing the rectangle representing one capability within the rectangle of another one, specifies that the first one is a sub-capability of another. The same holds true on any level.
3. A sub-capability can only be in one capability (i.e. it can not span several capabilities on the same level).
4. Decomposing a capability leads to disjoint sub-capabilities. There is no functional overlap between these sub-capabilities.
5. Decomposing a capability should lead to at least two sub-capabilities. **Patient Exercise** in Fig. 2.12 is violating this rule.
6. The number of levels should be limited to three or four. Otherwise, the number of capabilities gets very large and unhandy.
7. The number of levels can vary (i.e. does not need to be the same for all capabilities on the same level).

Example 2.5 (Capability Map: Logistics Industry) Another example for a hierarchical capability map is provided in Fig. 2.13, representing a parcel logistics company with the overall capability **Manage and execute parcel delivery**. This requires capabilities for **Logistics operations** as we have already seen before. It deals with managing the transports (**Transport management**) and warehousing (**Warehouse management**). Transport management, in turns, is decomposed into performing bookings, performing business transactions and offering functionality for tracking and tracing shipments.

All capabilities need to be explained. Here are a few examples:

- **Track & Trace** is one of the core capabilities of a logistics company. It helps with monitoring all shipments and is also offered as a service to the customer. You as somebody who is waiting for a parcel can check its status like the expected delivery date. Logistics companies need tracking and tracing data (i.e. track events) for controlling and managing logistics flows.

(continued)

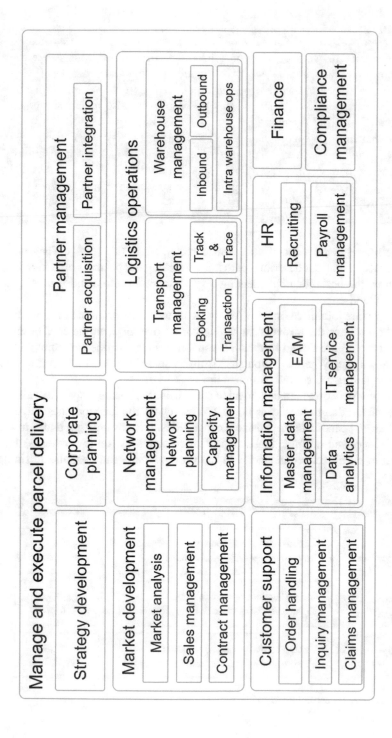

Fig. 2.13 Example capability map: parcel logistics company

Example 2.5 (continued)
- **Network planning** consists of managing the whole logistics network. A logistics network consists of hubs and transportation routes between them. Logistics panning will plan for required hubs and decide on how to set up transportation links between them. Transportation can be done by an external service provider so that this capability also includes contract negotiations with carriers.
- **Partner integration** beside the flow of physical objects, there is also a flow of information between logistics partners and government organisations. Hence, technical infrastructure for exchanging data with each individual partner needs to be set up. This includes agreements of data formats as well as protocols for data exchange.

Capabilities gained a lot of attention in recent years (cf. [6–8]). They are an excellent mechanism for describing and understanding the business on a high level. They can be the basis for implementing a governance structure and managing the application landscape.

When you are joining a company (either as a new starter or hired as a consultant) you might not have the business knowledge or an overview on the core business. Imagine that you are tasked to create a capability map for this company without proper knowledge. Where can you start from? There are a couple of sources you can use for getting a first draft as shown in Fig. 2.14.

If **business processes** are documented (i.e. business process maps are available) then you can use them as a starting point. You can check the functions used there and use them as first candidates for business capabilities. It is always a good idea to start on a high level and do investigation on detailed activities (on lower levels) later. You need to check for redundancies in the process maps and consolidate similar

Source	Description	Examples
Business processes	• Consolidation of common steps in processes • But: Risk of replicating redundancies	Customer data management
Business objects	• Identify business-relevant concepts • Determine what needs to be done with them	Customer, order, invoice
Reference architecture	• Existing capability maps as reference • Process frameworks or reference processes	PCF by APQC

Fig. 2.14 Sources for capabilities

steps from a functional point-of-view. If you just replicate the processes, there is always the risk of replicating existing redundancies.

Some methodologies use **business objects** for deriving business capabilities. They should not be confused with capabilities as discussed below. A business object refers to a relevant entity or concept within the business domain. Typical examples for business objects in a corporate environment are

- customer
- order
- invoice
- parcel

Business objects can relate to documents, physical objects, actors, or data that is being processed or used within a company. They are a pivotal element for developing a capability map according to the Business Architecture Guild in the BIZBOK, [9]. Roger Burlton provides an example for creating a capability map in the banking industry in [5]. The concept of business objects will be explained in more detail in the following Sect. 2.3. There will be a definition as well as further requirements.

There are also already **reference architectures** containing capability maps. Some people started creating reference architectures not only for an individual company but for certain industries. This kind of architecture comprises the commonalities of all companies within that industry and leave out the details. Such a capability map can then be reused for similar companies of that industry. It is called a *reference* because it is valid for being reused by other companies. The concept of reference models already exists for business processes. There is a standard available called the *Process Classification Framework* (PCF) by the *American Productivity & Quality Center* (APQC). Please, just open your browser and enter the following URL www.apqc.org/pcf. The PCF is a hierarchy of processes that is for example used for comparing different companies (by mapping individual processes to the PCF). But when looking at them and the naming, it is always referring to some kind of activity. And in fact you can reuse parts of the PCF also for defining business capabilities. To be honest, I also did it in my professional career in the following ways:

1. Getting ideas for new business capabilities
2. Checking existing capability maps with respect to completeness
3. Standardising capability maps of different corporate divisions

A quality check against the PCF can help us in identifying gaps in our own work and also identifying issues that can be eliminated.

2.3   Business Objects

In the course of this chapter, we discussed business processes and their relevance for
EA. We explained why business capabilities are better suited for architecture work.
Business capabilities are introduced by a definition and then further explained by
examples and general requirements. Let us now elaborate further on the second core
concept[10] that we will use for EAM, it's called *business object*.

Definition 2.2 (Business Object)   A business object (BO) is a static abstraction in
the business architecture for representing an entity or concept of the company and
relates to the business model. Even though they are less detailed than a data type,
business objects can be used as the basis for developing a data model in system
development.

While the capability is a *functional* abstraction (i.e. referring to some activity),
a business object is a *static* abstraction in the business architecture. It represents
an entity, or any kind of concept that is relevant for the organisation. It also has a
relationship to the business model. In fact when identifying business objects on a
high level together with business people in many cases the business object model
can then be a starting point for describing a data model for the company. Business
objects are on a high level while data types and models for system implementation
are very detailed (i.e. low level). Nevertheless if you have the broad overview on
the entities and the concepts you can use this for defining your data types, refining,
then handing it over to software development activities which then will develop the
database for the company.

A few examples for business objects in the logistics industry are listed on the
left-hand side of Fig. 2.15. We can apply the same distinction as we already did
with business capabilities: corporate, core, and support objects. Core objects within
logistics companies are the customer, the customer order or the transport service
provider. This is another logistics company performing a part of the logistics chain
on behalf of us. A very important concept is the booking. This is the order between
us and other logistics companies. If a logistics company wants to move a container
with an airline, they need to provide a booking to the airline. And a very common
business objects that you will find in most companies is the invoice.

Please note when looking at the names that it is always about entities (e.g.
documents, roles, objects) or any kind of static thing. Business objects are not
representing activities. The business object *customer* only refers to our customer. It
does not say what we are doing with the customer. It is the same with the customer
order. It just represents the document or the data set but it does not say what we
are doing with a customer order. Business objects and business capabilities are
complementary as

- *Business object* represents a concept from the business that we are using
- *Business capability* represents the function being performed on a business object
  or having a business object as a result

---

[10]We will mainly use business capabilities and business objects for EAM in subsequent chapters.

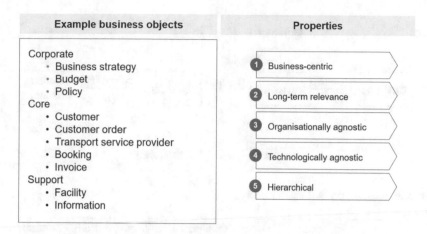

Fig. 2.15 Business objects: examples and properties

Figure 2.15 shows requirements for business objects on the right-hand side. Similar to the business capability, they need to be **business-centric**, they need to reflect the language of the business. If the business is calling the booking a *booking* then it is a booking, and it is not a transportation order or any other term. IT people tend to push their own wording towards the business as it seems to be more precise or even logical. Even though *transportation order* might be more specific as it states the fact as it is about an order, we should not use it as long it is not an established business term. We should not think like a database designer who clubs data types together for having less redundancies. In this case, we need to reflect the business language.

Business objects also need to have a **long-term relevance**—similar to the business capability. They should also be independent of any **organisation**. In the same way as the business capabilities, we should not introduce business objects just because we have **systems**. The business object should be the same no matter if the process later on will be manual or automated.

And last but not least, they can also be **hierarchical**. Each of those business objects you can cut into smaller objects. You can cut the customer into financial details, delivery addresses and sales agreements. You can have additional details for order execution. You can even have standard operating procedures just specific for customers.

Business objects can be listed and described in a text document—similar to a glossary. They can also be specified using a so-called *business object model* (BOM), which is similar to a map describing all of the business objects together with their relationships. In fact, a business object model looks like a high-level *Entity Relationship Model* (ERM). An example business object model is shown in Fig. 2.16. It contains familiar business objects that we already mentioned before. It shows, for example, the customer order (just named **Order**), **Customer**, **Booking** and the **Service providers** for transportation services.

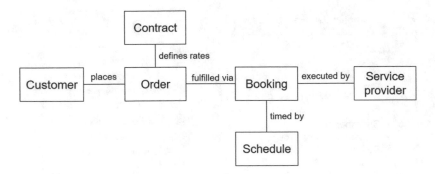

Fig. 2.16 Example business object model

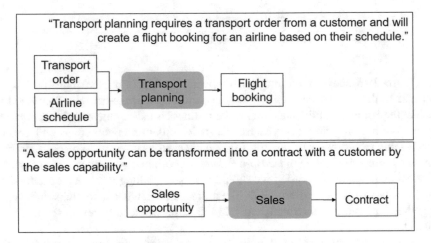

Fig. 2.17 Business objects related to capabilities

Showing business objects in such a model allows for showing relationships between them (which would not be possible in a glossary). We can, for example, specify that the rates used for the order (the price that the customer needs to pay) are defined within the contract: Relationship **defines rates** between **Order** and **Contract**. Further relationships describe that the customer who **places** the order and that orders are executed or **fulfilled via** bookings that we place with a service provider. Each booking is not just a document sent to an airline, but needs to fit to the airline's schedule: **timed by**. We can only book capacity on air planes that are really flying at the time and between the expected locations. It is just a small example for giving an impression of a business object model. You can find more examples in the literature, for example [10, pp.162] and [11, pp. 227].

Business objects and business capabilities are two different things. One is a static abstraction the other one is a functional abstraction. The first one describes the entity, the other one describes an activity. However, those are complementary, so they perfectly fit to each other. We have two examples in Fig. 2.17 for showing the relationship between objects and capabilities. The business capability **Transport planning** requires some input and will create an output. The arrow heads at the end of the lines indicate the direction of the object flow. The output is represented by the business object **Flight booking** as this is the value created by the capability. For creating the booking, the capability requires two business objects as an input. The **Transport order** provides the details for the shipment as provided by the customer (e.g. information on cargo, origin and destination). It further requires information on available flights, represented by **Airline schedule**.

The **Sales** capability (Fig. 2.17, bottom) deals with establishing new contracts with (new or existing) customers. It starts with a **Sales opportunity** as an input. A sales opportunity is a combination of a (potential) customer and a product that a company is aiming at selling to this customer. The **Sales** can consist of smaller capabilities like customer communication, performing sales activities or contract negotiation (not shown in the example).[11] If sales is successful then there will be a **Contract** with the customer. The example is showing the transformation from opportunities to contracts by reusing existing concepts: capabilities and objects.

The examples show an important aspect of EA: The architecture does not consist of different diagrams but the information provided by them is also connected with each other. We can create a capability map and a business object model and then establish a bigger picture by linking objects with capabilities. We will follow this principle throughout this textbook. We will introduce new concepts and also set them into context by showing relationships to other concepts.

2.4   Business Architecture Concepts

Business capabilities and business objects will remain the key concepts for business architecture within the textbook at hand. This is why they have been introduced in such detail. Nevertheless, business architecture can consist of many more concepts that help with understanding the business. This section will provide a brief overview so that you will get some understanding of the possibilities of business architecture. Only a few of them will further be used in this textbook.

Figure 2.18 shows an overview on common business architecture concepts. The underlying structure is provided by an experienced EA consultant in a paper published in [13]. This book is covering various aspects on business architecture and also contains some case studies. The structure is divided into three parts.

One of them is the **Business Motivation** which is providing a strategic view on the organisation:

Why are we doing business and what do we want to achieve?

---

[11]We are not considering how those activities are performed but only recognise that they exist as business capability.

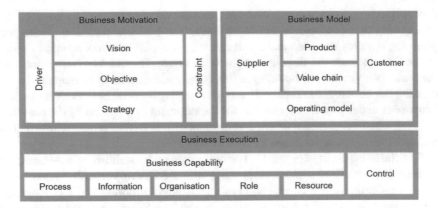

Fig. 2.18 Overview: business architecture concepts (based on [12])

Drivers cover the reasons for the motivation for starting and performing the business. They can be internal (e.g. product idea or personal motivation) or external (e.g. market opportunity or high demand). The **Vision** provides a high level description of the purpose and differentiators from other market participants. The vision is something like a leading principle for the organisation and can even be unrealistic. It can be written in an emotional way for making the company more attractive for shareholders and customers. The vision will then be the starting point for deriving **Objectives** that express concrete targets. Those targets need to be specific, measurable and time-bound so that we can determine whether they have been achieved.[12] *Key Performance Indicators* (KPI) will then be used for measuring the extent of the target achievement. The **Strategy** provides a high-level plan on how to achieve corporate objectives. It is like the company's roadmap for creating value.

Vision, objectives and the strategy reflect the internal view of our company. It is not operating in an isolated way but acting on a market so that we also need to incorporate external factors. There are certain drivers for making business, like markets, customers or the competition (especially lack of competition). A need for innovative products that are not available yet can be a special motivation. It will directly influence the creation of the vision. **Constraints** restrict the options for acting on the market. The market already has constraints but there are also legal and industry-specific regulations as well as physical restrictions. Company laws define how to perform business and industry regulations define business transactions between partners.

The **Business Model** provides the plan for transforming the strategy into value:

How do we provide value and which are our business partners?

---

[12]Objectives need to be SMART which stands for: specific, measurable, achievable, relevant and time-bound.

Concept	Description
Driver	Motivation for setting the vision and achieving objectives
Vision	Guiding image for the enterprise, providing direction
Objective	Desired result—specific, measurable, achievable, timed
Strategy	General course of actions and business priorities
Constraint	Political, economic, social, technological or internal

Fig. 2.19 Business motivation

It describes **Products** together with the **Value Chain** required for creating them. A value chain encompasses major process steps that will transform input resources into the final product for the customer. Products are supposed to have a value to the **Customer** (i.e. value proposition). Therefore, we also need to have a common understanding of the customers represented by customers segments. **Suppliers** provide resources (e.g. raw material, machines, services, information human resources) required in the value chain for creating the product. Strategic suppliers are key for the business model and require maintaining a long-term relationship. The **Operating Model** below describes restrictions for our business, for our infrastructure. The business model is derived from the business motivation and the elements are related to each other. The value chain, for example needs to consider the strategy and achieve corporate objectives.

Business Execution focuses on an operational view on the organisation. How do we execute our business? The business execution has a relationship to the value chain. The value chain is a high-level description of how to execute processes and the business execution refines processes so that they can be executed. **Process** performance relies on the availability of **Information**, **Roles** and **Resources**. Process execution is also embedded in an **Organisation**. **Control** mechanisms are implemented for monitoring the performance of business processes. Figure 2.18 also contains the notion of the business capability. Daniel Simon follows a slightly different interpretation of the term *Business Capability*. They see it as a bracket encapsulating the other concepts rather than restricting it to a functional view (as presented in Sect. 2.2).

Figure 2.19 summarises descriptions for business motivation concepts like the driver being the motivation for setting the vision and how to achieve the objects. We have the vision as some kind of guiding image for the company, providing directions for people within the company but also for communicating a good idea to shareholders that might fund the company in the future. We need SMART objectives that are specific, measurable, achievable, relevant and time-bound.

Concept	Description
Supplier	Partner providing resources or services
Product	Product or service with value proposition for customers
Customer	Business customer or consumer grouped by segment
Value chain	Main value adding stages from supplier to customer
Operating model	Business blueprint for implementing the value chain

Fig. 2.20 Business model

Concept	Description
Information	Information objects required for performing processes
Organisation	(Hierarchical) structure of executing business units
Role	Human actor or skill required for a specific activity
Resource	Any tool or material required for business processes
Control	Measures for controlling compliance and performance

Fig. 2.21 Business execution

We had the business model (Fig. 2.20) with suppliers referring to partners that help us with providing the service. We have the product as a description of what we are providing to the customers, including, very important, the value proposition. We need to represent the customer so that we can understand his or her needs. We can describe the high level value chains or what are the basic steps for creating the products for the customer. And we can also already have a link to end-to-end processes and then the operating model as some kind of a blueprint how to implement the value chain by using concrete resources and partners.

With business execution level (Fig. 2.21), we had concepts that you already know from IT-related classes. Information is representing data objects or any kind of information and knowledge that is required for performing processes. Organisational units build the structure of the company and execute business processes. Roles represent skills or competencies needed for performing activities. We have resources, which can be tangible resources like physical resources, but also intangible ones like information. And last but not least, the control enables us for measuring the execution of our business, also controlling compliance, and especially the performance of our business.

2.5 Further Reading

There are some recommendations for further reading: If you want to learn more about end-to-end processes, there is a very good textbook provided by Alex Sharpe and Peter McDermott called *Workflow Modelling*. The second edition is available from 2008 [14]. Alex is a consultant in the process industry, also providing workshops and tutorials about processes. He offers training, so that people can document processes. But he also works as a consultant helping top executives with improving their processes, having a very strong focus on end-to-end process, together with the trigger and the result.

The book by Simon and Schmidt on *Business Architecture Management* is a collection of papers, all of them having some more details about business architecture and how business architecture can help with managing the IT that is within a corporation. It is a pretty good reading for getting more information [13].

The Business Architecture Guild is an organisation consisting of people interested in business architecture. They provide a handbook on business architecture as well as methods for developing it. The BIZBOK Guide [9] is available to members of the guild only and will be updated frequently. An overview on the work of the Guild is published in [15].

The Open Group published a white paper on the notion of business capabilities and how business capabilities can help with EAM[16]. It is available for free in the internet.

Reference [5] is a blog post written by Roger Burlton, a consultant specialised on business architecture. He is quite popular also in the business process community. Roger is conducting conferences and organising conferences with respect to business process management. He is a consultant for companies who want to improve their processes. A while ago, he started writing a weblog, providing his point of view on business architecture, business processes, and so on. He published a very good article on the notion of business capabilities—just a short reading. I recommend having a look at this one because Roger perfectly describes how capabilities can be linked to the business processes, what is the difference, and how do they relate to each other, and also introduces a method—how to identify your business capabilities from your business objects. He is doing it by using examples, but also has some additional hints.

	Business Object	Business Capability
Description	• Static abstraction • "There **is** something."	• Functional abstraction • "Something is **done**."
Similar concepts (business)	• Concept, entity • Examples: physical object, product document, information, resource	• Business function • Examples: transformation, activity, (process) step
Similar concepts (computer science)	• Data type (programming) • Entity type (ERM) • Class (UML)	• Function, operation, method (programming) • Use case, activity (UML)
Naming	Noun	Noun + activity (noun)

Fig. 2.22 Business capabilities and objects compared

2.6   Summary

That's it so far concerning the business architecture within this chapter. We just want to summarise the most important concepts:

- *Business processes* are a common concept for describing the business. However, business process maps might not be available or tend to be too high level.
- *Business capabilities* are a functional abstraction for describing what a company is doing. It is one of the most important concepts for EAM.
- *Business objects* are a static abstraction representing entities or concepts of the business. They are a starting point for a data model and can be linked to business capabilities.

It sometimes seems to be hard to distinguish between the two concepts *Business Object* and *Business Capability*. They tend to describe the business on a very high level of abstraction (i.e. they are abstract) and may even have a similar naming. The word *Booking* can refer to the booking document (i.e. business object) or the activity of performing a booking (i.e. capability). This also shows that a consistent and adequate naming is of paramount importance for mapping business objects and capabilities.

An overview on differences between the two concepts is provided in Fig. 2.22. Beside a short description, the figure also provides information on similar concepts in both, business and IT. Business concepts can be used as a starting point for identifying business objects or capabilities. Typical sources for business objects are documents or physical object. Business capabilities can be derived from activities or corporate functions. The rather IT-related concepts (*computer science*) already provide an outlook on which concepts objects and capabilities will be mapped to. Business objects can be a high-level representation of an enterprise-wide data model, mapped as an entity-relationship diagram. Business capabilities can be implemented as functionality in a software system or as a web service.

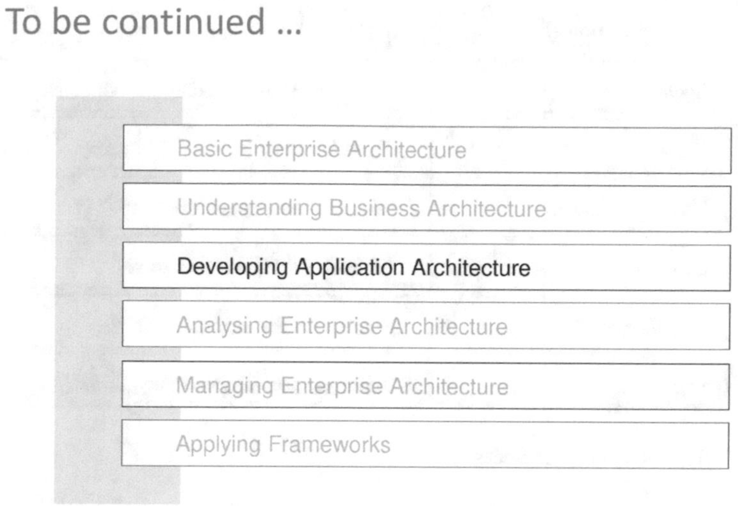

To be continued ...

Basic Enterprise Architecture
Understanding Business Architecture
Developing Application Architecture
Analysing Enterprise Architecture
Managing Enterprise Architecture
Applying Frameworks

Fig. 2.23 Following next: Developing application architecture

There are many more business architecture related concepts as provided in Sect. 2.4. Most of these concepts are derived from business and management disciplines and aim at having a complete view on the company. The next Chap. 3 will continue from here and have a closer look at the application architecture (Fig. 2.23) by covering the following topics:

- How can applications and application architecture be described?
- How do applications relate to business capabilities?
- How should an ideal application architecture look like being derived from the business capabilities?

2.7 Exercises

Exercise 2.1 (Core Processes) Identify and describe at least *three* core processes of the following businesses:

1. bakery producing and selling pastries
2. postal company for international parcel logistics
3. university
4. hospital
5. restaurant offering home delivery
6. car manufacturer
7. farming company producing fruits

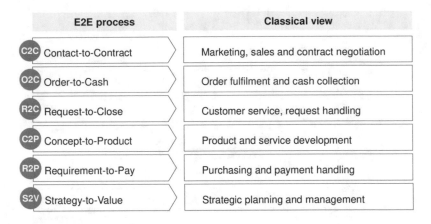

Fig. 2.24 Typical end-to-end processes

Each description should include the following information:

- result of the process
- major process steps or activities
- main resources and input

Exercise 2.2 (End-to-End Processes) Please, examine the end-to-end processes provided in Fig. 2.24 and determine for each of them:

1. *trigger* starting the process
2. *result* being the value add provided by each E2E process

Exercise 2.3 (Processes of a University) You are the Chief Process Officer (CPO) of the Deakin University and your first task is to create a high-level process map. Identify relevant end-to-end processes of the university and cover at least the following topics:

1. Defining and executing the strategy
2. Hiring staff (academic and administrative)
3. Developing new subjects for studying
4. Scheduling courses for a trimester
5. Executing a course within a trimester
6. Performing examinations

Describe each process by around five major steps.

Exercise 2.4 (Capability Map of a Logistics Company) Given is the business capability map of a parcel logistics company in Fig. 2.25.

1. Study it carefully and try to identify at least three missing capabilities.
2. Classify each capability on top level as cororate, core or support capability.

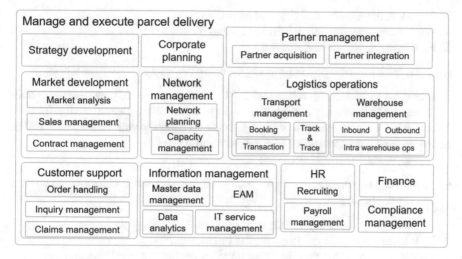

Fig. 2.25 Example capability map: parcel logistics company

3. Provide a written description for each capability based on your knowledge of the parcel logistics industry.

Exercise 2.5 (Capabilities of a University) You are the Chief Process Officer (CPO) of the Deakin University and are now tasked to create a capability map of the university. You should address the task in the following way:

1. Create a first draft of your map
2. Identify relevant sources for capabilities
3. Refine your draft based on your sources

Create a capability map with exactly two levels (meaning having several capabilities that are further decomposed into sub-capabilities).

Exercise 2.6 (Business Objects and Capabilities) Your line manager is getting confused with the concepts of *business object* and *business capability*. Please, explain in your own words major differences between the two of them. Your explanation needs to include:

1. characterisation of each term
2. examples illustrating differences
3. purpose of either of them

Exercise 2.7 (Business Objects of a University) You are the Chief Process Officer (CPO) of the Deakin University and you are tasked to create a high-level business object model. Identify relevant business objects of the university and cover at least the following domains:

1. University management and strategy
2. Managing human resources (academic and administrative)

3. Course management, studying and examinations
4. Performing research and publishing research results
5. Facility management and finance

Describe each business object properly by using complete English sentences.

Exercise 2.8 (Vision, Objectives and KPI) You are about to found a new consulting company in the supply chain business. In order to have a clear direction for your customers and employees, you should provide a vision for your business as well as objectives and corresponding KPI for determining your success.

Please, write down the following:

- *Vision* for providing guidance to your staff but also tell prospective customers about your business.

  1. What are you aiming at with your business?
  2. Why are you different from similar businesses?
  3. Which impact will your business have on the environment and society?

- *Objectives*, showing what you want to achieve within the next year
- *KPI* for measuring whether you achieved the objectives

References

1. M. Dumas, M. La Rosa, J. Mendling, H.A. Reijers, *Fundamentals of Business Process Management*, 2nd edn. (Springer Berlin, Berlin, 2018)
2. J. Liker, *The Toyota Way, 14 Management Principles from the World's Greatest Manufacturer* (McGraw-Hill Education, 2004)
3. R. Whittle, C. Myrik, *Enterprise Business Architecure, The Formal Link between Strategy and Results* (Auerbach Publications, 2005)
4. M. Hammer, J. Champy, *Reengineering the Corporation: A Manifesto for Business Revolution*, updated edition, ser. Collins Business Essentials (Harper Business, 2006)
5. R. Burlton, *Developing your capability architecture: It's all about being able to get things done*, 2017. [Online]. Available: https://www.bptrends.com/essentials-of-business-architecture-developing-your-capability-architecture-its-all-about-being-able-to-get-things-done/ (visited on 03/12/2021).
6. P.A. Khosroshahi, M. Hauder, S. Volkert, F. Matthes, M. Gernegroß, Business capability maps: Current practices and use cases for enterprise architecture management, ed. by T. Bui, ser. in *Proceedings of the Annual Hawaii International Conference on System Sciences, Hawaii International Conference on System Sciences* (2018)
7. M. Wißotzki, *Capability Management Guide, Method Support for Enterprise Architectures Management* (Springer Vieweg, 2018)
8. P.A. Khosroshahi, Using business capability maps for application portfolio complexity management, Doctoral Dissertation, Technische Universiät München, München, 2018
9. Business Architecture Guild (ed.), *A Guide to the Business Architecture Body of Knowledge, BIZBOK® Guide*, V 8.5. Business Architecture Guild, 2020
10. P. Desfray, G. Raymond, *Modeling Enterprise Architecture with TOGAF, A Practical Guide Using UML and BPMN* (Morgan Kaufmann, 2014)
11. J. McGovern, S.W. Ambler, M.E. Stevens, J. Linn, V. Sharan, E.K. Jo, *A Practical Guide to Enterprise Architecture*, ser. The Coad Series (Prentice Hall, 2004)

12. D. Simon, Introduction, Demystifying business architecture, in *Business Architecture Management: Architecting the Business for Consistency and Alignment*, ser. Management for Professionals, ch. 1 (Springer International Publishing, 2015), pp. 1–17
13. D. Simon, C. Schmidt, *Business Architecture Management: Architecting the Business for Consistency and Alignment*, ser. Management for Professionals (Springer International Publishing, 2015)
14. A. Sharp, P. McDermott, *Workflow Modeling: Tools for Process Improvement and Application Development*, 2nd edn. (Artech House, 2008). ISBN: 978-1596931923
15. W. Kuehne, S. Marshall, A. Randell, D. St. George, W. Ulrich, *The Business Architecture Quick Guide: A Brief Guide for Game Changers*. Business Architecture Guild, Ed. (Meghan-Kiffer Press, 2017)
16. TOGAF Business Architecture Work Stream, Business capabilities. The Open Group, Tech. Rep., Jun. 20, 2018

Chapter 3
Developing Application Architecture

The previous chapters introduce the notion of EA and architecture management (Chap. 1) as well as the business architecture (Chap. 2), which deals with providing mechanisms for describing the business. This chapter will have a look at the application architecture. We basically deal with concepts for describing applications, which information about applications are quite relevant, and how applications belong to business capabilities.

Learning Objectives

After completing this chapter, you will be able to . . .

- . . . explain the relationships between business and application architecture
- . . . create an application landscape
- . . . classify and document interactions between applications
- . . . explain the notion of data architecture

The learning objectives are given above. After finishing this chapter, you should be capable of explaining the relationship between business architecture on one side and application architecture on the other. We will basically focus on the relationships between applications and business capabilities. Section 3.2 will further present a method for deriving an ideal application landscape from the business capability map. You will also learn how to create an application landscape for a company. This will be drawing a map showing all the applications of an organisation, including their relationships. These relationships are not anonymous but can be of certain types. We will use data flows and services for describing interactions between applications. You will be capable of identifying them and also classifying interactions according to those types. Section 3.4 introduces the notion of *data architecture* as being part of an EA. It will base on the business object model

© The Author(s), under exclusive license to Springer Nature Switzerland AG 2021
J. Jung, B. Fraunholz, *Masterclass Enterprise Architecture Management*,
https://doi.org/10.1007/978-3-030-78495-9_3

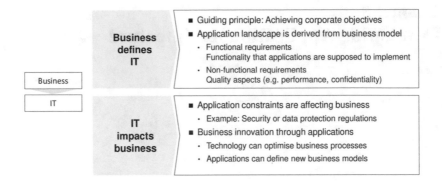

Fig. 3.1 Business-driven IT

introduced in the previous chapter (Sects. 2.3 and 3.4 cover more implementation specific data models).

3.1 Application Architecture

Let us reiterate, what EAM is all about as depicted in Fig. 3.1. As emphasised in Chap. 1, we want to derive our application landscape from business needs on a holistic basis. We want to understand the business needs so that we can define the IT landscape—more specific: the applications—required for supporting our business. The basic direction so far was from top understanding the business to bottom we define the IT. Nevertheless, we should always keep in mind that software systems and innovations in IT can also influence the business. For example, by introducing a process-based system, we can automate our business processes. There will be less manual work which will impact the work people are supposed to do.

We will see in Chap. 4 that any kind of change in the application landscape will have an impact on the business side. The direction from top to bottom for us will be the driver. The requirements from the top will drive how IT needs to change or needs to behave. But at the same time, we are always aware of the fact that IT will have an impact on the business side.

The basic artefact discussed in this section is the *application architecture* as defined by Definition 3.1. Sometimes it is also referred to as *application layer* as already introduced in Sect. 1.4 while describing the three-layered structure for EA. It encompasses all software applications of an organisation together with their relationships—interfaces between applications and relationship to the business context. We will not discuss applications as a means on their own, but keep their value for business in mind.

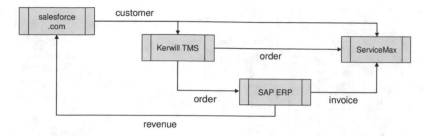

Fig. 3.2 Example application landscape with data flow

Definition 3.1 (Application Architecture)   The application architecture (also referred to as application layer) encompasses all software applications of an organisation together with:

- relationship to the business architecture
- interfaces between applications

Chapter 1 already introduced typical EA maps as for example, process maps for showing business processes. There is the so-called application landscape, which is a map showing the application architecture, including all the relationships, and including certain data that is required for managing applications. We will now use these maps for explaining application landscapes by example.

The example in Fig. 3.2 shows an application landscape consisting of four systems exchanging data. Data is represented by business objects assigned to lines between applications. The arrow head at the end of each line indicates the direction of the data flow. It is the same kind of business objects we introduced in Sect. 2.3 as part of the business architecture. There are business objects **customer**, **order**, **invoice** and **revenue**.[1] Business objects have special meaning and relevance for business people, but can also be used for describing information flows between applications. In this case, the customer relationship management system called *salesforce.com* provides customer data, represented by the business object customer, to a transport management system and a customer service system.

I am sure you also remember the map in Fig. 3.3 as it is one of the examples from Sect. 1.3. It shows applications assigned to individual organisational units (i.e. application is used by an organisational unit). We have three organisational units. One is representing the global headquarters and we have subsidiaries in the two regions Europe and Asia-Pacific. The map can be used for getting an overview on applications used in various organisational units. They might share common software systems but there might also be clear redundancies. If subsidiaries are allowed to procure their own IT, this usually leads to huge amount of individual

---

[1]Customer, order and invoice have already been introduced before. *Revenue* represents the income of a company.

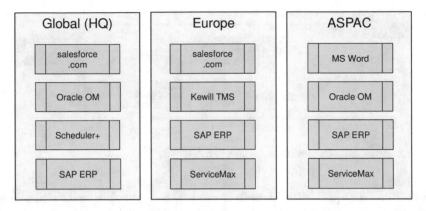

Fig. 3.3 Application landscape—Example context

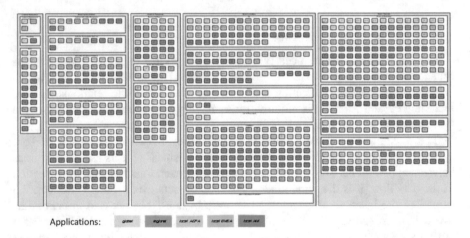

Fig. 3.4 Example application landscape

software.[2] The map in Fig. 3.3 can be created easily—manually or by an EA tool. Applications located within the box representing an organisational unit then this organisational unit is using this application.

We should not forget that real-world application landscapes tend to be large[3] and complex.[4] Even though most of the examples in this textbook are rather small, they are only focusing on showing you the concepts and how to use the concepts. They

---

[2]We should not forget the vessel in Fig. 1.6 on page 11. Having no strict Governance on IT can result in a plethora of (redundant) systems and, therefore, increase IT budgets.

[3]Corporate application landscapes can have a couple of hundred or more than thousand software applications.

[4]Each application is potentially connected to several others, resulting in thousand of interfaces.

are far away from the size of real-world maps and this is why we are using the map in Fig. 3.4 again.

It is showing applications (represented by the small coloured rectangles) mapped against business capabilities(grey and rectangular white areas as the background). You can also see the strengths of having structured maps. You can already get an overview on the functional distribution of applications. There are capabilities with many applications while others are only supported by a single one. If you have an additional colour coding, as provided here, you can even show some more information. The example here is showing whether it is a legacy application, a global application, specific for a region, or if it is only needed for certain products.

And in fact, this is an application landscape that was the result of a project. And this application landscape, you could see in each office of each of the top management people. They were using it as an overview for having an indication about the complex IT they are managing. During that time, the poster was showing the current situation, hence, it was an *as-is* application architecture. The same kind of visualisation can also be applied for showing how the application architecture should look like in the future. This is then called *to-be*. In the following section, we will introduce a method that will help with defining an ideal application landscape. It does not involve the as-is architecture but aims at deriving applications from business capabilities. Therefore, the relationship between capabilities and applications will be shown, following the direction *business drives IT*.

3.2 Deriving the Application Landscape from Capabilities

The focus of the notion of EA within this textbook is on business-IT alignment. We want to understand how to implement an IT landscape that will support the business adequately. The concept of business capabilities has been introduced as one of the key concepts on how to describe—and understand—the business part of the company (cf. Sect. 2.2). We will now further elaborate on how an *ideal application landscape* should look like.

This ideal landscape will be derived from the business capabilities. The method presented here will not incorporate any existing applications but derive the applications from the business capability map only. This might look a bit unrealistic as companies usually have an application landscape in place. However, the method here aims at . . .

- . . . creating an ideal state that can also be used as the long-term to-be architecture.
- . . . demonstrating how decisions on applications can be made just based on business needs.

The simple example in Fig. 3.5 illustrates the example of what the method is aiming at. The map shows four business capabilities we already used in previous sections. It contains **Market development** with all the marketing activities, **Logistics operations** for planning transports and moving parcels, **Supplier management**

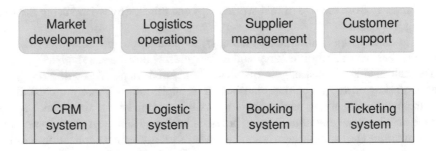

Fig. 3.5 Example capabilities and applications

for monitoring and controlling external partners, and the **Customer support** capability. This is a common map for showing the links between capabilities and aplications, showing the capabilities on top and supporting applications directly below each of them. A **CRM system** supporting marketing development, our **Logistics system** supporting logistics management, **Booking system** for supplier management, and a **Ticketing system** for customer support.

The map looks very straight forward as we have a dedicated system for each business capability. There are no redundancies or overlaps and each application has a distinct set of functionality.[5] Furthermore, each capability is supported by an application so that we are not experiencing any gaps in the application landscape. This example illustrated what we would expect from a method for deriving an ideal application landscape from business capabilities.

There are two drivers for an ideal application landscape for supporting business capabilities:

1. each automated capability is supported by a corrcsponding software application
2. avoid redundant applications for individual capabilities

The first one ensures that we are *effectively* supporting the business with applications. We do not miss any automation potential and provide quality systems for the company. The second driver enforces **efficiency** for application support. We are reducing run cost by avoiding redundant systems. We want to support making a conscious decision on how a minimal application landscape should look like—minimal with respect to minimising cost—but still making sure that all the automated capabilities are supported by IT.

---

[5]Needless to say, that such a map is rather the exception as real architectures are much larger and contain a lot of issues.

Application Architecture – Development

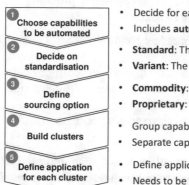

- Decide for each capability if it can to be automated by IT
- Includes **automation potential**

- **Standard**: The capability is the same for the whole company
- **Variant**: The capability can differ amongst business units

- **Commodity**: The capability is very common
- **Proprietary**: The capability is specific for the own business

- Group capabilities that are highly coupled
- Separate capabilities with only a few relationships

- Define applications based on clusters
- Needs to be aligned with available systems

Fig. 3.6 Developing an application architecture (overview)

3.2.1   Method Overview

The method presented here is not a standard methodology from a textbook. It has been developed in the context of an international logistics corporation. The company has a large IT department and can also develop software for core processes. An overview on the method is shown in Fig. 3.6 and will be explained here. Subsequent sections then have a spot on the details of some of the activities.

It starts with a complete business capability map of the organisation. The first step is to determine all capabilities that will have to be supported by IT applications (step 1 in Fig. 3.6). There is no general rule for such a decision as each organisation is different. This decision needs to be made together by business and IT people and has to be aligned with corporate strategy. Application support does not mean that the capability is fully automated but only that applications are required—among other resources.

First step: Assess for each capability if it needs application support or not.

After we made this decision on automation for each and every capability the next step will address standardisation (i.e. standard software for the whole company) as shown in step 2 in Fig. 3.6. It will be decided upon the answers to the following questions:

- Is the capability the same all over the company?
- Is the capability the same, independent of the corresponding country, organisational units or product?
- Is the capability always associated with the same business objects as input and output?

It is basically about making the decision whether we should prefer to have only one standard system. Benefits of a standard system as opposed to providing various redundant systems for the same capability are as follows:

- Reduced run cost (e.g. hosting, support, incident handling) as only one system needs to be supported
- Standardised training material and user trainings throughout the organisation
- New requirements only need to be incorporated into one software application instead of several ones
- Single source for all information related to the capability instead of data being spread over several applications

However, a standard system might not be sufficient for supporting the whole corporation. There might be legal requirements or physical restriction that require a differing application support for a single capability. This can be illustrated by some examples:

- Each country has legal requirements of its own for customs processing. This can not be provided by a single system globally but requires individual systems in each country.
- Automation of mail sorting differs between letters and parcels. Different software will be required for each.
- Payroll management has to follow local legislation so that country-specific systems will be required.
- Industry-specific compliance rules can impose special rules for different products.
- Different business partners may request for different systems for e-business integration (different formats and protocols)

An example for the last bullet point is a logistics company. They are doing bookings with external transport service providers. There might be two different systems necessary; one for airfreight bookings for interacting with the airlines and another system being responsible for making bookings with ocean lines The capability *Booking management* is the same but there are some differences. Especially the standards for interacting with airlines are different from the ones interacting with ocean freight carriers.

Second step: Go for a standard system unless there are relevant business reasons.

The next step (step 3 in Fig. 3.6) will consist of a make-or-buy decision. This step is only valid for organisations that have skills and capacity for developing a system on their own. If this is not the case, then it can be skipped. However, large corporations usually have their own development teams or can manage the development of custom-built systems together with external software development partners.

Buying a standard software system is usually a more cost-efficient option compared to a complete new development. Let us assume that most companies are trying to reduce IT-related cost, so that buying is supposed to be the preferred option—

even with own development capacities. A CRM system is, for example, a standard software system and there are many products available on the market, fulfilling requirements of different kinds of companies. Sales and marketing activities are very much standardised in the way how they are performed all over the industries. Consequently, there might not be a strong need for having a completely different customer relationship management systems. We are going for the standard by introducing a commodity system. You know the cost for it, and you know what the system can provide and also what it is not providing.

However, there are some capabilities that have an outstanding business relevance: business capabilities that make a difference between us and the competition, different industries or companies. There might be no system available, or we want to have a better system for this capability because this is a differentiator for us from the competition.

Developing a system on your own is more expensive than buying a commodity. You need to have software development skills and competencies. You need to manage the requirements. You have to manage risk during development because the development project might fail or being out of scope or not achieving the objectives as expected. In order to make a make-or-buy decision, you need to find a balance between business relevance on one side (make) as well as cost and risk on the other side (buy). If you need more flexibility or if you want to be different, developing your own system will accrue more cost and will also be some risk. But we will then have the benefit of a unique system that helps us with differentiating from your competition.

Third step: Software applications should be acquired on the market unless there is a clear business reason for having a unique system.

At the current stage we made decisions on which capabilities to support with IT. For those to be supported we decide whether we are going for a corporate standard system or allow for local variations. We might need different systems for a single capability in certain cases. We also made a decision on either buying or making the system. After making those decisions we should check if there are clusters of similar decisions (step 4 in Fig. 3.6). There should be capabilities that belong together because we made similar decisions or because they are very similar from a functional/data perspective.

One example might be marketing, sales and customer service capabilities. Even though they are three distinct capabilities, they are still closely related because marketing is generating all the contracts that are required for sales. Sales can be tightly coupled with customer service as they both interact with customers. They share a common business object: *customer*. And while sales is focusing on generating new orders, customer service is dealing with supporting the customer after or while buying a product. Both are working on the same kind of data, the customer accounts, they both need the same kind of information.[6] In today's world many CRM systems combine marketing, sales and customer service functionality.

The same usually holds true for other capabilities. Transport management, logistics operations and booking are closely related to each other because they are working with the same kind of business objects. We can make decisions on capabilities that relate to each other that build a group that cannot be easily separated from a business perspective. Each groups of related capabilities will build a cluster.

Fourth step: Build clusters of capabilities based on:

- same decisions made during previous steps
- related functions
- shared business objects

Decisions on potential software applications for each cluster will be made during step 5:

1. Each cluster with standard capabilities will be supported by a single application.
2. Each cluster allowing for local variants can have several applications of the same type.

The resulting application landscape can consist of concrete applications (e.g. *salesforce.com*) or application types instead of specific product names (e.g. *Customer Relationship Management*). An example landscape is shown in Fig. 3.10 on page 89. Before discussing it, we will have a look at three of the activities here. Let us start with step number two, the decision on the standardisation of applications.

3.2.2 Standardisation

Driven by the idea of cost reduction for the application landscape, we aim at reducing the number of systems and reducing the complexity of the whole landscape. The driving factor is in getting rid of systems for many IT organisations. One option is having one standard system for the whole corporation. This is not easy to achieve as software applications are directly connected with business processes and, therefore, are used for generating value. Please, remember the complexity of the IT landscape after a merger, having a company that has been merged by buying several other companies. This might lead to the fact that we have redundant CRM systems or systems for payroll management.

One indication for a standard system might be if this is a system that requires collaboration throughout all organisational units. Whenever those indications are given, then the recommendation for the application would be: implementing one central application. You can imagine the saving potential if we decide for a stan-

---

[6]The decisions should be made on business objects. We refer to data as business objects as it represents business data on a high level. We will further elaborate on this in Sect. 3.4.

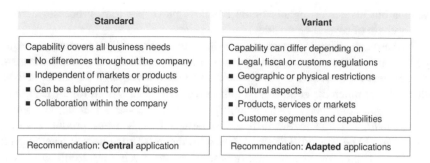

Standard	Variant
Capability covers all business needs ■ No differences throughout the company ■ Independent of markets or products ■ Can be a blueprint for new business ■ Collaboration within the company	Capability can differ depending on ■ Legal, fiscal or customs regulations ■ Geographic or physical restrictions ■ Cultural aspects ■ Products, services or markets ■ Customer segments and capabilities
Recommendation: **Central** application	Recommendation: **Adapted** applications

Fig. 3.7 Application architecture: Standardisation

dardised CRM system. Unless there is a relevant business reason, an organisation should introduce a system that can be used throughout the whole organisation—especially for those capabilities that . . .

- do not have any differences throughout the company
- are independent of any markets or products
- serve as a blueprint for a new business

Let us take a parcel logistics company as an example. It has a delivery network already in Europe and now wants to establish business in further countries and regions—for example in the Middle East or South-east Asia. Having a standard capability and a related delivery application can be the blueprint for establishing new businesses in these and further regions.

Some criteria that help with making the decision for standard or variants is given in Fig. 3.7. As you will see, there is no black-and-white. Criteria from both sides may apply at the same time. The enterprise architect then needs to make a judgement together with business experts. They need to evaluate which criterion is stronger than others.

We should not forget that there are certain reasons for also allowing variances in local applications. If there are **legal** requirements, *fiscal* requirements, or especially customs regulations that require different systems, then you cannot go for a global standard system. Example international trade and logistics: It is not possible to have one global standard system because the requirements on customs processes are different in each country. You are not even allowed to use a system that has not been certified by the country's customs organisation. Consequently, you cannot introduce a single system, but need to have a system for each country. Such systems are required for submitting customs declarations electronically and support clearance processes with customs organisations.

There might be other restrictions, like **geographic** or **physical** limitations. Further on, cultural differences need to be considered. Keep in mind that *applications systems* also includes user interfaces or customer portals. A global web portal might be adequate for one country, but might not respect cultural aspects of another country. Cultural differences will always influence user interfaces of software systems but also inter-organisational business processes (e.g. processes across a supply chain of several companies).

Furthermore, different **products**, **services**, or serving different **markets** require specific application support. In a logistics company, the software used for logistics management for mail delivery is different from the one required for parcel delivery, which also is much different from a logistics system that is used for air freight and ocean freight containers. Each capability is the same, like for example *Logistics management*, but due to the differences between the various products, various systems might be needed. The same goes with markets. Imagine you want to go for e-business. E-business requires not only that you are having electronic workflows, but also that you have electronic channels for interacting with your partners.

Simple capabilities (e.g. *Order handling*) already have differences between **customer segments**. For example a logistics company providing digital services for creating the shipment labels need different channels depending on private or large corporate customers. The result of such a service is a file containing the shipping label that can be attached to a parcel or container. A private customer only having a parcel once in a while definitely needs a web portal with an HTML user interface. It can be used for entering the shipment data and then get the label as a PDF or any graphic file for printing.

The use case looks much different for large corporate customers, big companies sending hundreds or thousands of parcels every day. They cannot have dedicated employees that enter data into a web portal and then print PDFs. They need a webservice that can be integrated with the customers' IT. It will support sending data for all parcels and then providing the labels as PDF electronically. The capability is the same for both customer segments: *Shipping label provision*. Due to differing levels of technical systems of the customers, the capability cannot be supported by a single label creation system.

Nevertheless, these criteria should be evaluated very carefully. Variances will result in redundant systems and, therefore, lead to higher run budgets and support effort. But an inadequate standard application can hamper the business. Of course, we are looking at this decision from a theory perspective. Having criteria makes it look simple. It will get very complicated when being in a corporate environment and talking to people because they feel very special. They always find a way for telling that they need a different system as the others because they have specific requirements. Therefore, the default should be marking each capability as standard so that it can be supported by a single application. Only if people provide evidence for a variant, then the recommendation will go for variants.

3.2.3   Make-or-Buy

The third step in the methodology, after standardisation, is considering make-or-buy. What is the best option for introducing the application? Is it better to develop an application on our own (because of the business relevance of the capability)? Or

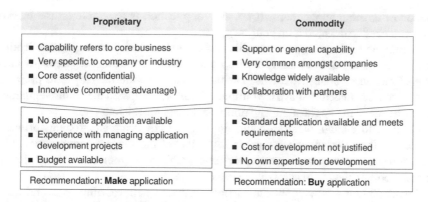

Fig. 3.8   Application architecture: Sourcing

should we just buy a cheaper standard system (in order to minimize expenditures and risk)? The default is *buy*, because it is cheaper. But many business stakeholders will have a saying in this one for pushing for developing a system on our own.

Let us have a look at the criteria summarised in Fig. 3.8. The capability should be considered as proprietary, if it refers to the **core business** (i.e. it is a core capability). Core business means that it is the heart or the core of our value chain. These capabilities directly contribute to revenue generation. Other capabilities (e.g. guiding and supporting) only indirectly contribute to value creation. In a large logistics company, this might be the system for making the route planning—how to transport parcels and containers. The capability is industry specific and the system helps with optimising business performance.

Requirements that are very specific to a company (or an industry) can justify a proprietary application. Some super sorting algorithm for parcel distribution, or for planning our logistics network, can be a **core asset**. They might be unique for the company and significantly improve business performance. A company does not want others to know about it or share it with them.

Developing something very **innovative** (based on artificial intelligence) for the core business (e.g. routing optimisation for network) will provide a competitive advantage. It is not recommended to buy a standard system as it will be available to everyone. A company might also consider developing it internally and not with external development partners as the knowledge is strictly confidential.

I talked to a major airline a while ago and they are thinking of using artificial intelligence (AI) for optimising their network. It is supposed to optimise their schedule and the routing of the fleet. It provides an advantage for being better than others and can optimise business efficiency. From a pure business perspective, this is a core asset and very special to the company. Such a system is not available on the market and would provide a competitive advantage.

The method emphasises a pure business point of view by just looking at the capability and its business relevance. At the same time, one also has to consider the market of existing applications. If no such application is **available** on the market then you need to develop it on your own.

A company also needs to have skills and **experience** with managing application development. It needs to have the implementation workforce. It needs to have project managers being experienced with IT and software development projects. And of course, it needs to have the **budget**. If this is given, then the recommendation would be make the application, and don't try to buy an existing one.

On the other hand, there are valid reasons for procuring an existing software. Especially for a very common commodity. Most of the support commodities (like human resources, finance, IT, customer relationship management) are very similar in many companies, even across industries.

Implementing a new application would compete with existing ones and most probably not be that innovative. Criteria supporting such an option are listed on the right-hand side of Fig. 3.8. We first need to check if the capability common amongst companies. Customer Relationship Management is a well understood function and there are mature solutions available on the market. They are also supported by textbooks on marketing, sales and customer service. There is plenty of research in academia and practice that constantly improves the discipline. Furthermore, the same concepts are applicable for any kind of company or industry. If it is common knowledge provided within this capability, or even if it requires collaboration with partners, then rather think of deciding for an application to be bought on the market.

An application can only be procured if it is available on the market (which holds true for most supporting capabilities) and if it meets requirements. If the effort for development is not justified (because expenditures exceed the benefit by far) or the expertise in development is not available, then rather go for buying an existing application.

Honestly speaking, the world is never black and white. There will never be hard facts for making the decision for either make or buy. It will always be about checking and weighing the criteria, one against each other, prioritising the criteria, and then make that decision. Some criteria are stronger than others. If no system is available on the market, then you don't have any chance. You need to develop it, or if it is too expensive and does not justify the benefit, then there might even be the decision we are not going for an application at all. Developing an application providing a smaller benefit compared to implementation cost, does not make sense.

If you don't have software development expertise you should still consider buying an application—even for core capabilities that are very specific to your company. There are some start-up companies developing software for niche markets that tailor their system to specific customer needs. Such applications are either already configurable or the small company wants to increase their customer base. It will then also spend effort on adding additional functionality that can later be sold to further clients. Instead of buying it, having a partner that can customise an existing software with respect to your needs, can be a good choice. Even though it relates to the core business, and even though it should be a differentiator, you can let the partner develop the application.

Those criteria here should be seen as a rule of thumb that you can keep in mind. They are not hard facts. You always need to have the big picture. And then at the end, make a decision based on all relevant facts.

3.2.4 Clustering

The last step was dealing with building groups of capabilities or building clusters of capabilities. A capability map can be very large by having specialised capabilities and a very deep decomposition level.[7] It is not reasonable to have a software application for each individual capability. Consequently, capabilities need to be grouped so that we reduce the number of applications by only having one per cluster.

Clustering can follow some simple rules:

1. Only automated capabilities are relevant for clustering
2. A top-level capability (or to be more precise: all its automated sub-capabilities) can already be a cluster.
3. A top-level capability cannot mix standard/variant or proprietary/commodity. In this case it needs to be split into two or more clusters for the respective decisions.
4. Top-level capabilities can be clustered if they are similar.
5. Any capability can be a cluster if all its sub-capabilities are similar.
6. Capabilities are similar if ...

   • ...they have similar functions
   • ...work with the same business objects

Clustering is based on similarity which covers the decisions for standard vs. variant and proprietary vs. commodity. You cannot mix them in a cluster as we would then have a conflict for the application. Similarity can also be decided by functionality (which should be the case for a decomposition of one capability) or common business objects. Also the complexity of the application landscape should be considered during clustering. One should, for example, reduce the number of interfaces between applications. Splitting common functionality or business objects across several applications will lead to interfaces for data exchange or service requests (cf. Sect. 3.3).

Applications can be derived from clusters as shown in Fig. 3.9. It does not necessarily mean that you need to have a certain product in mind. You can at least

---

[7]Imagine having a capability map with ten top-level capabilities that are decomposed by two more levels. If each (sub-)capability is in average decomposed into 5 sub-capabilities the we will have around 310 capabilities (10 on level one, 50 on level two and 250 on level three).

Derive applications	Application landscape

• Define a potential application for each capability cluster
• Each automated capability needs to be supported by an application
• There can be several applications for a non-standard capability
 	
➤ Existing or anticipated applications should not drive cluster definition!
	• Application name can be …
	  • … abstract but similar to capability name
	  • … the name of a standard software (in case of commodity)
	  • … the name of an existing system (proprietary)
	• Application has same sourcing option as capability
	• There can be a different sourcing options for each variant

Fig. 3.9 Application architecture: Derive applications

have an abstract name or an application type. It can even have the same name as the capabilities. For customer service, you might decide for example:

1. *salesforce.com* (concrete application)
2. *Customer Service System* (derived from capability name)
3. *Ticketing system* (class of application)

Large companies already have an application landscape in place. If those systems are supposed to be reused, then you can already put it there as a representative. For each application, you need to make sure that they have the same sourcing option as their capability.

If the capability is standard, then you can have one standard application throughout the company. If the sourcing option was *buy* based on the capability, then you can procure the application. In case of the variants, you might have different sourcing options for the same capability. Let's reconsider the example with the customs processing. Some countries have established customs systems available that you can procure on the market. If no such system is available for other countries, you can develop it on your own, even considering selling it later on. But this is a different story.

3.2.5 Resulting Application Landscape

A simple example for showing the result after applying the method is shown in Fig. 3.10. We are not seeing the decisions here, but the result of this method. Those capabilities are on a very high level, we have different systems for market development, which includes marketing and sales, we made the decision we want to have one integrated **CRM system** supporting all our marketing activities, and then also directly drive sales.

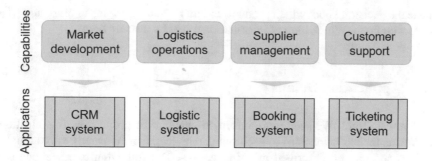

Fig. 3.10 Application architecture: Result

For logistics operations we made the decision we want to have one integrated **Logistics system**. It can be different from the CRM system and operates on different data. We want a different system for the supplier management because we are having systems that are integrated with the systems of our partners. We are not only managing our bookings, but also use the **Booking system** for sending booking data towards our partners, like airlines and ocean freight companies.

The last one is a **Ticketing system** for our customer support. Most probably, for the capability market development we decided on going for a global standard, because we also want to have one repository with all the customer data so that we can use it throughout all our marketing departments globally. Marketing and sales are not that much different across industries, so we can buy an existing CRM system. We did not make the decision on which one yet, but we made the decision we want to have a standard system.

It is different for logistics operations because here, even though systems are available, we can implement better systems that are more suited for our products and our customer segments. It is a differentiator from other competitors. This system will be developed on our own, so it will be a proprietary system and also a global standard system. We are going for an existing booking system because we have several partners and we don't want to implement integration with other partners. We want to have existing systems that already enable us sending booking data to partners. And we can also allow for variance here because there is one system for airlines and another one for ocean lines. The differentiator here are our products. We have airfreight and ocean freight products. They are very different with respect to partner integration. Hence, for the one capability, we need different booking systems. But we can buy them on the market as this functionality is publicly available.

Having those systems is the starting point for developing our application landscape. At the current stage, we used the business capabilities and derived some kind of the best application landscape we can imagine from the business capabilities. Do you think this is enough for talking about applications? Will just having the symbols on the map help us optimising the application landscape? If you say yes, it is enough, then you are too fast. Just consider being the CIO that now needs to make the decision about which products to buy or which systems to reuse and what to do with them. Which kind of information might be missing here?

3.3 Application Details

Yes, you are right. We need more information about the properties of applications as well as their relationships to each other. Applications are usually very complex entities and can be described in various ways. The following two sections will provide an overview on ...

- ...relationships between applications
- ...properties relevant for managing applications

3.3.1 Relationships

While remembering the examples for application landscapes, we know that applications are not only working on their own. Usually, a whole process is supported by several applications and those applications need to work together. An overview on typical relationships is given in Fig. 3.11. One of the previous examples specifies the exchange of business objects between applications.[8] Salesforce.com providers information on customer accounts to the transport management system and also to the ticketing system in Fig. 3.2 on page 75.

Application landscapes are not only about showing a system we own but also the collaboration between applications. In the past years, there was also some hype on service oriented architectures which is now superseded by the notion of micro services. We will not stress this buzzword here.[9] However, the notion of providing services is still a dominant mechanism in today's application landscapes. It encompasses applications *providing* services and others *using* them.

There are some examples on the very right-hand side of Fig. 3.11. The order data being maintained in the order management system will be required for billing, so it will be sent to a billing system. The same can happen with the customer accounts, as already discussed. Any business object can be subject to **data flow** between applications.

---

[8]We will transfer this principle to data objects as well. In the remainder of this section, *data flow* and *exchange of business objects* will be used synonymously.

[9]The service-oriented paradigm is heavily recognised in software development as it fosters reuse of application functionality. There is a popular book about Service-Oriented Architecture (SOA) by Erl [1]. There are several books available on microservice-based architecture, like for example [2].

Relationship	Explanation	Example
General	Two or more applications collaborate in an unspecific way. This relationship might be used instead of data flow or service if details not known.	"uses" or "requires"
Data flow	Data maintained in one application (data provider) is transferred to another (data consumer) for further processing.	Order data from OMS to billing
Service	Functionality is implemented in one application (service provider) and offered as a service. Others (service consumer) use it by invoking the service.	Calculate price

Fig. 3.11 Application relationships (overview)

A **service** represents some self-contained unit of functionality implemented by or within one application. This service can be provided so that other applications can use it. It works similar to a function call in any programming language. A service has a name as well as input (data provided during service invocation) and output parameters (result returned after finishing execution). For example, we can have an electronic product catalogue that helps with calculating prices for a product. The calculation can be based on the amount of ordered products, additional services or further product properties. This kind of service might be required for creating the offer to the customer and later for processing the order. Finally, it will be used by the finance system for generating the invoice. The rules for calculating the price are always the same and it makes sense having a single software system for this service. This functionality will be reused by others. A service can be implemented for exchanging data (i.e. data flow) but also implement functionality for reuse.

Especially during an early stage, while getting an overview on the application landscape, people only know *that* one system works with the other. They are aware of the relationship but do not have enough knowledge for classifying it as a service or data flow. Details are missing very often. But it is important to document the relationship so that we are aware of the connection. In this case, we got the concept of a **general** relationship between applications.

Figure 3.12 presents an application landscape showing data flows between applications. It is very similar to previous examples in this textbook. It represents a customer portal that can be used by our customers for entering order details. The customer order is then transferred to the order management system (data flow **customer order** between the two applications). Order data is then also sent to the billing system. It is a simple description, but still very powerful. It is used in many organisations for showing how applications are working with each other. Integrating e-commerce processes and companies along a supply chain is based on well defined data flows.

This is one of the most important map when describing the application landscape. Yes, this example is simple. But let us always keep in mind, maps of real world

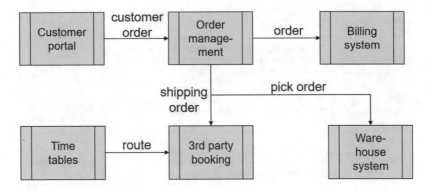

Fig. 3.12 Example: Data flow

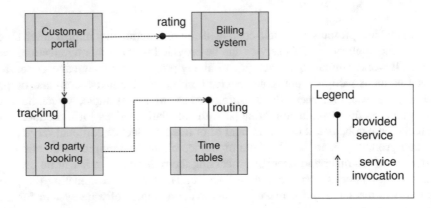

Fig. 3.13 Service-oriented relationships

companies are much larger and complex. They are not only having six systems, but a couple of hundred, or even more than a thousand software applications. Understanding how they relate to each other can only be done with a good overview map. The map can also be considered as *best practise* visualisation for showing how applications work with each other.

The notion of service provisioning might sound a little bit abstract. We want to explain it with a quick example in Fig. 3.13. The application landscape has a **Billing system** which provides the **rating** service for other applications. This service is supposed to calculate the rate (i.e. the price) of a product. Other applications, like the customer portal, can use the rating functionality by just invoking the service.

Imagine the customer entering the new order in the customer portal. This portal shows all relevant information for the product and also automatically calculates the price by just using the rating service of the billing system. The functionality for price calculations is only implemented in the billing system and not in the customer portal. The rating service can also be used by other systems, like the order management system or the customer relationship management system. The benefit of having those services is economies of scale: You implement them once and then they can be reused by other applications.

There are two more services

1. **tracking** service in the **3rd party booking** system
2. **routing** service in the **Time tables** system

Monitoring logistics flows requires an overview on the status of each shipment. Status information is generated whenever a certain activity[10] has been performed on a shipment or it has been handed over between logistics partners. A logistics company provides those *track events* by itself but also receives them from their logistics partners.

Parcel logistics companies need to receive tracking information, for example, from the airline. Did the plane with the parcel (or the container with all my parcels) already arrive at the destination? Did the shipment pass customs? Are there any delays? Instead of implementing tracking functionality in each system, we can implement it once in a single system (in this case the third-party booking system). It can then be reused by the customer portal so that the customer can track the status of the booking. The service can also be used by logistics management systems or order management systems (not shown in Fig. 3.13).

The **routing** service is implemented in the **Time tables** application. This service calculates the optimal routing for a new shipment based on available capacity and cost. Routing is one of the core capabilities of a logistics company. It aims at minimising the cost for shipment by evaluating different options for moving a shipment from A to B. Those options can compare direct flights with multi-stops or rates from different airlines. The service is only used by the 3rd party booking system in this example but can also be offered to further applications. It can support network optimisation, order management and order execution.

3.3.2   Properties

Let us now get a little bit more specific about what kind of information is needed for assessing the application landscape. It will be required for the following two scenarios:

- *as-is analysis* is about understanding the current application landscape. We need data that will help with identifying and documenting current issues. This will be the starting point for optimising the application landscape.[11]

---

[10]Example activities are: export processing finalised, customs clearance done, shipment sent to destination country, shipment on hold.

[11]Transforming the application landscape will be further discussed in Sect. 5.1.

- *to-be planning* will provide a map describing the future state of the application landscape. It is supposed to be *better* than the as-is, hence, we need criteria for comparing as-is with to-be.

There are two kinds of information that are relevant for the analysis of application landscape as provided in Fig. 3.14. First of all, we need to know the cost associated with existing (or planned future) application systems. This will cover on-time and periodic fixed cost for implementation and provisioning. Maintenance generates periodic variable costs for bug fixing and system updates based on new requirements. Costs are the key concern for most IT organisations as discussed in Sect. 1.1 (visualised by Fig. 1.6). Especially when facing an application landscape that has been growing in an uncontrolled way, people need to consider how to reduce the number of applications (and complexity). After identifying redundant software applications, the IT department needs to make a decision on how to consolidate them. Is it a good idea to keep the cheapest one and decommission the other ones?

Most probably not as you need to consider application quality during such a decision. This can be addressed by the following questions:

- What is the technical implementation platform of an application? Out-dated implementation environments can result in increased maintenance cost in the future. It is recommended to switch off applications on legacy infrastructure (e.g. mainframe computer) instead of modern server systems. This is referred to as **technical fitness**.
- How well does the application fit into your overall architecture? The implementation of applications in an organisation should follow the same principles (**architectural fit**). The structure of the application landscape should also fit to business processes.
- Can it easily exchange data with other applications or do we need a dedicated data translation system? This is a common symptom for an architectural mismatch. Value-add along end-to-end business processes requires a seamless flow of data. Translations can hamper this flow by information loss or inconsistencies during data exchange.

Fig. 3.14 Application properties

- How well is an application supporting the business? All business capabilities should be fully supported by software applications. Applications should help with performing business processes in an optimal way (**business fit**).
- How well is the application contributing to the corporate strategy? The prioritisation of software applications also needs to consider their **strategic relevance**. However, the strategic relevance of an application is usually determined by the capabilities it supports.[12] The strategic relevance does not only consider immediate effects but also investments into future business opportunities.

The properties from Fig. 3.14 can be taken into consideration when assessing existing applications and a complete application architecture. They help with making decisions based on hard facts like reducing cost or increasing quality. Beside the complexity reduction mentioned above, they can also substantiate a decision on an investment—including the replacement of an existing application.

Example 3.1 (CRM Replacement) We have a CRM system, but users are complaining about it. It is buggy and makes the work of customer service very cumbersome. It is also quite old and does not serve all the business requirements. The sales and marketing heads ask for a replacement but you have to provide the information for a making conscious decision.

Your first investigation starts with determining cost:

- What are the costs associated with the existing CRM system? (provisioning and maintenance)
- How much do we need to pay for implementing the new system? (either make or buy)
- What will be the run costs of the new system compared to the old one?
- Will we have less maintenance cost with the new one, compared to the old system?
- How much do we need to pay for shutting down the old system?

These are only a few example questions for a pure cost-related comparison between *keeping the existing system* or *introducing a new CRM application*. However, this is not only a cost-centric decision. You also need to consider quality attributes:

- Technical fitness of the new system should be better than the old one in order to solve one of the biggest pain points.
- The new CRM system needs to fit to the corporate application landscape.

(continued)

---

[12]Applications—as any resource—do not have a business relevance. Their relevance is decided by the business they are supporting as only value-add provides result in a corporate environment.

Example 3.1 (continued)
- Business support should be improved due to less frictions caused by insufficient IT.

The quality attributes can be applied for assessing one CRM system and also the comparison between several options. For example: Is salesforce.com better suited for us because it is a cloud solution? Would Oracle (or another customer relationship management system) be a better option as it will be hosted by us? And we also need to have technical support for the new application. At the same time, does salesforce.com really support our business processes better than Oracle?

All these information will influence your decision on changes on your application landscape. Therefore, it information needs to be collected and maintained for each and every application. Maintaining a repository with application data will be further discussed in Sect. 5.2 when describing the role of the enterprise architect.

Figure 3.15 provides some more detail on quality attributes of applications. Technical fitness is a view on the architecture and implementation of an individual software system:

- Is it an old system based on mainframes, or is it implemented using modern technologies?
- Or did we use modern web frameworks or user interface frameworks?
- Does it follow a holistic architecture?

The better the maintainability of a system, the higher the **technical fitness** will be. If the application only has a few bug reports and only requires a very few technical changes, then the technical fitness might be higher. This is something you can even measure for existing applications. You can check bug reports or incident

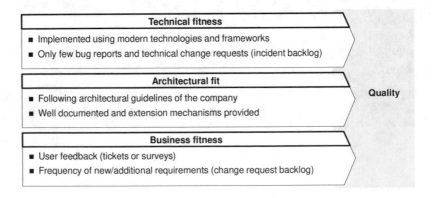

Fig. 3.15 Quality aspects

logs for applications. The number of incidents negatively affects the technical fitness (more incidents usually implies less technical fitness).

The **architectural fit** does not only look at the system (i.e. its technical implementation) but its integration with other applications. Does the application follow architectural guidelines that have been provided by the companies, or does it follow the rules provided by EA? If yes, it fits our architectural vision. At the same time, we also need to make sure that the software and its interfaces are well documented. Documentation will be required later on for any kind of maintenance activity (extension of integration). The better the documentation, and also the architectural quality, the better the architectural fit can be assessed.

Business fitness measures how well the application supports the business. Sometimes this is not easy to assess because different people can assess the quality differently. Some people might prefer a Windows-based user interface while others still prefer the old mainframe style with keyboard short-cuts. These users can be more efficient with entering data in the old mainframe-style than with mixed mouse and keyboard interactions. However, such an assessment can be subjective. There are some criteria that can help with measuring the business fitness of a system.

- *Survey*: First of all, we might conduct a survey concerning business fitness. We ask people how well the application supports their activities. A survey does not only address individuals but can be performed with many people.
- *Number of tickets*: The more business users are complaining about a software system, the worse the technical fitness might be. Furthermore, if the business fit is high, then we should expect that people are not complaining or opening less tickets with respect to a certain application.
- *Change frequency*: The more changes are required by business stakeholders for a specific application, the less it supports current requirements. Otherwise, they would not request the requirements.

In summary, a huge backlog of change requests is an indication (or a measure) for assessing the business fit. If the application is properly supporting the business, users would not open many tickets, and they would not have many change requests. The other way around, if you have a lot of tickets and change requests, then you should investigate further. The number of tickets and change requests can be a measure for poor business fit. However, this assumption can be wrong. Many change request might also be the result of the popularity of an application. Users might like it and, therefore, extend it with further functionality.

That's it so far about the core concept and the core information we need about application landscapes or concepts that we need to describe application landscapes. Most important, we have the application itself. We have relationships between applications, which might be data flows or services being used or just general relationships without further specification. We also need data about applications. Collecting data is quite tedious but required for doing analysis to make decisions on optimising application landscapes.

Concept	Description
Application system	Group of applications that needs to be used together (e.g. server system and different clients).
Application component	Part of an application offering an exposed functionality (e.g. interface to other applications)
Data object	Data in applications and data flows (more detailed than business object)

Fig. 3.16 Additional application concepts

3.3.3   Further Application Concepts

There is not much more to add to application landscape, except a few additional concepts, shown in Fig. 3.16. We will briefly present them here so that you are aware of them. Some EAM tools may require them. They will not be required in the remainder of this textbook.

Some tools provide concepts for **application systems**, which is a group of applications that relate to each other. SAP is, for example, such an application system, consisting of several applications. It encompasses an Enterprise Resource Planning (ERP) module, Transportation Management (TM), Customer Relationship Management (CRM) and some more. They build a whole software system working together.

There is another abstraction called the **application component**. An application can be further devided into several modules or components. This provides a more fine-grained description of functionalities implemented by such an application. A logistics management application can, for example, consist of a module for planning the bookings, for transmitting bookings to partners, and also for monitoring the transports. The application consists of three components. Even having interfaces to other applications might justify a dedicated component.

We will now have a look at the topic of data objects. When talking about the application architecture, people also relate it very often to data objects. And in fact, our examples for the application landscape already indicated that we have data flows between applications. And for describing those, we need the notion of a **data object**.

3.4   Data Architecture

I would like to remember the levelling scheme of EA as introduced in Sect. 1.4. Figure 1.20 shows the three-layered structure for EA, consisting of

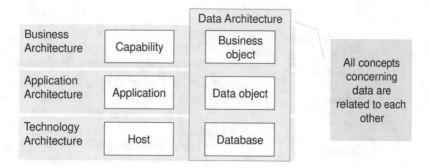

Fig. 3.17 Data architecture as cross-cutting view

- *Business architecture*: introducing business processes, capabilities, business objects and further business-related concepts.
- *Application architecture*: consisting of applications and their relationships.
- *Technical architecture*: will not be covered in this textbook.

We did not talk that much about data but only business objects. It was already stated that business objects can be a starting point for deriving data models for applications and software development. Some frameworks use the notion of the *data architecture*. We will not change the three-layered approach here by adding another layer. We will rather explain, how the notion of data fits into the current model.

Whenever we see, read or hear the term data architecture, we should keep in mind it refers to data on various level of detail in our enterprise as shown in Fig. 3.17. In this sense, the business object relates to the data architecture. It is the business view on the data represented by business objects. On application architecture, we also have a view on data, which is represented by data objects. Data objects represent data that is stored in applications and exchanged between applications. And going further downwards on the levels, we have the database as a representation of business objects in the technology layer.

We will not follow the notion of data architecture that much in the course of this textbook. We just introduced it here for showing the term also exists. Sometimes people interpret it differently. In our case, if we think of data and data architecture, it is a separate dimension over the layers. We already had concepts for representing data on the level of abstraction for each level. Namely, business object as the business architecture representation of data. Data objects are a more detailed view in the application architecture. The next level is considering the implementation of the technology. This comprises installing concrete application system that use databases making data persistent.

These three concepts represent the same kind of information, it is all about data. The difference is in the level of abstraction (Fig. 3.18). While the business objects are on a high level (business level), we only think of the most important terms that are relevant for the business. They are reflected by a name and can have a description in natural language (like a glossary). They can also already contain properties

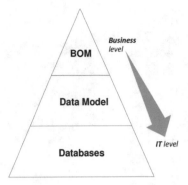

Fig. 3.18 Levels of abstraction of data

defining concrete information contained in that object. A business object model (BOM) shows relationships between them, and is usually driven by the terminology used by the business.

The business object model can be the starting point for an application-specific data model. A data model is a very common tool during software development, helping the software engineers, designing and implementing the software system. Ideally, the data model is not something completely new, but should refer to the business object model by reusing terminology from the business object model. It will define further data objects and provide more details on attributes and relationships between data objects.

If business people are talking about bookings, then there's no need for having an abstract name in the data model, something like XYZ5. Even if it is nicer for the programmers, it is not really helpful if business stakeholders do not recognise business concepts. The data model should link back to the business object model by reusing the terminology introduced by the business objects. There will be more data types as well. Defining the data model for the application, we need to introduce new data that is required for implementing the system. Implementation details should not be relevant on a business level.

A concrete database (technology architecture) being implemented in our corporate environment will contain specific information about primary keys, foreign keys, tables for implementing end to end relationships—very specific details that are required for database design. All those details are not required on the business level. Going from the business object model via the data model towards the database will result in more technical details on data objects required for system implementation

3.5 Further Reading

For further reading, there are three titles that I would like to recommend. There are two books available that deal with a language called ArchiMate. The first one by Lankhorst and co-authors, is now available in the fourth edition (the first edition being published already more than 10 years ago). It is very motivating and describes the basics of the ArchiMate modelling language, which is quite popular for describing EA. It offers a lot of concepts for modelling applications and application landscapes. Whoever needs to have an overview and then more details, [3] would be a recommended reading.

There's also some kind of textbook for teaching how to use ArchiMate, also published by a Dutch guy called Gerben Wierda. He has a very detailed book about how to use ArchiMate, how to describe certain architectures using the ArchiMate language and tools [4]. This book provides many examples on how to describe an application architecture and its relationships to the business architecture.

The third one is a blog entry by a German consultant called Stefan Tilkov, who's very popular in the software engineering community, and also in the architecture community. He provided some thoughts on something called a *canonical data model*. Starting from the business object model, we can think of having a standard data model for the whole enterprise. He provides a very critical discussion and comes to the conclusion that we should not aim at having a detailed enterprise-wide data model. If you're interested in this one, there's a discussion on this in the blog provided by Stefan Tilkov [5].

3.6 Summary

That's it for this chapter. It introduced application architecture concepts for describing the application landscape. It basically covered software applications together with their relationships and business context. We also introduced a method for deriving an ideal application landscape from the business capability map. More concepts have been introduced for describing information about software applications and their interfaces (data flow and services). They are required for describing and analysing the as-is application architecture. Analysis will be subject of the next chapter.

We should have an overview on what we covered so far in this book (Fig. 3.19). We started with the introduction into EA and EAM, providing the motivation why we are doing it in Chap. 1. This was followed by two sections describing special architectures. Chapter 2 covers concepts for describing the business architecture with the two core concepts, business capability and business object. Chapter 3 added the perspective on application architecture with the core concepts application and data object. We learned how to derive an ideal application landscape from our business capabilities. Additional information was introduced in order to further describe software applications. The subsequent Chap. 4 called *analysing EA* will address the following topics:

- How can we describe and analyse EA?
- What is the business support matrix and how can it help with improving our EA?
- Which typical problems can be found in an application landscape?

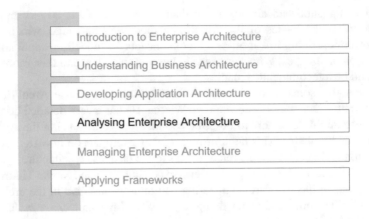

Fig. 3.19 Following next: Analysing enterprise architecture

3.7 Exercises

Exercise 3.1 (Application Interfaces) Please, describe in your own words the difference between *data flow* and *service* relationships between applications.

Exercise 3.2 (Commodity Applications) You are an enterprise architect in a pharmaceutical company. The marketing and sales head wants to replace the legacy Customer Relationship Management (CRM) system by a new one. He wants the IT department to develop a proprietary system so that industry-specific knowledge can be incorporated as well as modern data analytics functionality.

What would you recommend? Should they develop a new system or procure an established one from the market? Please, explain your answer thoroughly!

Exercise 3.3 (Standard Applications) You are an enterprise architect in a international banking corporation having subsidiaries in Australia, New Zealand, United Kingdom, Malaysia and Hong Kong. Your Chief Operations Officer aims at automating compliance and security check by introducing intelligent data analytics systems. As those compliance rules look very complicated, he wants to introduce an individual system for each country organisation.

What would you recommend? Should they introduce a global system or individual ones for each country? Please, explain your answer thoroughly!

Exercise 3.4 (Target Application Landscape) You are the Chief Information Officer (CIO) of the Deakin University and are tasked to create a target application landscape for the university.

You should address the task in the following way:

1. Use the capability map as a starting point
2. Identify applications for supporting these capabilities
3. Try to eliminate redundant applications

Create an application landscape with at least twelve applications and the respective capabilities. You should take the business capabilities you already identified as a starting point. Investigate for applications that are required for supporting these capabilities. Try to identify as less applications as possible as we want to keep the application landscape as small as possible.

Exercise 3.5 (Application Landscape Analysis) You are the Chief Information Officer (CIO) of the Deakin University and are tasked to optimize the as-is application landscape for the university.

You should address the task in the following way:

1. Identify potential issues. Keep the purpose of EAM in mind!
2. Determine which kind of information is required for analysing the issues.

List and explain any kind of information you will need about the applications.

Exercise 3.6 (Application Properties) You are an enterprise architect in a company and currently tasked with consolidating data on software applications. You are scheduling and conducting interviews with various IT and business experts in order to collect the data from them. They feel a bit uncomfortable by all your questions and would like to understand the purpose of the data collection. Please, explain in your own words, why the following kinds of data are needed:

1. Licenses and run cost of applications
2. number of users
3. data maintained by the application
4. number of changes and project related to the application
5. business processes or capabilities supported by an application

References

1. T. Erl, *Service-Oriented Architecture, Concepts, Technology, and Design* (Prentice Hall, 2005)
2. M. Amundsen, M. Mclarty, *Microservice Architecture, Aligning Principles, Practices, and Culture* (O'Reilly, 2016)
3. M. Lankhorst, et al., *Enterprise Architecture at Work: Modelling, Communication and Analysis*, 3rd edn.. The Enterprise Engineering Series (Springer, Berlin, Heidelberg, New York, NY, 2013)
4. G. Wierda, *Mastering ArchiMate: A Serious Introduction to the ArchiMate Enterprise Architecture Modeling Language, Version 3.0.1*, Edition III. TC1 (R&A, The Netherlands, 2017)
5. S. Tilkov, *Why You Should Avoid a Canonical Data Model* (2015). [Online]. Available: https://www.innoq.com/en/blog/thoughts-on-a-canonical-data-model (visited on 03/12/2021)

Chapter 4
Analysing Enterprise Architecture

Let us reflect what we learned so far in this textbook. In Chap. 1, we started with an introduction to the topic of EA and EAM and also presented idea goals of the purpose of EA and management. We then took a closer look at concepts for describing the business architecture in Chap. 2. We not only covered business processes, but placed strong emphasis on the notion of *business capability* and *business object*. In the subsequent Chap. 3, we looked at how software applications relate to the business architecture. We derived an ideal application landscape from business capabilities and had a look at additional information required for describing an entire application landscape in a corporate environment.

So far the majority of this book was focused on the descriptive aspect of EA. It contains concepts and maps that assist in developing a picture of the EA of an organisation. The application and analysis of those viewpoints will be introduced in this Chap. 4.

Don't worry. This does not require the application of complex mathematics and mathematical models for fancy analysis. Most of the analysis will be facilitated based on visualisations that you know already from previous chapters. We will extend this by presenting basic principles for new viewpoints. We will introduce one very important tool, the so-called business support matrix. This matrix helps with the analysis of the relationship between IT architectures on one side and the business on the other. After completing this section, the subsequent section called Managing EA will then deal with the role of the enterprise architect and how to set up an organisation so that EAM can be performed within an organisation. We will also have a look at typical activities in EAM.

Learning Objectives

At the completion of this chapter, you will be able to . . .

- . . . explain different kinds of maps for visualising EA
- . . . apply common visualisations for EA

© The Author(s), under exclusive license to Springer Nature Switzerland AG 2021
J. Jung, B. Fraunholz, *Masterclass Enterprise Architecture Management*,
https://doi.org/10.1007/978-3-030-78495-9_4

- ...create a business support matrix based on capabilities and applications
- ...discuss business support based on the business support matrix

---

As per these learning objectives , after completing this section, you will be able to explain different types of maps for visualising EA (cf. Sect. 4.2). You will further understand data required for creating those visualisations. You will gain an overview and able to apply common visualisations that are used in today's EAM disciplines to visualise the architecture, and also, drive decisions within the company.

Furthermore, we will take a look at a very special tool, the so-called *business support matrix* in Sect. 4.3. You will be capable of creating a business support matrix for a given domain. Based on this business support matrix, you should discuss the implications of what you see there. You will identify and discuss typical issues, and consider follow-up actions for solving the issues identified by the business support matrix.

4.1 Objectives of Enterprise Architecture Analysis

Let's start with the general challenge in today's world for an enterprise architect. Many enterprise architects still very much look like those architects building houses and large buildings: walking around with big blueprints depicting architecture and information. I still remember one of my superiors who was walking around with all the blueprints showing them to his boss. He was showing off the work his department did, and explaining what the top executives can now do with these designs to make decisions based on the information shown there.

It is still like that in many organisations. Especially those that introduced a dedicated EA tool will use it for generating the blueprint automatically. One of the most important hardware tools for architects is the large format plotter capable of creating plots for the large format documents that are then distributed. In fact, it often happens that those outputs are used by top executives. You might see some of the posters attached to the wall when entering their office.

Analysing the EA can cover a variety of aspects in an organisation, especially as some people have a very broad interpretation of EA,[1] it might even cover the analysis of business processes and the corporate strategy. However, this textbook follows a narrow perspective by concentrating on business-IT alignment. We will, therefore, restrict analysis to:

1. application architecture
2. the relationship between application and business architecture

---

[1] You still remember the three schools of thought on EA identified by LaPalme et al. in [1]. They are briefly introduced in Sect. 1.3 starting from page 18.

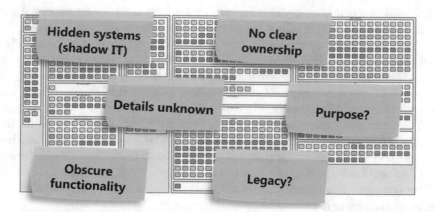

Fig. 4.1 Example issues for EAM

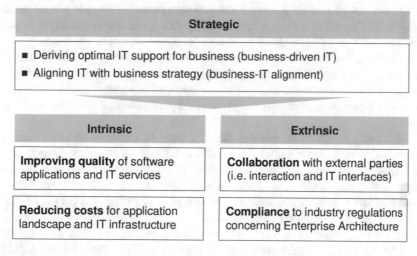

Fig. 4.2 Classification of objectives for EA analysis

We first need to discuss typical objectives that are part of the analysis. Analyse without a clear objective. You should know what you want to achieve with your analysis. It is usually based on some assumptions on existing issues (like for example in Fig. 4.1) that will lead to potential changes. We already presented a couple of objectives in Sect. 1.2, providing examples from current practitioners and decision makers. We will now put them into a structure, a taxonomy for objectives for EAM as shown in Fig. 4.2.

There are **strategic** objectives for applying EAM. This is an executive management decision within the company, because people recognised issues with IT support. We might have operational issues with business processes. Conversely we want to have a holistic approach for optimising our business. Many EA initiatives have been initiated in companies because of a strong need for transparency and business-IT alignment. Within the strategic section, companies want to understand the business so that they can derive their optimal IT support. This is the so-called *business-driven IT* within corporations as it is based on business requirements following a holistic approach. Another objective is making sure that anything we do within IT is properly aligned with the business strategy and business needs—the so-called business IT alignment.

There are also more **operational** objectives for EAM. These can be further categorised into two different types of objectives. One of them is called *intrinsic* because they are driven by the company and provide an immediate benefit. Beside this, we also have *extrinsic* objectives that are externally driven from the context of the company. Examples for these are legal requirements, industry regulations, business partners or markets.

Intrinsic objectives can be classified as either improving the quality or reducing cost. In the case of EAM this refers to improving the quality of software applications and IT services so that they support the business properly. Even if people are not explicitly talking about reducing cost, in many initiatives, this is one of the implicit objectives for many IT heads in typical corporate environments.

Further **extrinsic** objectives are divided into two categories. One of them refers to collaborating with external parties. This means we need to integrate information systems, but it also refers to changes in our business processes, in our procedures, in the way how we present data to our external parties so that they can work with them.

A company needs to be open to the exchange of information (also data and documents) with external parties. Especially in today's e-commerce environments, in e-business companies collaboration is one of the key capabilities. Companies are not managing the whole value chain for a specific service on their own, but only fraction of the supply chain. Imagine the use case of ordering a packet of tea in China at one of the popular marketplaces.[2] People are offering tea and you can order it on the marketplace. There will be some payment service involved, which is provided by an external payment service provider. This also involves logistics companies which will make sure that your pack of tea is transported from China to your home address.

This simple example already highlights a lot of parties involved in tea delivery. Firstly, the provider of the marketplace, then the company offering the tea on the market place. Then a different company providing the payment service. Then the local logistics service provider in China picking up all the parcels from the tea manufacturer. It will then hand them over to airlines so that airlines can send the parcels to your country. And then your local postal organisation taking the parcel and delivering it at your doorstep. This workflow is even more complicated in reality.[3] But this end-to-end process already involves six business partners. And

---

[2]Popular marketplaces are Amazon, eBay or tmall and AliExpress in China.
[3]We left out customs, for example.

they all need to interact smoothly so that you do not experience any delays or lost parcels. This simple use case already requires a lot of data exchange between those partners. Therefore, in a networked e-commerce environment, it is not only about checking internal factors for EAM, but also checking how do we connect with our environment.

Business is usually also constraint by legal requirements, fiscal requirements, and industry regulations. These constraints place restrictions on the design of our processes and IT systems supporting the business processes. Beside quality, cost and collaboration, we also need to achieve compliance. Being non-compliant will have a negative impact on the company. Examples of this could be loss of reputation or fines.

Strategic objectives defined by executive management will drive operational objectives. Strategy provides the guidance on how to achieve corporate objectives and also helps with prioritising different options while analysing and improving business performance.

4.2   Enterprise Architecture Visualisation

How is enterprise architect supposed to be working today? Do you remember the diagram in Fig. 4.3? We presented it briefly in Chap. 1 on page 17 when explaining the working mode of an enterprise architect.[4] The enterprise architect in corporate IT is working in a very similar fashion as an architect in construction creating buildings or developing huge maps. The enterprise architect is producing huge posters with information displaying the architecture of the company. Those maps, referred to as viewpoints in this model, are created from a plethora of information that is stored in an EA repository.

One can do it manually, like for example having all the information in office documents or tables, and then draw the maps using common drawing tools. There are also dedicated EAM tools available at the market that support this step automatically. You need to collect all the data about your applications, about your business capabilities, about business objects, and their relationships. It covers any concept presented so far in this book. Information needs to be stored in a structured way in the EA repository. And then the EAM tool can create certain viewpoints (the maps or the posters we are referring to). The visualisation is supposed to support stakeholders in the company with addressing their specific concerns.

---

[4]The diagram has been created based on a similar discussion in [2, pp. 35] and [3, pp. 5].

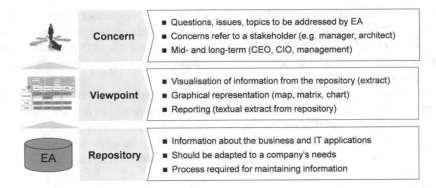

Fig. 4.3 Working mode of an enterprise architect

4.2.1 Types of Maps

There exists substantial research on the visualisation of EA with respect to stake-holders' need. One research group headed by Professor Matthes at the Technical University of Munich is working on providing a sound theory containing an EA repository and the generation of viewpoints. Among others, this group published a research report co-authored by Khosroshahi and others containing typical patterns for describing EA (cf. [3]). The theory encompasses a data model for EA, viewpoints and stakeholders together with their concerns. For the visualisation part, they are defining three different kinds of maps as shown in (Fig. 4.4).

The first type is called the **cluster map**. It is usually used for partitioning elements into logical domains, like for example assigning applications to organi-sational units or assigning applications to business capabilities. Sounds familiar? Just reiterate the examples provided in this book so far. By doing so you will find a couple of cluster maps.

A second type of visualisation is called the **Cartesian map**. While we can assign elements only to one background or to one kind of information in the cluster map, the Cartesian map is usually two-dimensional. We are mapping elements against two types of informations. Spoiler alert: The business support matrix as presented in Sect. 4.3 is a Cartesian map. You did not experience many examples Cartesian maps yet. These will be part of subsequent paragraphs in this section.

The third type of visualisation is called the **graph layout map**. It looks like a graph in software engineering, showing elements as nodes and the relationships as edges between these. Unlike cluster maps here we do not apply a visual background.

Most of these maps might already sound familiar as we explained EA by drawing on these examples. Such examples can be categorised as one of the types of maps introduced in Fig. 4.4. There will be some more examples in the following section (except for the Cartesian map as it will be introduced in the context of the business support matrix).

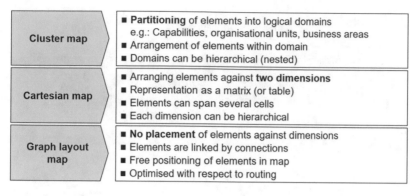

Fig. 4.4 Types of maps

4.2.2 Example Maps

An example cluster map is provided in Fig. 4.5. It might look very familiar as we have been using cluster maps from the beginning of this textbook.

The cluster map shown here is providing applications as elements and mapping these against organisational units. There exists an application called the **Customer portal**, others are called **Order management**, **3rd party booking** and a **Billing system**. An application is visually placed within the organisational unit where it is used. The sales department only requires one application, the customer portal. The operations team uses two applications supporting operations processes. And the finance department has one system, too. Clusters are built by organisational units of a fictional company and applications are mapped against these.

The graph layout map might look familiar to you because we used similar visualisations in this book previously. Figure 4.6 shows a different example for a graph layout map. The applications are the same as in Fig. 4.5. They are connected by data flows, showing which data object is flowing from one application to the other.

You are not restricted to a single type of map but allowed to combine views. Figure 4.7 shows the combination of the previous two maps (from Figs. 4.5 and 4.6). We have the cluster map in the background for detailing the organisational units and then adding arrows for the data flow. This is a combined cluster map and graph-layout map.

4.2.3 Software Cartography

Let us now take a look at the general structure of a map and elements for constructing them. It will be rare to create a pure cluster maps and a pure graph layouts map. Frequently you will mix these visualisations. Pure maps can be helpful

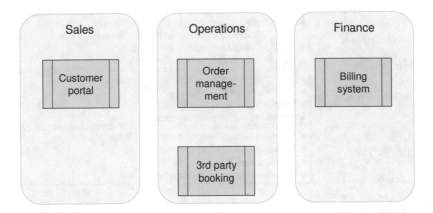

Fig. 4.5 Example cluster map

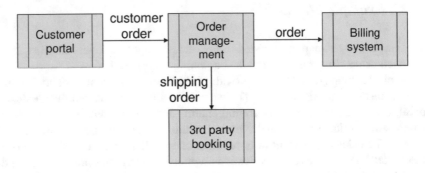

Fig. 4.6 Example graph layout map

(and are widely used), but you will frequently see complex maps displaying different types of information.

Based on the theory provided by André Wittenburg as member of Professor Matthes' team, the general structure for such a map is shown in Fig. 4.8. The background is represented by a **base map**. This could be clusters from a cluster map, for example. You can assign your **elements** against this background. These will be applications most of the time for the purpose of this book. These could also be any other types of element, including business objects, data objects, roles, people—in other words: anything that is relevant for the EA. a base map with clusters together with a layer for elements, we can already construct a cluster map.

An additional layer for **relationships** can be introduced for displaying connections between elements.[5] This results in a combined visualisation are shown in Fig. 4.7.

---

[5]The two layers for **elements** and **relationships** build a graph-layout map.

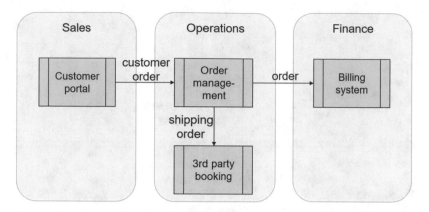

Fig. 4.7 Example combined views

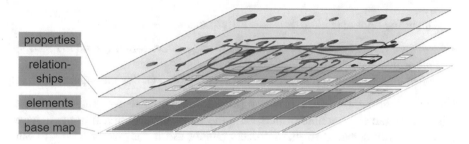

Fig. 4.8 Layers of a map (based on [4, p. 83])

Additional **properties** of the elements can be shown using a fourth layer. You can add for example information like:

- run and maintenance costs of each application
- quality attributes (e.g. technical fitness, business fit)
- planning status (e.g. *planned*, *in use* or *to be decommissioned*
- age of an application (e.g. *legacy*, *state-of-the-art*, *innovator*)

Most maps used in EAM will consist of these four layers. These will have a background and show elements, which are the focus of the investigation. They can display, but are not necessarily limited to, relationships between these elements. Further the properties can provide additional information for the elements shown on the map.

Let us explain this structure by the example map given in Fig. 4.9. This is an extension of the example from Fig. 4.7. The background is build by the three organisational units with software applications assigned to them. The relationships, again, show data flows between them. The top level—represented by the traffic light symbols—adds information on the applications.

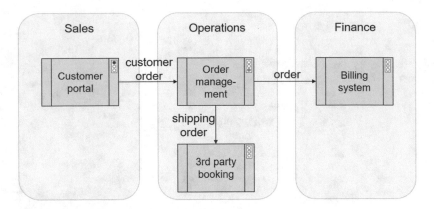

Fig. 4.9 EA viewpoints—example map

The traffic light may indicate the security status of the application:

- *red*: poor level of data protection and security (e.g. **Customer portal** in Fig. 4.9)
- *amber*: average security level and data protection policies
- *green*: high level of data protection and security (e.g. **Order management**)

The red traffic light on the **Customer portal** indicates a severe issue, because a customer portal is accessible from outside the corporate network. It needs to have a high security standard so that intruders cannot use it for getting access to our network.

Amber traffic lights, in this case, might indicate systems with an average security level. They are neither outstanding nor poor. However, the implications here are not clear by just looking at the map. You have to have more information for a precise assessment of the severity. Is it bad having an amber traffic light or not? Do we need to do something? Those symbols can only reflect a highly aggregated view on the application. However, they help in getting an overview on the whole application landscape. Simple visualisations can help top executives with getting a grip on the big picture.

There is no standard way for showing additional information on an EA map. We just provided a simple example using traffic lights. Traffic lights might be associated with statuses like low (red), medium (amber), and high (green) if *high* refers to a positive property. The interpretation needs to be defined by the enterprise architect or by the wider company, so that every person looking at the map can understand what is represented by green, amber, and red. This includes:

1. What does the colour mean?
2. How do we determine the colour?

There are further possibilities for displaying information, like the *Harvey balls* in Fig. 4.10. These are typically used for indicating progress or status of completeness.

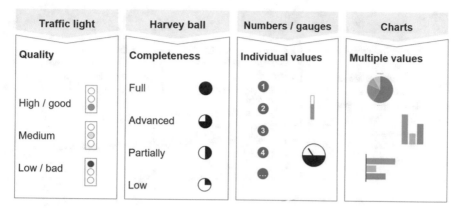

Fig. 4.10 Visualisation of properties

But it can also address a quality criteria with four different degrees. For example, the execution of a project can be indicated by Harvey balls:

- *low*: project just started
- *partial*: progressing
- *advanced*: major work done
- *full*: completed

They can also indicate quality:

- *low*: only a few quality criteria are met
- *partial*: half of quality criteria are met
- *advanced*: most quality criteria satisfied
- *full*: quality criteria fully satisfied

We can only provide examples on how to use Harvey balls and other visualisations. These can be adapted in any organisation just by defining their meaning. They normally will refer to existing properties or KPI.

Alternatively you can assign numbers. If you have security statuses based on numbers, or even if you want to show cost, then you can add numbers. You can even add text if you prefer, but the more text you include, the more complicated the map will become. Architects usually relate to graphical symbols which, of course, need to be interpreted. Further you can include gauges or progress bars to display relative values, like a percentage or some kind of relative values. Such values can, for example, show budget usage (i.e. budget used compared to the overall budget), or the running cost of applications compared to others.

Last but not least, you can also utilise charts for rather complicated maps. Example: The different cost types of an application (e.g. run, support, maintenance, training) can be displayed by a bar chart. Those charts can also provide a summary view on quality attributes (i.e. business fit, technical fitness and architectural fit).

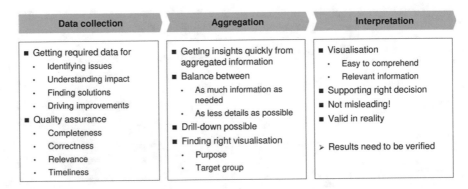

Fig. 4.11 Challenges with visualising properties

Creating these maps requires an EA repository with high quality data. This can be quite a challenging task in the corporate environment if no such repository pre-exists (cf. Fig. 4.11). An enterprise architect needs to start the collection of all data concerning applications, capabilities and business objects. This requires more than simply sending an email to everybody requesting them to provide that information. Architects usually spend a lot of time on sourcing information, contacting people, participating in meetings to obtain all relevant information. Business and IT stakeholders are normally busy with their own responsibilities or might simply refuse to collaborate with EA.

Analysis and optimisation of the application landscape in its business context requires a lot of information. This includes detailed cost figures, usage statistics of applications, number of users and business stakeholders. Obtaining all relevant data can become very tedious. You can keep an army of architects or external consultants busy with meetings to obtain all the relevant detail.

We also have to keep in mind that it is not only a one-time effort to populate the EA repository. We also need to ensure the data quality over time. This requires the data to be complete, correct, relevant and available on time. Furthermore, we need to make sure that we update this data over time. It is an illusion that you are only doing data collection once, and then you are able to simply focus on your EAM work. You need to make sure to update your data frequently whenever the organisation changes. To make matters more complex the application landscape changes too. Processes are also constantly changing. New products are introduced. All this needs to be incorporated into your repository, meaning you need to be aware of the change and constantly collect updated information.

Once you have all the details and data available, then you can think of how to aggregate these. You will never display all the details on one big map because this will be too confusing. You need to decide how to aggregate data, so that it will be helpful for the corresponding stakeholder. The stakeholder should see as much detail as required for addressing concerns. At the same time, you should display as much information as possible, so that all relevant facts are clearly visible.

The more unnecessary information you have, the more tedious it will be for the decision maker. If you show less detail this will adversely impact the decisions made. Aggregation must be planned, but should also be somewhat flexible, so that you can disaggregate data at a later stage. Displaying high level data on a dashboard or an EA map should also allow to drill down and show how this aggregated value has been calculated based on more detailed data. Each aggregation does not exist in isolation. You always have to keep the stakeholder in mind (referred to as target group) and also the purpose of the visualisation.

After you created the map, the stakeholder can use the map not only for visualising and understanding information, but also to support their decisions. Whenever you create the viewpoint, you need to make sure that the map is not misleading. It should not show anything that can be interpreted by the stakeholder in a wrong way. Data, even when aggregated, needs to correspond with the real world.

In real life the process never works by simply collecting data, creating a map, and everyone is happy. Whenever we needed to create maps, it was some kind of iterative process consisting of the following steps:

1. get initial data (might not be complete)
2. make a first draft map
3. discuss draft with stakeholder

   a. Can you use this for your work?
   b. Is it easy to handle?
   c. Is it easy to understand?
   d. Will it support your work?

4. collect additional data based on stakeholders' feedback
5. calculate aggregated data
6. improve data quality
7. refine draft map and continue with step 3

This process shows why traditional EA initiatives have a huge risk of failing. It is not simply an initial set up and then applying standard tools. It is an ongoing collaborative approach together with all stakeholders as organisations, concerns and perception differ vastly. There is no one-size-fits-all map.

Real-life corporations are very complex, thus we need a lot of information in order to properly understand business processes and software applications. You will not always obtain all the data you wish for in a professional environment. You need to start with what you managed to get and discuss first drafts with stakeholders. Their feedback will likely require changes to the map but also result in the need to collect more data (in case they require more information in the map). This is an iterative process until all parties agree on a map or abandon the idea. There is no fixed time-frame until you reach a result. It depends on your knowledge and understanding of the stakeholders for getting a result quickly. But it might also take a couple of months or more.

Many enterprise architects were driven by using existing EA tools. They simply collected the data required by the tool for generating pre-defined reports and maps. This can work but often bears the risk that top executives do not perceive the visualisations as helpful. Pushing for such standard visualisations that are not understood by top executives will be a guarantee for the project to fail. You need to listen to the customers of your work: stakeholders using your maps. This includes top executives, middle management and any relevant stakeholder required for the succesful adoption of EAM.

4.3 Business Support

Even though getting all the information is a challenging task, it needs to be done to support proper alignment between business and IT (as depicted in Fig. 4.12):

- *Effectiveness*: We need to understand the business so that we can provide an adequate application landscape.
- *Efficiency*: We need to know details about applications in order to become more cost efficient.

The world is not simply black and white. The views presented here reflect the perspective of a head of IT who wants to provide an optimal application landscape for the company. Optimisation on the business side is also required from a corporate perspective. With cost reductions, we can increase the efficiency of our business processes. Furthermore, IT is only effective if we make sure that the business is working effectively. From the IT perspective, we want to provide an efficient IT landscape. The remainder of this section will, therefore, provide a closer look at the relationship between business and application architecture. The business support matrix is introduced as a tool for visualisation and analysis.

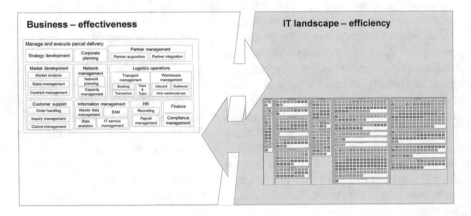

Fig. 4.12 Business and application architecture influencing each other

4.3.1   Business Support Matrix

Instead of starting with a definition, the notion of a business support matrix in
EAM is introduced by an example in Fig. 4.13. You might remember this kind of
visualisation from Sect. 1.3 like maps in Figs. 1.15 and 1.16. The matrix has two
dimensions:

- *Business processes*: value-adding business processes performed within the organisation
- *Region*: organisation of the company based on geographic regions

   The example contains the global headquarters and sub-organisations in Europe
and in the Asia-Pacific region. Within the matrix, you see applications. **Scheduler+**,
for example, is an application supporting **Execute order** in the global organisation.
SAP ERP is a standard application for cash collection across the whole company.
Don't be scared when reading the word *matrix*. We are not talking about mathematics and formal analysis. The matrix is a visual tool for describing, understanding
and optimising EA.

   A definition of *business support matrix* is provided in Definition 4.1. It is a
Cartesian map for putting applications in direct relationship with concepts from
the business architecture. This is what we exemplified in Fig. 4.13: applications
are mapped against processes and organisational units. We could have done the
same with business capabilities, corporate strategy, product or any kind of business-
related concept.[6]

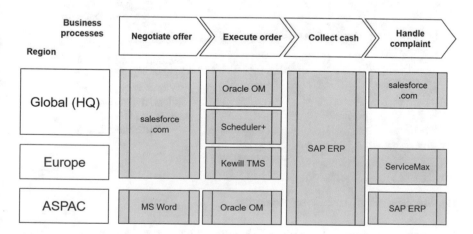

Fig. 4.13 Example business support

---

[6]An overview on business architecture concepts is given in Sect. 2.4 and in Chap. 2.

Definition 4.1 (Business Support Matrix) A business support matrix (BSM) is Cartesian map for setting applications in direct relationships with concepts from the business architecture (e.g. capabilities, processes or organisational units). There is no standard way but a variance of different matrix representations that can be applied. Hence, each of the two dimensions of the matrix can represent an individual business architecture concept.

There is no standard visualisation of the *business support matrix* or even the *standard matrix*. There is an example in Fig. 4.13 but there are various other representations. When studying textbooks and papers from the EA community, you will find a huge variety of visualisations for the business support matrix. It might not even be called a business support matrix but have a different name like *domain map*, *business map* or *application map*. We continue to use the term *business support matrix* throughout this textbook.[7]

We will now introduce a very specific kind of business support matrix that we will need to analyse the application architecture with respect to its business support. It has the following dimensions:

1. Business capabilities
2. Applications

An abstract example is provided in Fig. 4.14. A cell at the intersection of an application and a capability represents business support between them. If there

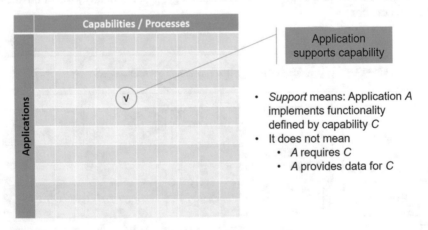

Fig. 4.14 Structure of a business support matrix

---

[7]This simple kind of matrix does not require a dedicated EA tool or a drawing program but can be easily created using a common spreadsheet application. We used this kind of matrix quite often when data was available in a (relational) database, SharePoint lists or Excel spreadsheets. It can be generated as a pivot table and then any kind of digram offered by Excel can be produced. It took a couple of years until this kind of visualisation emerged as the one most suited for all the stakeholders in the company for understanding the relationship of software applications and the business capabilities. Even though there was a dedicated EAM tool (planningIT), it was not flexible enough as people wanted to have different visualisations. We imported all the required data into an Excel spreadsheet and then used the pivot table to show the business support matrix.

is a tick, then the application does support the capability—otherwise it does not. This refers to the fact that the execution of the capability requires the respective application but not the other way. It does not show whether an application needs a capability. The matrix also represents a clear functional point-of-view: The application implements functionality that is used in the capability. It does not refer to data only.

4.3.2 Analysis Using the Business Support Matrix

Figure 4.15 shows a more complex, but still abstract, example for a business support matrix. It is not only displaying one tick but all relationships between applications and business capabilities. It lists several applications, named **a1** to **a8**, and 10 different business capabilities just having abstract names, **c1** to **c10**. The specific meaning is not relevant for this example because we just want to discuss the structure. What we can see in this matrix is that application **a1** is supporting capability **c3**, **c5**, and capability **c8**. In the same way, we can see that the business capability **c8** requires two applications, namely **a1** and **a5**.

We will use this example to explain typical issues in the EA that can be identified with the business support matrix. These are:

- *Gap*: missed automation potential
- *Redundancy*: too many applications
- *Orphan*: application without any business value
- *Monolith*: lack of modularity in the application landscape

The business capability called **c6** is not supported by any application. This does not necessarily need to be an issue but might be an indication for a missed

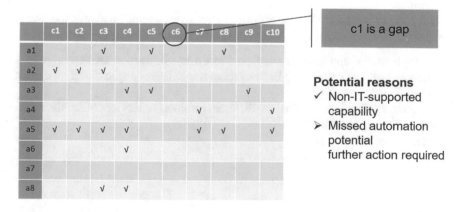

Fig. 4.15 Business support matrix indicating a gap

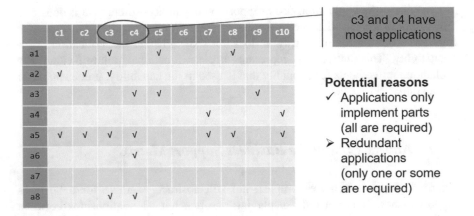

Fig. 4.16 Business support matrix indicating redundancies

opportunity for automation or IT support. We need to check the background to understand why it is not supported. Perhaps this is a capability that we do not want to be supported by IT because it is a pure manual activity (e.g. loading parcels into a truck). This root cause analysis requires human actors as the details are not visible in the matrix.

Another kind of typical issue to be identified using the business support matrix is determining capabilities that are using a lot of applications. You can do this very easily by simply looking at the matrix in Fig. 4.16. You can determine some capabilities (e.g. **c9**) only being supported by one application or by two (**c8** and **c10**). However, there are two business capabilities, each of them requiring a lot of applications. **c3** is supported by **a1**, **a2**, **a5**, and **a8**. **c4** is supported by four different applications. Looking at the matrix only allows us the neutral statement that each of them is supported by four applications and this is more compared to other business capabilities.

Is it good or is it bad? We cannot draw any reliable conclusion by just looking at the matrix. We need some more background information, like for example:

- Do each of the applications only perform a small fraction of activities in a complex business capability? Each of them might be very specialised on certain tasks.
- Are these applications required for different products or services? (e.g. manufacturing cars vs. motor bikes)
- Or, are they *redundant*?

Example 4.1 Let us assume **c3** being *Customer Relationship Management.* Having four different CRM applications would in fact reveal a redundancy. CRM is a commodity and we should have one integrated standard application. We should have only one database with customer data. We should not maintain sales training or sales-related training for four different systems, but only have one. In this case, **c3** would be supported by redundant applications.

Example 4.2 Another example is that business capability C4 refers to *logistics operations.* There can be one system for *network planning,* another system for *monitoring* the logistics network, one system for making the *bookings* with external service providers, and one system for *managing customer orders.* In this case, even if it is within one business capability, each of them has a different purpose, and then, four systems might be justified.

Observation number three is that application A7 is not supporting any business capability as highlighted in Fig. 4.17. This means we are maintaining and providing an application that does not provide any business value. This will, of course, hamper efficiency and most heads of IT would challenge this application. *Why are we paying for something that is not useful?*

EAM often identifies applications without supporting any business capability. This will usually drive initiatives investigating for reasons. Such an initiative

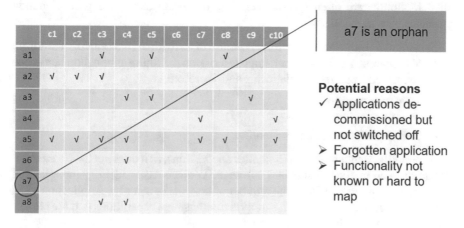

Fig. 4.17 Business support matrix indicating an orphan

will analyse the background of that application and provide a decision for its decommissioning:

1. It is a forgotten application that is not used any more. It can be decommissioned.
2. It is used for activities without business relevance. It might be decommissioned.
3. It is required by relevant business applications (e.g. an integration backbone). It should be kept.
4. It is directly or indirectly required by all capabilities (e.g. office suite). It needs to stay.
5. A business capability is missing (e.g. business collaboration). The capability map needs to be updated.

The business support matrix can support finding certain observations very easily. It is a simple but very powerful tool with respect to identifying common inefficiencies in the application architecture. It takes some effort to obtain all the information required for creating it. But summarising it on one single chart will be a visual aid for decision makers. They start finding issues by counting ticks and perceiving patterns (e.g. empty rows and columns) in the matrix. Also an accumulation of ticks (in a row, a column or a certain area in the matrix) are easy to grasp visually.

However, let us not forget about the fact this is only a highly aggregated representation of a complex system. It only displays aggregated information while leaving out significant detail. An observation in the matrix is primarily only an indication that there might be an issue. A careful analysis has to be conducted in order to reveal valid reasons or proof that it really is an issue. We do not know the reason or the business rationale behind it.

The fourth kind of observation is called a *monolith* as shown in Fig. 4.18. A monolith is a large and self-contained software application with a lot of functionality. Monoliths are often grown over time or introduced in the past. Common problems with monoliths are:

- No modular design and, therefore, no reuse of individual functionality (services)
- Hard to maintain and, therefore, impose a risk on the future application landscape
- Implemented using legacy platforms and, therefore, ...

  - inefficient for users
  - security risk
  - limited performance and scalability

A monolith cannot be split into smaller applications, as it does not have a modular design or is an integrated standard software. You can easily identify monoliths in the business support matrix by the number of tick marks in a row. Application **a5** in Fig. 4.18 is a monolith because it supports four business capabilities that are closely related to each other (**c1** to **c4**) and more.

When recognising a monolith, this observation should be neutral in the first step as with each observation from the matrix. Even though the term *monolith* has a negative connotation, it might be acceptable in many cases.

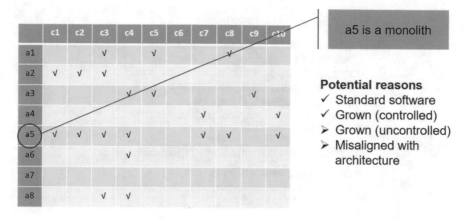

Fig. 4.18 Business support matrix indicating a monolith

There might be a conscious decision for having a monolith in the company. A proprietary core operations system[8] might be developed by the company as a competitive advantage. If you are developing it on your own, you can ensure modularity and maintainability with respect to future business needs. In such a case this is not an issue.

Also an integrated commodity application procured on the market is less of an issue. For example, a customer relationship management suite supports marketing, sales and customer service. If it is a conscious decision that you need only one dedicated system for these capabilities, then it is okay to have a monolith. Before making any judgement about the monolith being good or bad, you need to understand its purpose and why it is there.

4.3.3 Implications from the Business Support Matrix

Let us summarise the implications. The observations[9] from the business support matrix are listed on the left-hand side of Fig. 4.19 together with recommendations how to handle them:

- gap being a business capability without application support
- redundancies, having business capabilities with many applications
- orphan applications or application, not supporting any business capability
- monolith, supporting many business capabilities that are related to each other

---

[8]The term *core operations system* does not refer to a computer operating system but to an application being used for execution a company's core business processes.

[9]This is only an excerpt of observations you can make in corporate environments. Schlör and Jung [5] introduces some more, which are some kind of special and also require some more detailed analysis.

	Recommended actions	Overall
Gap	• Check automation potential and benefit • If beneficial: Plan new or extend existing application	Align with IT strategy and architecture guidelines
Redundancy	• Determine reason for redundancy • Shut down or reduce redundant applications	
Orphan	• Determine application status • Shut down unnecessary application • Update capability map and BSM if application required	
Monolith	• Analyse circumstances for monolith • Plan for refactoring in case of pain points	

Fig. 4.19 Implications from analysing the business support matrix

In case of a **gap**, we need to check whether the business capability is a completely manual one. If not, there might be missed automation potential. There are two options for filling the gap:

1. introducing a new software application just for this business capability
2. check for an existing application that can support the business capability—even if it requires extensions

The same pattern holds true for **redundancies**. We first need to check the reason behind the it. And if it is perceived as an unnecessary redundancy then it should be eliminated by replacing applications. The same logic applies to **orphans**. Orphans without any reasons can be decommissioned. However, the analysis of the business support matrix may reveal some potential orphans that are still required (see above).

The implication in case of a monolith might be slightly different. You start with its identification in the matrix and then the analysis of the reasons. But, in case of an issue, you cannot get rid of it easily. You need to plan for a step-wise replacement of it. There are some common strategies for this:

1. re-factoring the monolith, which means dividing the software into smaller units
2. introducing one new system as a replacement (in case you need to replace a legacy monolith)
3. introducing several applications, each of which supports a fraction of the functionality (i.e. based on sub-capabilities)

The first option is easier to perform (and less risky) as it is only a redesign of the software. It does not need to be replaced and existing business processes are not affected as they continue using the same system. However, the benefit is quite low as the (legacy) software is still in use. It can be an initial stage before performing option number three.

The second option will consist of a large scale change as also the business processes need to be adjusted to a new software system. Further interfaces of the old monolith need to be re-established with the new one so that data flows continue to work. This also bears the risk of hampering business during the transition and missing features of the new monolith.

The third option implies a program consisting of individual projects, each of which replaces a part of the monolith. It can be seen as a chance as the application landscape can be optimised by introducing several specialised applications. This *best of bread* approach consists of choosing the best application for each task and integrating them. The division of the monolith (assuming it supports a single capability) can be based on sub-capabilities, hence, the functional split of the software application is derived from the capability tree. the method introduced in Sect. 3.2 can be used here. The complexity of managing this program is quite large as the introduction of several systems need to be aligned and all dependencies must be managed properly.

4.3.4 Dimensions in Business Support

The business support matrix introduced in this textbook consists of two dimensions, allowing for only two concepts from the business architecture. The example provided above was limited to applications and business capabilities. But, what about the other concepts? The business support matrix is a valuable tool showing high-level information. However, we will most likely need additional information for further analysis. This can be incorporated by having additional dimensions for business support (i.e. more information behind each tick) as shown in Fig. 4.20.

Each cell in the matrix (i.e. each business support) can have additional details on time, organisational context, customer segments and products. It also allows for quantifying the degree of business support (e.g. the application only supports the capability by 25%).

Dimension	Application supports capability
1 Time	For a given time **period** (from .. to) or **plan** (as-is, to-be)
2 Organisation	In an organisational unit (including **countries, regions**)
3 Customer type	For specific customer segment (e.g. **consumer, business partner**)
4 Product type	Capabilities may require specialised applications for different products
5 Degree	Degree of business support (partially, completely)

Fig. 4.20 Business support—dimensions

The **time** dimension allows for distinguishing between several stages in the roadmap. A business support can be indicated as *as-is* (the application is currently supporting the capability) or *to-be* (the application will support the capability in the future). Time can also be given as concrete periods of time if there is already a plan for decommissioning an as-is application or when to introduce a to-be application.

We also need to know the **organisation** which is using this application. Remember, there might be a variety of applications for one and the same business capability.[10] We need different applications for the same functionality because of legal or physical reasons. We discussed it in Sect. 3.2 based on customs processing, because of different customs regulations resulting in different requirements. These kinds of redundancies are justified and it would be helpful to have this kind of information included in the business support matrix.

Another piece of information we needed to add to the business support matrix is the **customer type**. There exist significant differences in applications for business customers compared to private customers (i.e. consumers). Order taking for a private customer can be done by phone or a web interface. A corporate customer, submitting thousands of orders every day will ask for an e-business solution.

Product type can results in different requirements for the same capability. Delivering a letter requires a different application compared to delivering a parcel, compared to delivering a huge ocean freight container. Difference in size is not the only reason. It is also the difference in how the delivery is handled. Therefore, different applications are required, but still it is one and the same capability— delivery.

And last but not least, we needed to introduce something that is describing the **degree** of business support. Is this application fully supporting the business capability? Or only half, because they are missing requirements, or there are still some manual steps, or because there are more features required but we cannot extend the application for whatever reason?

Example 4.3 Figure 4.21 shows two examples for business support with different dimensions. The business support matrix is the same as above. Application **a3** is supposed to support business capability **c6**. It is not supporting this capability now. There is a plan (**to-be**) that this application will support the capability beginning May 2022.[11] If you remember the previous version of this business support matrix (Fig. 4.15), the business capability **c6** was a gap as there was no application support. The updated matrix in Fig. 4.21 now indicates the plan to close the gap with application **a3** on a **global** level. a3 is becoming the standard application for **c6** in the entire

(continued)

---

[10] Reasons for variant applications and common criteria are described in more detail in Sect. 3.2.
[11] Which is in the future when writing this textbook.

Example 4.3 (continued)

company. However, the application is only relevant for **business customers**. It is not intended for private customers. Its usage is also restricted to a certain product type, **production facilities**. But as **a3** is already about to be extended, the objective is to support this capability 100%.

To summarise the example: We identified the gap **c6** and made the plan to extend the application **a3** so that it fully supports the business capability. The change will need some time, so we are planning to support this capability starting May 2022 globally. It will be used by all organisational units for the interaction with business customers only, buying production machinery.

There can be several business support relationships between the same pair of application and capability. The example in Fig. 4.21 also shows the plan for using **a3** for the same capability for private customers (i.e. **consumers**) in **Europe** buying **home appliances** from **January**. Interactions with private customers is less standardised, so that the application only supports the capability to 80%.

This example demonstrates that the real business support behind one tick can be rather complex. In this case one tick already indicates two sets of details for the business support. The requirements for business customers do not apply for supporting consumers—and vice versa.

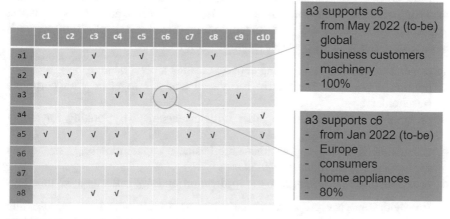

Fig. 4.21 Example dimensions for business support

4.3.5 Summary of Business Support Matrix

There are many more tools and visualisations available for EA. The chair of Prof. Matthes already performed two evaluations of tools showing the range of visualisation in [6] and [7]. Some researcher summarise existing visualisations together with a critical reflection (e.g. [8]) or propose their idea of a complete set of maps (e.g. [9, 10]). We will not discuss these in this book but rather refer to existing publications. Further references will be provided in Chap. 6 as part of the EA frameworks.

Why are we specifically looking at the business support matrix in this book? Because it is a powerful visualisation which can be implemented using a standard spreadsheet application. There are also not many publications presenting it in such detail. A more elaborate comparison of benefits and draw-backs is provided in Fig. 4.22.

It is a very simple tool allowing for high level analysis. It can be used to identify potential issues in the application support and lead to further analysis. Such analysis consists of drilling down into more details—provided in further documents or repositories. Analysis is not only restricted to the current state of your architecture. You can also make decisions for a planned to-be. You can even show intermediate steps for your planning if you want to change your applications landscape step by step. You can have several versions of the business support matrix for then showing also the changes over time (similar to the roadmap presented by Figs. 1.17 and 1.18 in Sect. 1.4).

Most corporate users already have a software tool available for creating and analysing the business support matrix. It is Microsoft Excel or any other spreadsheet application. Microsoft Excel (as an example for a spreadsheet application) supports several scenarios with the business support matrix:

1. creating the matrix from existing data by creating a pivot table
2. printing a poster of the matrix for visual analysis together with corporate stakeholders
3. performing visual analysis together with management by looking for empty rows/columns or clusters of ticks
4. calculating KPIs for applications and business capabilities (e.g. *size of an application or* magnitude *of redundancy)*
5. recording (potential) changes to the application landscape after analysis meetings

It provides an easy graphical visualisation as a table with ticks representing business support. It can be used during workshops hosted by the EA team, business experts or with top executives to indicate improvement potential for the application landscape. The matrix can be used to facilitate face-to-face workshops. You can print it. You can attach it to a wall in a room. You can have a group of people discussing it. And if you printed it, people can draw on it, make comments or highlight issues. A print-out improves interaction between people and can even be extended by sticky notes so that people add comments to the matrix. Having the matrix as a poster on

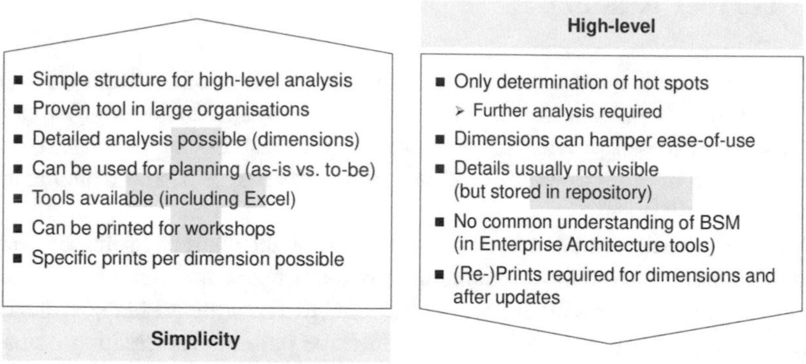

High-level

- Simple structure for high-level analysis
- Proven tool in large organisations
- Detailed analysis possible (dimensions)
- Can be used for planning (as-is vs. to-be)
- Tools available (including Excel)
- Can be printed for workshops
- Specific prints per dimension possible

- Only determination of hot spots
  - Further analysis required
- Dimensions can hamper ease-of-use
- Details usually not visible
  (but stored in repository)
- No common understanding of BSM
  (in Enterprise Architecture tools)
- (Re-)Prints required for dimensions and
  after updates

Simplicity

Fig. 4.22 Business support matrix—critical review

the wall makes workshops very interactive so that participants can come up with ideas on how to improve the EA.

Nevertheless, it is only a high level view. Even though it can be complemented by some details, more information is required for decision making. To show the five dimensions introduced above, can make reading the matrix cumbersome. If you show all the details on a hardcopy then it can get very complicated. Consequently, a poster should not contain all the information (applications, capabilities, dimensions) but only what is relevant for the corresponding stakeholder or purpose.

Introducing the business support matrix takes a long time as it relies on data and needs to be established within the corporation. It should also not be pushed by EA but rather be introduced as a tool that can also provide benefits for business people. One might start with simple versions or a matrix for one organisational unit only. If people perceive a value by using the matrix, it can be transferred to other units as well.

There is no standard definition for the business support matrix in the literature. You can find similar visualisations, sometimes by another name. It can also be created with any concept from business and application architecture (e.g. processes and data objects) as well as differing dimensions (e.g. create, read or update data objects). You will have to develop your own version of the standard business support matrix tailored to your organisation.

Using prints to facilitate workshops can lead to some time delay when posters need to be reprinted after a session. When reprinting too often, it may become a waste of resources (paper and print colours). Several versions of out-dated prints may pile-up in offices. Sometimes you need to update your information digitally and then throw away the print-outs.

4.4 Further Reading

There is a conference paper that describes the application of the business support matrix [5]. It was published at a conference on EAM in Stockholm (Sweden) in the year 2018. It will provide more details on the business support matrix, what you need to do in order to establish it, how you can analyse it, and which research questions are still open.

The theory we described in Sect. 4.2 is applied by the chair of Professor Matthes at the Technical University in Munich. This team has a number of publications around this topic. One of them we would like to recommend here is the EAM Pattern Catalogue [3]. In this paper they describe patterns for creating maps and visualisations for EAM. Some of their theory we describe here, like—the layering and the types of maps that are introduced there. In addition to that, Matthes and his team performed evaluations of EAM tools. These evaluations (cf. [6, 7]) are based on typical scenarios and provide plenty of examples for common visualisations.

The third title written by Op't Land, Proper, and others is titled *EA—Creating Values by Informed Governance* [2]. We already recommended this in the first chapter because this provides an overview on the purpose of EAM. They also talk about the analysis and typical objectives when analysing your EAM.

Finally the last book already recommend in the third chapter [9] is on how to describe EA—especially the application architecture. It is a book published by a researcher in Melbourne, who completes a lot of literature reviews and also research about views for EAM. His book, *The Practise of EA—A Modern Approach to Business and IT Alignment* is full of maps and types of maps that can be used within EAM. As we are only capable of discussing a very few within this course, whenever you are interested to check additional maps and visualisations, this book might provide a good starting point.

4.5 Summary

This is the end of the fourth chapter on EAM. We were dealing with the analysis of EA through visualisations, by using maps. We provided some theory on creating maps for EA with respect to analysis. We provided a more detailed view of the business support matrix indicates the business support and helps us with the identification of typical issues. However, the business support matrix is a rather high level tool that—after identifying typical observations—will require more detailed analysis and reasoning of those issues.

The next section will continue as shown in Fig. 4.23. After describing and analysing the EA, we now need to discuss:

- How can we manage the EA?
- How can we make sure that we have an organisational unit that will create all the maps and maintain them?
- How does the organisation look, which will then conduct the changes on the EA?

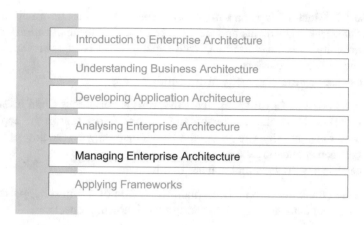

Fig. 4.23 Following next: managing enterprise architecture

It is not enough having the architecture captured in maps. We also need an organisation for planning and conducting changes on any architectural layer.

4.6 Exercises

Exercise 4.1 (Objectives for Analysis) You are owning a company that is specialised on delivering medical supplies to clinics and hospitals in Greater Melbourne. The current pandemic situation leads to an increase in demand and a shortage of materials from your providers. You are aiming at extending your business so that you also cover imports of supplies from international partners.

Against this background, you have to analyse your EA as you add new capabilities (e.g. import and customs processing) and will have to introduce new application systems for integrating new business partners (e.g. providers or government organisations). List concrete objectives for your analysis. Use the structure given in Fig. 4.2 on page 107 and define an at least two objectives for each category:

1. Strategic
2. Intrinsic

   a. Quality
   b. Cost

3. extrinsic

   a. Collaboration
   b. Compliance

Exercise 4.2 (Cluster Map of a University) You are the Chief Information Officer (CIO) of the Deakin University and are tasked to visualize the application landscape of the university. Create a cluster map with capabilities as clusters and applications as elements within the clusters.

You can use any drawing tool you are familiar with.

Exercise 4.3 (Graph-Layout Map of a University) You are the Chief Information Officer (CIO) of the Deakin University and are tasked to visualize the application landscape of the university. Create a graph layout map showing the flow of business objects between applications.

You can use any drawing tool you are familiar with.

Exercise 4.4 (Business Support) Explain the notion of *business support* in your own words. Your explanation should address the following aspects:

1. What is it used for?
2. Which concepts is it related to?
3. Which properties does it have?
4. When should it not be used?

Exercise 4.5 (Business Support Matrix) Explain the notion of *business support matrix* in your own words. Your explanation should address the following aspects:

1. What is it used for?
2. How does it look like and which kind of information does it rely on?
3. Which kinds of issues can be identified by using the business support matrix?
4. Which limitations exist with respect to its application?

References

1. J. Lapalme, Three schools of thought on enterprise architecture. IT Professional **14**(6), 37–43 (2012)
2. M. Op't Land, E. Proper, M. Waage, J. Cloo, C. Steghuis, *Enterprise Architecture, Creating Value by Informed Governance*. The Enterprise Engineering Series (Springer, Berlin, London, 2009)
3. P.A. Khosroshahi, M. Hauder, A.W. Schneider, F. Matthes, Enterprise architecture management pattern catalog, Version 2.0. Software Engineering for Business Information Systems (sebis), Technische Universität München, München, Technical Report, 2015
4. A. Wittenburg, Softwarekartographie: Modelle und methoden zur systematischen visualisierung von anwendungslandschaften. Dissertation, Technical University München, 2007
5. R. Schlör, J. Jung, Analysis using the business support matrix: elaborating potential for improving application landscapes in logistics, in *2018 IEEE 22nd International Enterprise Distributed Object Computing Workshop (EDOCW)* (IEEE, New York, 2018)
6. F. Matthes, S. Buckl, L. Jana, C. Schweda, Enterprise architecture management tool survey 2008. München: Techn. Univ. München, 2008
7. S. Roth, M. Zec, F. Matthes, Enterprise architecture visualisation tool survey 2014, Technische UNniversität München, München. Technical Report, April 2014

8. S. Kotusev, Enterprise architecture: a reconceptualization is needed. Pacif. Asia J. Assoc. Inf. Syst. **10**, 1–36 (2018)
9. S. Kotusev, *The Practice of Enterprise Architecture: A Modern Approach to Business and IT Alignment* (SK Publishing, Carlton, VIC, 2018)
10. G. Wierda, *Mastering ArchiMate: A Serious Introduction to the ArchiMate Enterprise Architecture Modeling Language, Version 3.0.1*, Edition III, TC1 (R&A, Utrecht, 2017)

Chapter 5
Managing Enterprise Architecture

What did we study so far during the course EAM? We started with an introduction into the topic of EA and EAM, and also discussed, what it is good for in Chap. 1. We then had a look at concepts for describing and also understanding business processes and business architecture with a strong focus on business capabilities and business objects in Chap. 2. We then looked at, how to develop the application landscape from the business architecture in Chap. 3. It starts with having the business capabilities so that we can then decide for an optimal application landscape. We also looked at concepts and information that is required for further describing a detailed application architecture. Based on this, we looked at methods and tools for analysing EA in Chap. 4.

In this chapter, we will now have a look at the organisational aspects behind EAM. We will present skills of an enterprise architect (starting from page 153) and discuss options for setting up an organisational unit for EAM (Sect. 5.2). As most of the work is dealing with performing changes, we will start with an overview on change management in Sect. 5.1.

Learning Objectives

After completing this chapter, you will be able to ...

- ...explain typical changes in the application landscape and their impact on the business
- ...create a roadmap for describing changes in the application landscape
- ...describe the role of an Enterprise Architect, including tasks and skills
- ...discuss different approaches for establishing an organisation for EAM

The learning objectives are as follows: After completing this chapter, you should be capable of explaining typical changes in the application landscape, and also, the impact of those changes on the organisation. Furthermore, we will have a look at

© The Author(s), under exclusive license to Springer Nature Switzerland AG 2021
J. Jung, B. Fraunholz, *Masterclass Enterprise Architecture Management*,
https://doi.org/10.1007/978-3-030-78495-9_5

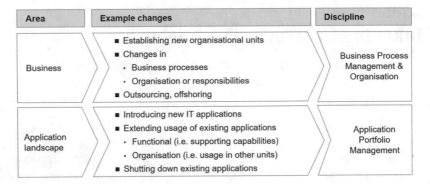

Fig. 5.1 Typical changes in an EA

one typical kind of map or some typical representation called the roadmap, which is used for describing changes not only on your application landscape but also in general. We will create certain roadmaps, and you should be capable of creating such visualisations in the future on your own. Concerning the organisational aspects, you should be capable of describing the role of the enterprise architect, including typical tasks and skills that are required from an architect. The section will end with an overview on options for setting up the EAM organisations, so we will look at different options. And you should be capable of discussing them in your future job environment.

5.1   Managing Changes

Which kind of changes are we facing when dealing with EA? Figure 5.1 shows some examples for typical changes that can occur on the business side. As the environment changes, our company needs to adapt to new situations. This might require that we will set up new organisational units for new products or new businesses that we want to achieve. There might be changes in business processes and also changes in the organisational structure. We might shift responsibilities from one person (or role) to the other. Furthermore, a typical kind of change is subject to outsourcing or off-shoring of certain activities. When a company decides not to execute certain processes on their own but rather hands them over to an external company for service provisioning. Typical examples are IT outsourcing or offshoring of customer service (i.e. the helpdesk) to a country with lower wages.

Those kind of changes can be triggered by any kind of change in the business, but to be honest, also changes in application will trigger changes in business processes. Changes in business or IT will influence each other. Changes in business also often imply changes in the application landscape. Even though we have two different domains (business and IT), changes are not performed in an isolated way. One change in business might imply several changes in the application landscape and also the other way around. Changes in business are usually subject to other disciplines, like business process management, strategic management, and others.

We will not talk about business changes in very detail within this book on EAM. We will rather focus on changes in the application landscape, their management and alignment with business processes. Changes in the application landscape may consist of introducing a new software application that needs to be integrated with existing processes and with existing applications. A new system does not only mean a new IT application, but implies new processes, processes changes and even changes in the organisational structure. Further kind of changes in the context of the application landscape consist of modifying existing systems, like extending an existing software application with further functionality or even extending the usage of an existing application to other organisational units. Last but not least, as we are driving cost savings within IT, most of the changes will address shutting down existing applications for saving the costs usually associated with hosting, maintaining, and using them.

The discipline of *application portfolio management* (APM) deals with such kinds of changes, so it is closely related to EAM. Based on analysis and visualisations from EAM, application portfolio management also establishes the link to financial accounting and to project management for managing all the projects dealing with those changes. We are not discussing the interdependencies of those changes but rather look at them individually in the remainder of this chapter.

5.1.1 Example Change

We have a Cartesian map showing the application landscape of a fictional company in Fig. 5.2 as a simple example for illustrating changes. It is a matrix showing the applications against the following business capabilities: *purchasing*, *goods in*, *invoice verification* and *payment handling*. It is only a fraction of the business capabilities—showing a snapshot of the application landscape. And on the other side, it maps the applications against organisational units within the company so like the headquarters the European organisation and the SAP organisation in the Asia-Pacific region. We only see five different systems, reflecting a small example. Please always keep in mind real life application landscapes are much larger, consisting of a couple of hundred and even more than 1000 applications.

What do you think when looking at this application landscape? Is there anything that you see that you think might not be optimal and should be changed. We don't know the exact background, but it looks like that there are a couple of redundant systems. There are two inventory management systems on the left-hand side—the one called system A being used in the headquarter and the European region, and another one called system B being used in the Asia-Pacific region. Let us assume

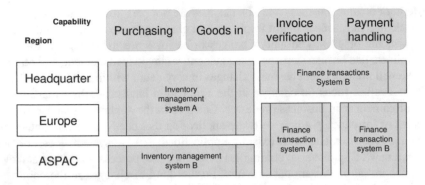

Fig. 5.2 Example map subject to change

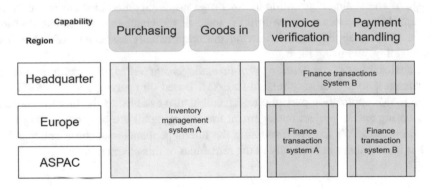

Fig. 5.3 Example map showing result of first change

that the company did some analysis and found out we can replace one system by the other, and then made the conscious decision to club the two systems together. The to-be architecture only contains a single inventory management system.

The result of the optimization is shown in Fig. 5.3. The decision was to only use System A for inventory management throughout the whole corporation. What we see here is just the result. System B is not available any more and the scope of System A has been extended so that it can also be used in the Asia-Pacific region. Looks better, doesn't it? Or is there anything else you would consider in this application landscape?

Obviously, there are two redundant finance transaction systems in Figs. 5.2 and 5.3. One of them is covering the invoice verification and the other one payment handling in Europe and the ASPAC region. Another change consists of getting rid of one of the finance transaction systems and replacing it by another one (Fig. 5.4). It looks like just a small change, but let's keep in mind that switching off applications is not an activity that can be done from today to tomorrow. It does not only require

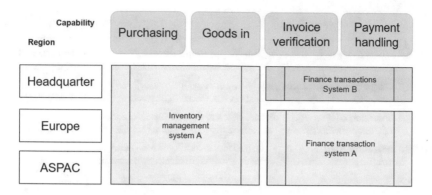

Fig. 5.4 Example map showing result of second change

switching off a computer. There are more implications behind it. Just to mention a few:

- We need to check if there's data in the system to be switched on that is needed by others or we need to move the data from one system to the other.
- We need to cut interfaces between systems so that the one that is about switched off cannot be used anymore.
- We need to train people so that they can also use the new system and that they are not using the old system anymore.
- When switching over systems, we need to change other systems as well.
- We need to inform business (and potentially business partners) and change they way they work and collaborate.

In fact, we have a lot of implications from shutting down a single software application. What happened here within seconds from one picture to another takes a long while. These are major changes within the corporation.

5.1.2 Managing Enterprise Architecture Changes

Have you ever been subject to a change? Changes are not done easily in a corporate environment, especially when you think of changing people's behaviour. People need to change the way how they work—usual or common practises that they know from the past which will not be valid after the change. Sometimes the organisation role changes. It might have an impact on the role of individuals, their salary, their importance, or even their self-esteem.

If you ask for issues in an organisation, there will be many people who can tell about the issues they perceive. It will be issues they see anywhere else, and of course,

Reason	Examples
➊ Lack of awareness	Underlying problem & details not defined or communicated
➋ Change-specific resistance	Workload or wrong methodology
➌ Uncertainty & fear	Loss of power, status, influence or compensation
➍ Lack of leadership	No guidance or missing trust in leadership
➎ Change saturation	Too many or even unsuccessful changes in the past

Fig. 5.5 Reasons for resistance to change

people always have an idea of how to make things better. Similar to going to a pub and asking people about politics, they will always have an opinion.

In the same way, people in a corporation might be supportive with changes in order to get rid of issues. But motivation often looks very different when you ask people to change their own behaviour or situation. It is not only about solving an issue you identified in a rational way. Changes in the company are needed, and this might also require individuals to change. They need to change established habits and beliefs that they trusted in and that might not be valid any more. And what you can see in many companies is that the motivation of change decreases when people are being faced with changing themselves.

The reason is not that people just want to avoid change, or just want to make the management look bad. They have tangible reasons for opposing changes. A couple of typical reasons are provided in Fig. 5.5.

One reason might be that people do not agree that a certain change needs to be done (i.e. **lack of awareness**). It is always easier to say, *the other person needs to change*, instead of, *I need to change*, because of being comfortable with the established way of doing things. Sometimes, people are not aware that they are part of the problem, or that they are working within the problem, and that they should be aware that they also need to change.

A typical **change-specific reason** for resistance is that people are already busy with the day-to-day work. They have a lot of work, they are busy, and in many companies, people are doing overtime hours—perhaps because of inefficient processes. But at the end, what they are saying is, I don't have time for spending work on making plans for conducting a change. This will will increase the workload of people. They are resisting to change because they just cannot handleplanning and performing the change.

Reason number three is a little bit subtle, because this addresses an emotional aspect. For many people, it will remain **uncertain** what will happen to them if the company changes:

How will my process change?

What happens if the system I'm using since 20 years is switched off? Am I capable of using the new one? Will I be overwhelmed with the new software?

Perhaps they don't need my work anymore. Perhaps I get fired, or perhaps I just lose my status, I lose influence, and so on.

Changes can lead to loss of power or a loss in status for some stakeholders. However, they tend to preserve their personal status within the company.

Another reason for opposing change is that the company lacks establishing clear leadership for performing the change (i.e. **missing leadership**. There needs to be a strong leader who will guide the change, who will also talk to people, who will try to address all the other reasons. Hence, a person is required that makes people aware of the reason for change as well as the anticipated result of the change initiative. Urgent changes sometimes need to be pushed in order to avoid, for example, bankruptcy of the company.[1] The leader needs to explain the options, emphasize the urgency and enable people for performing a change. This includes making sure that people get additional time, that they know why to spend working on changes, and that they get rid of other tasks that are not as urgent as performing the change.

The leader needs to be a manager that can also influence the day-to-day work of people. There is also leadership required for managing uncertainty and fears. He or she also needs to provide a proper vision to people in order to provide some guidance for what the change is heading for. You need to tell them what will happen. In many companies, people get aware of changes, but nobody informs them properly. People may get really fearful in such a case because they are afraid of the consequences. A lack of transparency combined with information hiding will hamper any change initiative. A change leader should properly communicate what the change is about and what will it mean for people, so that they can understand what will change for them. In many companies, it is a big issue that management is not properly telling about the implications, because they want to hide. They are afraid of further resistance. But planning a change somewhere in the Ivory Tower and not talking to people will increase their resistance.

Reason number five listed in Fig. 5.5 is **change saturation**. This does not happen in all cases, but there are organisations that already performed a couple of change initiatives in the past—whether successfully or not. I once joined an organisation that already terminated three major initiatives for the same kind of change. All of them failed, and we were about to start project number four. The biggest resistance we got is that people got annoyed as they were expected to support another change initiative—again: They perceived a new team that will again, steal valuable time.

---

[1]Mooney provides several examples and small case studies from his professional experience in [1]. He works as a consultant in the change management area.

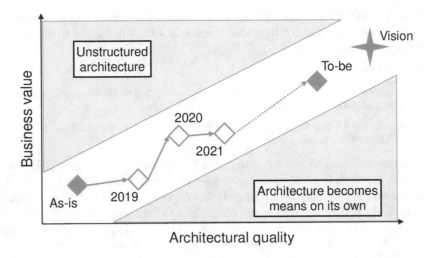

Fig. 5.6 Managed evolution

Again, it will lead to nothing. They did not expect reasonable results from that change as the previous three initiatives already failed. Even though the change management team was explaining the urgency and the innovative change method, people did not believe in that change. Gaining so much experience with unsuccessful changes in the past made them really fed up with new change initiatives. Of course, being saturated by change is not an excuse for not changing. But for a change leader, this is a topic he or she needs to keep in mind and also address during managing the change.

The text book at hand does not provide a chapter on change management.[2] The previous paragraphs are just meant to emphasize the fact that changes cannot be done easily in most cases. The remainder of this section will now address planning and envisioning changes in EA. There will be a strong focus on the application architecture.

5.1.3 Managed Evolution

In EAM, there is one principle for changes called *Managed Evolution*[3] (cf. Fig. 5.6). Changing the whole EA of a company is not a short-term task—it will not be done within the course of a single project. Usually, changing several applications, changing the processes related to this change in the organisation, will take a couple

---

[2] A plethora of text books is available like for example [1–3].

[3] The notion of *Managed Evolution* is further explained in [4].

of years. The planning will start with having a clear understanding where the changes are heading at. What are the objectives of a change? We need to establish a clear **vision** that will provide guidance with respect to the anticipated optimal state. A guiding vision will help everybody to understand the big picture. A vision does not exactly describe the to-be, but a rather optimal EA that might never be achieved. It serves as a light house for providing guidance and direction so that all involved people are working towards the same objective. It can be quite high-level and show the ideal future we can just imagine. Nevertheless, having a clear vision is very important as it will help us with getting started with planning several iterations for achieving an ideal architecture.

Let us start with analysing the as-is architecture in the year 2018 (as shown in Fig. 5.6). Instead of planning how to change the whole organisation in order to achieve the optimal architecture (i.e. the vision), we need to perform changes incrementally. The organisation can only deal with small changes while still doing business and the its environment will constantly be changing. We cannot predict the future, like the situation in 10 years or more. Enterprise architects will start with planning the first step in a very detailed way and also already anticipating future iterations. This will mainly cover the application landscape for the next planning period (e.g. next year). We already did this in the small example starting from page 139. We did not perform a big change, but rather doing small changes step by step. This also happens in a corporate environment when performing EAM.

After finishing one iteration (i.e. at the end of the planning period) we need to assess the situation and plan for the subsequent one. The vision will serve as our guiding principle. There are two drivers that will basically influence how the architecture looks like. One of them is the quality of the EA determined by architectural principles and quality criteria. Those criteria will support assessing the quality of the application landscape and how the idea business capability map should look like—just to provide two examples. This might look very academic to business people and only helps with improving the architecture.

However, the company needs to earn money at the same time. Whatever we do with our EA has to provide value for the business (i.e. earning money). This is indicated by the *business value* dimension in Fig. 5.6. At the beginning of each planning period will be decisions about new software applications or new functionality so that we can have a new product, or improve customer relationships. Business stakeholders will provide many requirements from their perspective that aims at making the business impact of our EA better.

Just following business requirements often leads to an unstructured architecture because it is all about having small changes, additions, and not controlling them properly. You remember one of the first pictures we discussed in Chap. 1, the one with the Titanic on it (Fig. 1.6 on page 11), showing that missing guidance for the architecture can lead to unstructured architecture. This would result in an application landscape that is not manageable any more, with a lot of cost, increasing maintenance cost, like an iceberg that are endangering our cruise. If you just follow business value, then you are not controlling your architecture any more. You are just adding the functionality in any way that is required by the business. This is why you need the architecture quality dimension for making sure that any kind of change also fits to our architecture. This will drive us towards improving the EA, and also makes sure that we have a maintainable structure in the future. This will also foster flexibility with respect to adjusting our architecture easily based on new requirements.

However, working on the quality of the architecture does not always provide immediate business value. By only following IT or EA principles, we are in danger of just having the architecture becoming a means on its own: Having the perfect architecture, but but no success on the market. None of the extremes—having the best architecture or providing most business value—will lead to overall success. Each of them might be achievable individually. But for the whole company, both of them are not desirable.

Therefore, planned changes should happen within a corridor between *unstructured architecture* and *architecture as a means on its own*. It should not focus too much on on business value and not too much pushing towards the ideal architecture at the same time. Concrete objectives for the next iteration will be decided at the end of the previous planning period.[4] The example in Fig. 5.6 is assuming a decision every year. Plans for the next iteration will cover one year and set objectives that can be achieved with in a one year's period. The objectives will always be a compromise between the two dimensions.

The first iteration is starting from the as-is and moving towards improving the architecture by 2019. It is not supposed to add much business value. For the following year, it looks like people agreed on adding more business value and only slightly improve the architectural quality. The next iteration improves architectural quality by end of 2021. Further iterations for reaching the *to-be* are not planned in a detailed way, yet. This might be some kind of state we want to achieve within 10 years after starting the transformation. The to-be architecture depicted in Fig. 5.6 is not carved in stone. An organisation usually has to adjust it based on changes in its environment or due to internal changes. New products or changing market will lead to adjusting a company's understanding of the notion of *business value*.

Managed evolution is emphasising two aspects:

1. Changes in the EA are performed iteratively towards a to-be state.
2. Each iteration will balance the improvement of *business value or* architecture quality.

The vision will provide a clear direction for planning the iterations. Decisions on the objectives for each iteration will be made at the end of the preceding iteration. The vision will remain the same while the to-be architecture might vary.

Performing a transformation based on managed evolution, consequently, requires thorough planning and flexibility with respect to adjusting plans. Figure 5.7 provides

---

[4]The decision of the duration of each planning period is done by the organisation. It tends to be a full or a half year. The duration needs to incorporate the ability of the company to adjust to new requirements and objectives.

an overview on various aspects of different phases during the transformation as being defined managed evolution:

- **Definition**: What is the scope of the phase?
- **Time:** What is the envisioned time horizon for the phase?
- **Stability:** How stable is the description of the architecture in the respective phase?
- **Detail**: Which level of detail is required for the plan?

The *as-is* shown as the first phase in Fig. 5.7 describes our current architecture. Analysis of the as-is usually reveals issues in the architecture that will have to be fixed during the whole transformation. The as-is architecture, therefore, is not stable as it will be subject to changes. Its description will not be very detailed as we just need to understand the current situation as a starting point for subsequent iterations. Its level of detail should be medium or high as we need as much information as required for documenting the issues. More detailed information is then required for planning the next iterations (phase **Plan** in Fig. 5.7). Such a plan will include, for example, the following information:

- detailed target application landscape
- changes to business processes and organisation
- projects (including project management documents) for performing changes
- budget and resources required for executing the iteration
- KPI and targets for measuring success of each iteration

The level of detail for the next iteration will be high, while subsequent iterations require plans with less details. Their plans might change after each planning period—including the to-be. The vision (right-hand side of Fig. 5.7) is some kind of ideal architecture and has less details than other phases. The level of detail should be very low. It is not about having a plan, how it should look like, but rather having a story to tell. The vision can also be written in an emotional way. We want to be better, or we want to be the best. We want to have the most optimal architecture, so it is more for encouraging people for changing. Because this is the bright future we are aiming at. Knowing we will not achieve it, because we need to face reality. There is no plan for ever achieving the vision, because we know that the way how to achieve the vision (i.e. the iterations) might change over time. Hence, there is no timeline associated with it. However, the vision should reflect what is decided by the corporate strategy. Whenever our business strategy or the IT strategy has some objectives that needs to be achieved, of course, this has to be reflected in the vision for our future architecture. The vision will incorporate a future business motivation and capability map including guidelines for an optimal application support.

For all the steps in between, we have different level of details. The intermediate steps will achieve partial results of the overall transformation. They are steps that we have to do in order to achieve the to be. The result of a complete transformation is usually due in many years. We can think of in 10 years or even in 15 years, meaning, we are talking about a long time horizon. Many of things can happen within 10 or 15 years, so cannot predict the exact state we will achieve in 10 years. Each and every

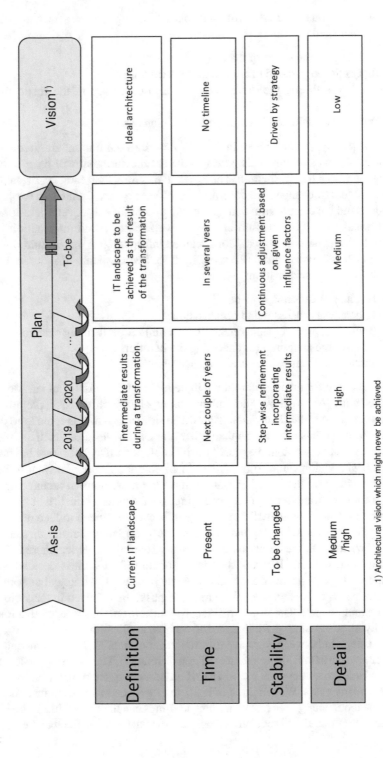

Fig. 5.7 Planning transformations

year, we need to reassess our to be and adjust it to changes that might happen. If we lost a certain market or don't want to offer a certain product any more, having a new product, even making a strategic decision (e.g. going away from a classical business model to a e-commerce business model), those kinds of changes and decisions can happen within 10 years. Which then also implies that we need to adjust our plan for the to be. Also the intermediate steps that are planned for next year, for in two years, and so on, they need to be refined step by step and also adjusted whenever we change the to be vision or the to be landscape.

5.1.4 Application Roadmap

This current section covers the management of changes in an EA. We already looked at a simple example and discussed different phases during a transformation during a managed evolution. As enterprise architects are using various maps, there is also one kind of map describing the roadmap of a transformation. An application roadmap lists all applications and initiatives that are performing changes on the application landscape. Please, keep in mind that EAM also includes changes on the business side (e.g. business processes, organisational structure). We will not cover those kinds of changes here as they are subject to different disciplines.[5] We will now focus on how to manage changes in the application architecture by considering dependencies to business architecture.

Definition 5.1 (Application Roadmap)   An **Application Roadmap** is a visualisation of (intended) changes to the application landscape of an organisation. It focuses on change initiatives working on applications, each of which …

- … has a planned start and end date
- … **implements** a new application, performs a **change** on an existing one or **shuts down** a legacy application.

Changes to the application landscape can be visualised using by an application roadmap (Definition 5.1). It shows intended changes to the application landscape in an organisation and focuses on initiatives that are supposed perform the changes (i.e. projects, programs or a small initiative). Each of those initiatives has a planned start and end date. Each of those initiatives can do one or more of the following activities:

- A **new application** is introduced (developed (i.e. make) or procured and configured (buy). This will most probably be subject to a large project.

---

[5]There is a plethora of textbooks on business process improvement like for example [5, 6].

- An existing application can be **updated**. The size of the change can vary from very small (initiative) to large (program). Modifications can consist of:
  - adding new functionality based on ne requirements
  - changing functionality based on updated requirements
  - rolling out the application to another organisational unit
  - reducing the scope of an application (i.e. disabling functionality

- An existing application is **decommissioned** (complete or partial)

Most initiatives will refer to updating existing applications, but also shutting down applications happens quite frequently. Running applications is associated with cost and if it does not provide any business value or needs to be replaced by a better application, then we need to initiate projects for shutting down such an application. Please keep in mind, shutting down an application is not like we are doing at home with our computer, uninstall and then it is done. An application in a corporate environment is used by many people, by hundreds of people who are trained with this application, who know how to use it, how to start it. They know all the specifics about it. There are further applications receiving data from one being subject to decommissioning. Therefore, we need to make sure that there is no other application depending on an application before switching it off. And we also need to make sure that business processes will be adjusted so that they are not using the old application any more but either switch to another one or do not require application support.

These kinds of changes, especially when thinking of reorganising the corporation, will take a long time. And any kind of change concerning decommissioning an application has to be done as a project.

Graphical visualisations are a central tool for EAM as already introduced in Chaps. 1 and 4. We already showed a couple of examples representing capabilities, business processes, applications and business support. Of course, there is also a

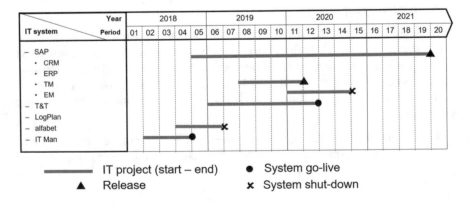

Fig. 5.8 Example roadmap

map or a visualisation for showing transformations, which is called the *application roadmap* as defined in Definition 5.1.

It can be visualised by a map like the one in Fig. 5.8. It indicates the time horizon on top of the map, starting with **year** 2018 until 2021. Software applications are listed on the left-hand side (named **IT systems**): The example consists of an *SAP system* comprising several applications for *Customer Relationship Management* (CRM), *Enterprise Resource Planning* (ERP), *transportation management* (TM) and *event management* (EM). It has a *track and trace* (T&T) application, an application called *LogPlan*, *alfabet*, which is an EAM tool, and a tool called IT management, short *IT Man*.

The main part of the roadmap shows several initiatives (i.e. **IT projects**) that are working on those applications. A very long project already started in 2018 and will last for almost 3 years, leading to a new release of the CRM application. The new release is indicated by the black triangle at the right end of the project time line. As given by the legend, a project can terminate with the **go-live** of a new application, a new **release** of an existing one or a system **shut-down**. The transportation management software is subject to a short project resulting in a new release. What happened to event management? For some reason, there was the decision that it is not required any more. Consequently, a project is started in the beginning of 2020 which will decommission EM before the end of the year. It cannot be used any more from then on and will be replaced by **T&T**. In parallel decommissioning *EM*, a project has already been started beginning of 2019 with the objective of having a new track and trace application by around mid of 2020. The black circle at the right end of the project time line indicates the system go live. The same holds true the EAM tools *alfabet* and *IT Man*. There is a plan for switching off *alfabet* and introducing *IT Man* in parallel. Such replacements are usually planned with some buffer between go-live and decommissioning. Planning has to avoid switching off an application before the substitute is in place in case of any unexpected delay.

It is just an example, but maps like this exist in many corporations. It is a very common representation for showing several initiatives like projects that work on changing the application landscape. It visualises information concerning:

1. time line of individual projects and desired result
2. dependencies between related initiatives

The example is very simple and is meant to show the underlying structure. It can be further annotated with additional information, like:

- project milestones or phases for more detailed planning
- resource requirements and financial aspects for resource planning
- business contacts and responsibilities of inter-project coordination
- dependencies from other applications as provided in the application architecture
- affected business capabilities or processes

The application roadmap provides an overview on changes being performed on the application landscape but is also connected to other architectural view.

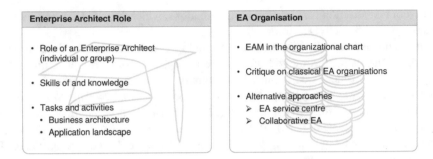

Fig. 5.9 Enterprise architect and organisation

It is, furthermore, the link towards project management or program management (i.e. coordinating several interrelated projects). As projects progress over time, the roadmap has to be updated in case of any change during project execution (e.g. a delay).

5.2   Enterprise Architect Role and Organisation

The previous sections of this chapter provide an overview on conducting changes in EAM. This topic is quite important as EAM does not only describe architecture but also aims at its improvement. Those improvements will then be executed as projects changing the application architecture or the business. Both are interrelated as business changes imply different application, and application changes cannot be done without affecting business processes. Who is responsible for doing all those changes? this will be the role of the enterprise architect as the one preparing, planning, making decisions, and also supporting conducting changes.

The section at hand will describe the two aspects as shown in Fig. 5.9

- **enterprise architect role:** skills and responsibilities of people acting as enterprise architect
- **enterprise architecture organisation:** classical organisational unit providing EA in a company

An enterprise architect does not just exist somewhere in the company. EAM has a place in the organisational chart. This is what we will look at after having a common understanding on the role of the enterprise architect. We will have some options, how to set up and what architecture management in the organisation and compare them against each other.

The following Sect. 5.3 will then provide an overview on critique on EAM as it is implemented in many organisations today. It will also provide an outlook on current and future approaches for a more collaborative working mode of EA—as opposed to classical methods. We will check for organisations that can be set up in a more service centred way or even establishing a collaborative approach for EAM within a company. Just to state it very clearly, EAM in the past was rather seen as a governance approach and this is still the case in many organisations. If you want to achieve a holistic optimization—i.e. large changes—you need to enable it from top down by using tools and methods from governance. However, EA can also be implemented on a smaller scale. And there is a lot of criticism, especially because of this governance approach. Therefore, you will find new approaches that do not only use governance mechanisms for setting up EA but also adopt collaborative and service oriented ideas.

5.2.1 Enterprise Architect Role

Let us start with understanding the role of the *enterprise architect*. It can be an individual but usually will be a group of people providing EAM in a company.[6] This section cover the following aspects:

- skills and knowledge required for EAM
- tasks and activities performed by an enterprise architect

Definition 5.2 (Enterprise Architect) The **Enterprise Architect Role** (short Enterprise Architect) is an abstract description of skills and knowledge for performing EA work. It also refers to responsibilities of an enterprise architect in an organisation.

Figure 5.10 provides an overview on the responsibilities of an enterprise architect. Depending on the company's size, the EA group can be a large team. Team members (each of them having the enterprise architect role) can share or divide responsibilities.

Enterprise architects need to help with **creating** the artefacts that we discussed so far.[7] We are talking about a lot of maps that need to be created including collecting information required for creating them. All of this is typically done by the enterprise architect who is feeding the EA repository with information and then can create the maps as required by stakeholders. The enterprise architect is not only responsible for collecting the data but also for ensuring the correctness of the data or quality assurance for all the EA artefacts.

The enterprise architect does not only maintain the artefacts but also support stakeholders with **applying** them. Each stakeholder needs to get an adequate visualisation and they need to be informed whenever data and a map changes. An enterprise architect also needs to make sure that new maps are published within the

---

[6]The term *enterprise architect* will be used for referring to an individual, a position or even a group of people throughout this book.

[7]We covered for example the following artefacts: business capability map (Chap. 2, application landscape (Chap. 3), business support matrix (Chap. 4) and application roadmap (Sect. 5.1).

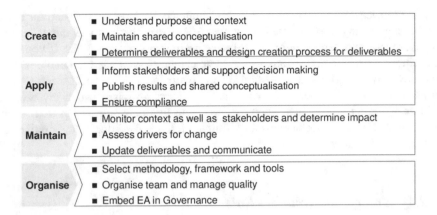

Fig. 5.10 Enterprise architect role: responsibilities

corporation and that anybody who needs to have an overview of certain aspects will have a corresponding viewpoint. Publishing includes making sure that compliance rules are met. The enterprise architect cannot just show all the information to any stakeholder in the company due to data protection and security reasons. The viewpoints have to be created based on a stakeholder's authorisation.

Maintaining data and artefacts (i.e. maps) is usually an underestimated task. I still meet people telling me about introducing an EAM tool. They assume that we just need to install the tool, gather any required data and can then generate architecture viewpoints automatically. This will then provide value to the organisation as depicted in Fig. 1.9 on page 17. Those people (usually sales staff of an EAM tool provider) are very enthusiastic about the tool and the method. What they are very often forget about, is that the company changes frequently. Even worse, the enterprise architect is not always getting aware of all those changes. It is very tough to keep the EAM repository updated over time. The enterprise architect needs to establish mechanisms for monitoring the organisation and also the stakeholders so that the enterprise architect gets informed about changes so that the drivers for the change can be understood. The EA repository can then be updated and also corresponding maps regenerated and provided to the stakeholders.

Generally speaking, the enterprise architect needs to **organise** all the work around EA. It starts with selecting and defining the proper methodology or a framework, selecting a software tool for EA work, adjusting existing frameworks, configuring methodologies so that they fit to organisational needs. A team needs to be set up for doing EA work. In many organisations, they still do not have an EA team. The EA discipline was not that popular in the 1990s. Starting from 2000, many organisations recognised its value and got busy with setting up such an organisation. Forming a team, setting up the organisation, establishing it in the company, and then also managing the team over time are quite important tasks. Also existing governance mechanisms need to be aligned with EAM. Both need to use common tools and mechanisms for guiding the corporation.

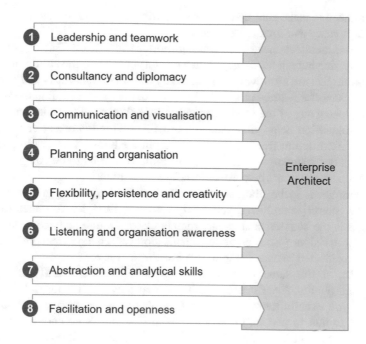

Fig. 5.11 Enterprise architect role: Skills

Bad news for specialists: EAM is a job generalists. Being a successful enterprise architect requires a lot of different skills that you need to offer for managing your day-to-day work (cf. Fig. 5.11[8]). One of the most important skills is *communication*. There is a study by Banaeianjahromi et al. investigating critical success factors as well as reasons for EA initiatives to fail (cf. [8]). They come to the conclusion that *communication* and also *collaboration* are key for being successful. The other way around, if communication does not work properly between enterprise architects and stakeholders, then it will not be successful.

EAM is not only about drawing and publishing pictures. It is not only about having a solid IT knowledge, but also being very good at communication. The chief enterprise architect needs to be very good at **leading a team** and each member needs to be good in working within a team. EAM is a holistic approach covering the whole company. Therefore, problems need to be addressed on corporate level rather than fixing small problems. This can only be achieved by working as a team.

The work of the enterprise architect sometimes resembles the one of a **consultant**. You need to know how to talk to people and listen to their concerns. You also need to know how to explain them required actions in an adequate way. At the same

---

[8]The overview provided in Fig. 5.11 has been compiled from [7].

time, you need to make sure that you are not irritating people. It therefore requires a bit of diplomacy and social intelligence.

Enterprise architects need excellent **communication** skills. This does not only refer to applying human language (written or oral) but also to the ability of creating visualisations that are intuitively understood by stakeholders. This is one of the soft skills that cannot be learned mechanically. It is not only about reading the EA book and then picking any of the existing visualisations. You need to make sure that the chosen visualisation helps your stakeholder with solving his or her concern. This might be very different from the standard way in the book. It is very important to not create just a standard visualisation, but to make sure that you can provide the map that top management perceives as useful for their work.

EA work needs to be **planned** and **organised**.It requires organisational skills and as the enterprise architect, you need to be very **flexible**. You need to adjust to changes in the business and its environment.Even though managed evolution is striving for a vision, priorities in an organisation can change frequently and this needs to be reflected in each iteration in a transformation roadmap.

However, at the same time, you also need to be **persistent** for ensuring architectural quality. Even if people tell you that they don't want to follow your advise. If you exactly know this is the best way to do it, then you should also know how to talk to people, to convince them that there's no choice, or that the other choices are not better than the one you are heading at. Of course, persistence is not just being stubborn and isolated. Being persistent also means that you have communicative skills, that you are some kind of diplomatic that you have some leadership skills, that you can define and communicate a vision. All the skills provided in Fig. 5.11 relate to each other.

When talking to people or conducting meetings, you need to be a good **facilitator**. This also requires being neutral as a facilitator. Even though you have a preference for a certain solution, the facilitator should not for pushing for one solution, but helping people with finding a common solution.

As most IT people, you need to be skilled in **analysis** and have a good understanding of **abstraction**, so that you are not getting dragged too much into the details. You are not the system architect—you are not building a house—but the town planner. You need a high level view on the architecture in order to have the overview on all applications together with their business context. An application landscape depicts all software applications and not details about their internal algorithms.

And last but not least, an enterprise architect needs to **listen** to what people are saying. You will never be successful if you don't listen to people and understand their concerns. You need to listen to them for understanding which kind of visualisation they need. You need to listen to them for understanding which kind of message you need to provide to them, in case of consultancy. You need to listen to them for also doing the facilitation. This will require a balance between appreciating people's concerns on the one hand and being persistent with solid solution on the other hand. There is no easy solution for this balance except for experience. Listening is one of the key skills you need to have as an enterprise architect. And of course, organisational skills and **organisation awareness**. You need to make sure that you are connected within the company and get informed by other people, or even getting contacted by other people. A successful enterprise architect will profit from his/her network.

What are the typical tasks that can happen in day-to-day work of an Enterprise Architect? An overview is provided in Fig. 5.12. It is not meant to exhaustive or complete but rather provide an impression of the spectrum of EAM activities. The overview is structured by the following two dimensions:

1. Activities can affect the **application layer** or the **business layer**. As these layers are interconnected, some activities can have an impact on both. We will locate them in that level in which activities will have an immediate effect.
2. Any activity can have a long-term relevance (i.e. being **strategic**) or being subject to daily routine (**operational**), providing immediate results.

Let us start with *operational* activities that enterprise architects may perform or might get involved in with respect to the *application layer*. We already talked about some of those activities in previous sections. Enterprise architects need to ...

- ...collect and maintain data about applications (cf. Sects. 3.3 and 5.2.1, page 154).
- ...connect applications to the business layer, i.e. describing the business support (Sect. 4.3)
- ...provide maps describing the application landscape for business and IT stakeholders (cf. Sects. 4.1 and 1.3, page 20)
- ...assist with performing EA analysis (e.g. by using the business support matrix as shown in Sect. 4.3)

Analysis can be performed by the EA team, but can also involve management from the IT side or people from the business side. In many organisations, enterprise architects are also involved in application portfolio management. Therefore, they also have to assess proposals for IT projects. Such an assessment will help with selecting projects with the most potential for success. Each project will be evaluated with respect to effort, benefit as well as its risk so that it can be compared to others. An enterprise architect will also get involved in facilitating, conducting, or managing changes in IT.

There are activities that are not part of day-to-day work, but have a *strategic* relevance. Maintaining the IT architecture or the *application landscape* needs a common methodology. This needs to be defined and implemented on corporate level so that we have tools and visualisations available for managing the application landscape. This includes the kind of viewpoints required by stakeholders for their concerns. Do you remember the posters showing application landscape?[9] These need to be defined, not on a day-to-day basis, but on a long-term basis so that we

---

[9]For example in Sect. 4.2.

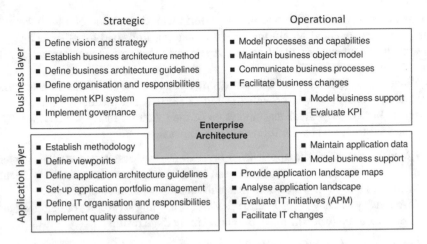

Fig. 5.12 Enterprise architect role—tasks

can make sure we have the resources for creating those posters whenever they are needed.

Managing the architecture does not only mean we are describing and making plans about how to get there. We also need to provide quality criteria for the evolution of the application landscape. Those guidelines will act similar to KPI in the business. They provide information on how to assess a good architecture compared to a not so good one. These guidelines are not changed every day. They are defined once and only rarely updated. They are meant to be valid for a long period of time.

The same holds true for setting up a methodology for application portfolio management. It is not only about performing decisions, but also defining the methodology for managing the application portfolio. The enterprise architect is involved in defining the responsibilities that need to be covered by the IT organisation. This especially holds true in the case of partial outsourcing if part of the activities of the IT organisation are outsourced to a third-party provider.

And last but not least, we need to have quality assurance in IT. This certainly bases on the guidelines for good architecture defined by the EA role. Therefore, the architect also gets involved in implementing measures for assuring the quality of IT landscapes.

Even though we are talking about applications and IT very often, and talk about changing the IT landscape, of course EA still refers to a holistic approach that also incorporates activities on the *business layer*. An enterprise architect can be part of a business process team or can get involved in activities for describing business processes and business capabilities, together with the business specialists. The enterprise architect can also get involved in maintaining the business object model (cf. Sect. 2.3). This is not a task that can be done in IT or by IT people alone, but definitely requires skills and knowledge from the business perspective.

New business processes or changes in existing processes need to be communicated. And if we agree on changes, then they also need to be facilitated. There might be a dedicated business process management team. Business process management teams and enterprise architects are often working closely together for making sure that they are not having two different versions of the company, but having one common understanding of business processes, capabilities and objects. Modelling of the business support—which might look kind of redundant, because here it is on the business layer, and it is here on the application layer–is definitely a shared responsibility. Business support can be managed or maintained from two directions, either from the business side or from the IT side—or both in a coordinated way.

There are a couple of activities that have a *strategic* implication for the organisation. Somebody needs to define the vision and the strategy for the whole corporation. As this is part of top executives or the top management, it will be covered by them and their staff departments. Nevertheless, EA can get involved into those activities. Architecture guidelines, quality criteria for architecture and ideas for business process improvement can influence the definition of the strategy.

The business architecture method needs to be defined and implemented on a corporate level and aligned with the one for the application landscape. We also need guidelines for the business architecture, guidelines describing good business processes, and also how to describe good business capabilities. EA can get involved in organisational design and also assigning responsibilities to organisational units. EA can have a consulting role in establishing a KPI system. Such a system of key performance indicators is necessary for measuring the performance of individual organisations (based on their responsibilities) and measuring the performance of business processes.

5.2.2   Enterprise Architecture Organisation

The previous section describes the role of the enterprise architect by explaining responsibilities, skills and typical activities. We should now have an understanding about what an architect is doing. The current section will describe the EA organisation and where EA is located in the organisational structure. This organisation is defined as follows:

Definition 5.3 (Enterprise Architecture Organisation) The Enterprise Architecture Organisation (EAO) is an organisational unit enabling EAM in a company. It consolidates people with EA skills and knowledge. The organisation can be set up in one of the following forms:

- **enterprise architecture team**: consisting of enterprise architects performing EA work
- **competency centre**: for disseminating EAM knowledge

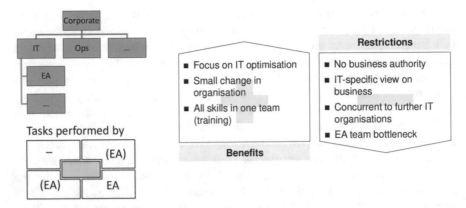

Fig. 5.13 EAM organisation as part of IT organisation

The classical perspective is that EA needs to be implemented top-down as an organisational unit supporting the management. Depending on sponsor, it can be part of the IT organisation (sponsored by the IT head) or on corporate level (driven by a top executive). The current section will present four options for setting up EAM in the organisation. Each option is characterised by its benefits and also drawback. We will also indicate which kinds of activities are performed by different organisational units against the structure of Fig. 5.12. The figures describing each option will show, which set of activities is performed by EA, IT teams or business specialists. This will not represent a strict assignment of tasks but rather serve as a rough characterisation of responsibilities.

A simple option for setting up EA **within the IT organisation** is shown in Fig. 5.13. This reflects the situation when I started my carreer in EA. The EA team is one among others in IT. This allows for a close collaboration with other IT teams but EA is disconnected from other departments (e.g. operations, marketing and customer service) and far away from corporate management. Having this set-up in mind, I think you can imagine that the power of people working here is quite limited. And effectively, my team was just performing activities on application landscape and being involved in application portfolio management. We were only slightly involved in strategic aspects within IT (in the same extent as other IT departments). We were basically expected to execute what was defined by the CIO together with other IT heads.

Even worse, we were mostly disconnected from business people. This made it impossible to to understand business processes, capabilities and objects. We were asking the business departments for providing information about the business architecture. Some of them refused to follow the request because they did not want to or did not have any business process maps at hand. And we could not force them to maintain such kind of information and hand it over to us. Chances are also very low with respect to getting actively involved in activities concerning business architecture—especially no activities with strategic relevance. This just summarises experience from my perspective. However, this experience is quite common in other companies with a similar set-up of EAM within the IT organisation. Other people reported similar experiences. Even though there might be differences in collaboration (perhaps supported by the company culture) but the basic disconnect still remains.

There might be differences in data, but the general restriction is that those departments do not have any authority in business. And they are focusing very much on an IT-specific topics without properly understanding business priorities. Honestly speaking, this does not reflect the basic idea of EA aligning business and IT. Business capability maps are often created by (senior) IT people who are familiar with the organisation. Nevertheless, it will still remain an IT point of view on the business and not the real business perspective. Also the alignment with further IT departments can become cumbersome. Identifying and eliminating redundancies in the application landscape relies on other departments' support and collaboration. If they do not collaborate, there is no way for forcing them to performing required changes.

The EA team is accountable for performing most of the architecture-related activities, as shown in Fig. 5.13. Architects maintain all information about the application architecture, try to get an overview on business architecture and can only slightly influence strategic aspects. They can easily become a bottleneck if they are not staffed sufficiently or are busy with understanding the business context without (or only minor) support by business departments. If you only have a small team which is located somewhere in IT, your scope of work can get restricted to tasks like drawing maps, collecting information, and do not get any support from other departments.

However, the benefits of such a kind of organisational set-up lies in its simplicity. Imagine the situation not having EA at all in the company. Introducing EA as one department within IT is a small change. The CIO can push for this change and in setting it up. And you can make sure that all the skills that are required are within one team. We don't need to train other people.

But against the restrictions of having limited impact, we should check how could we set up EA differently. Instead of being one department, it can be introduced as staff department directly supporting the CIO. This option—as shown in Fig. 5.14— shifts the responsibility of the EA team from operational activities towards strategic aspects in IT. Collecting information on the application landscape is not only done by architects but can be delegated to IT teams. Maintaining the application landscape is now shifted towards those people who are also performing the changes on applications (i.e. executing IT projects).

However, even though being closer to the CIO, there is still the tendency of being disconnected from business stakeholders. Chances are still high, that the representation of the business capabilities only reflect an IT-specific view and not the view how business people see what the business is doing. And instead of only having skilled enterprise architects within one team, you also need to start training other IT staff so that they can collect and maintain data about applications. They need to understand EA so that they can also create the viewpoints required by

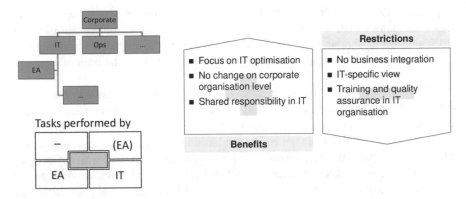

Fig. 5.14 EAM organisation as staff department to CIO

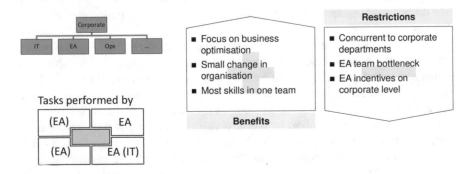

Fig. 5.15 EAM organisation as corporate EA division

various stakeholders. If you want to get other peoples involved, you also need to enable them so that they can perform the tasks as expected.

If training is done properly, then the EA team can share the workload with other IT departments. EA is a shared responsibility within IT. At least you do not need to change the organisational chart on a corporate level, as the change is still within IT, and you can focus on a broader optimization of IT.

In order to improve the business relevance of EA, the team can build an organisational unit on corporate level and not restricting EA to IT. From the beginning on in this book, I was emphasising the fact that EAM is not just IT management. It is a holistic approach, enforcing business IT alignment. It is deriving an IT landscape that is optimal for supporting the business. It also fosters (IT) innovation in the company, so that business can be more efficient in the future. If you want to achieve this, you need to make sure that EA is perceived as part of the whole organisation. The corresponding organisational chart is shown in Fig. 5.15. EA is one department on the same level as IT as well as other business departments (e.g. operations, finance, sales). being the enterprise architect, you can collaborate with business people and you can align with IT people. You can define guidelines that are relevant for the whole organisation.

When checking the tasks that need to be performed, we have a shift of activities on the operational side for the application architecture. Again, EA tend to get involved because they are not part of IT—even not as staff members for the CIO. They cannot influence other IT people or define their responsibilities. However, as EA is on the same level as IT, they can find some working agreement between EA and IT. Ideally, EA should maintain the EA repository together with IT people. Of course, as they are not part of the IT department, they can only get partially involved in strategic activities for IT and the same for business strategy. The CEO on corporate level will certainly not only ask EA about how to define the corporate strategy. He or she will also involve IT heads, operations heads, marketing heads— i.e. all his or her direct reports.

EA now at least gets in charge of all the activities that are related to maintaining the business architecture. I experienced being in such an organisation at a later point of time during my professional career. The department was not called EA but *Performance Management* and supporting a strategic program for improving business performance. Although being tasked to monitor and improve business performance, this department was also accountable for aligning business and IT.[10]

The benefit of this kind of organisation is that you are on the same level as other departments and it is easier to establish a collaborative working mode. You can focus more on business optimization and not only on managing IT landscapes. Introducing such an team in the overall organisation is a small to medium-sized change. You just create a new department on corporate level and do not impact changes in other department. You can consolidate EA skills and competencies within one department which needs to consult and work with other departments.

However, this might lead to conflicts as the EA team is concurrent with other corporate divisions and departments. You can provide guidelines and justify them but incentives for others to obey them are limited. The EA organisation can become a bottleneck like in the second option (Fig. 5.14). All the EA skills are bundled within one department that needs to support the whole organisation. EA is basically defining the objectives, but cannot provide any restrictions or guidelines for other departments as being on the same level (Fig. 5.15).

Ideally, EA should be directly consulting and supporting the CEO.[11] What I am describing here is the ideal form of EA (Fig. 5.16). EA is not just in IT or on the same level as others. The enterprise architect is directly supporting the CEO with managing the corporation. EA is supposed to be a corporate staff department, describing, prescribing, enabling changes, standards, guidelines for all the other departments.

---

[10]The team was managing business requirements for IT developments and providing training for business people. As they had they expertise on business and software applications, the team got also involved in activities typical to EA.

[11]I've never been in such an environment. There is a book published by Chris Potts, a consultant in EA: [9]. It is nicely written as a story and explaining the idea that the CEO is the real enterprise architect.

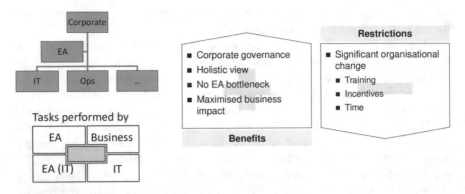

Fig. 5.16 EAM Organisation as corporate staff department

The benefits is that you can then implement a corporate governance approach for EA. You can enforce the holistic view as you are in top of all the other organisational units. You can involve any other department. It is not about performing the work, but defining how the whole organisation should work. This approach can maximise the business impact of EA work.

However, restrictions are clear. If you involve other departments in EA work, you need to enable them. This will result in a lot of changes. You need to implement an EAM method. You need to train people. You need to set proper incentives for people to make sure that we have a corporate, holistic, EAM. Each person working in any department needs to spend some time on EA work.

When looking at it from the task perspective, it really looks like EA can get involved in defining business strategy, setting up KPI, defining measurements, and, also defining the EA method on a corporate level. Business units are in charge of describing business processes, performing business changes, and provide transparency for others. The IT department is in charge of planning and executing changes in the application landscape. Furthermore, EA can also get involved in defining the IT strategy. The IT strategy can be derived from the corporate strategy. IT will still have a stake on defining the IT strategy, but EA can have a leading role.

As I have never been in such an environment, I cannot provide any hands-on experience. But, this is the idea of EAM. It is a holistic approach. It needs to be implemented company-wide. It is addressing each and every part in the company. And if you want to set it up as a corporate responsibility, you need to have it on corporate level and not just as part of any of the other departments.

5.3   Collaborative Enterprise Architecture

The different options for setting up EAM in an organisation base on the assumption that it needs to be implemented top-down. It is supposed to be driven by a leader (e.g. top executive on board level) that pushes for achieving a holistic view. We can

Critique on classical EA organisations	Requirements for collaborative EA organisation
• Implemented top-down (Governance) • Bureaucratic working mode • Controls, approvals and sign-offs • Working in silo as another IT function • Group of people in the ivory tower • Requesting participation from others • Adapting complex frameworks • Establish strict method and many artefacts • Focussed on prescribing future architecture • Producing plenty of documents and maps • Artefacts hardly understood or appreciated by non-EA people • Perceived as not providing relevant outcomes or value • In fact, many ambitious EA initiatives failed	• Implemented by and with stakeholders • Collaborative working mode • Support, results and value • Being open for business needs • Being involved across the organisation • Participating in stakeholders' activities • Adopting Lean and agile techniques • Develop flexible method • Supporting changes in objectives • Focus on necessary documents • Provide information and visualisation as needed by stakeholders • Having a clear value proposition based on business needs • Hence, foster business success

Fig. 5.17 Critique on classical EAM approaches and requirements for collaborative EAM

see that EA can be assigned to different levels in the organisational chart which will have its benefits and drawbacks. However, they all reflect the classical perspective on implementing EA in a company.

In the beginning, the EA function was very often driven by IT departments. They understood that they need to have a good understanding of the business in order to provide optimal (and cost efficient) IT support. It was also motivated by classical IT organisations that were only focussing on IT (technology and networking) and rarely considering business needs. Even though this already provides an improvement, there is some criticism on EAM. The criticism is addressed towards the discipline itself but even more on how organisations introduce and perform it today. Figure 5.17 provides an overview on how EA is perceived in a negative way on the left-hand side[12]. The right-hand of the figure derives requirements for an improved EAM.

The EA organisation is very often perceived as being set up **top down** with a very **bureaucratic** working mode. Because of being a governance function, classical EA initiatives were setting up controls and procedures (including **approvals** and **sign offs**) in order to control changes. Those overhead activities tend to delay projects and production processes.

The prospect of EA is providing a holistic view but in some cases EA just created an additional **silo** if the EA organisation did not establish a collaborative working mode with IT and business units. How can you establish proper controls if you are disconnected from others? Silo thinking and controls rarely foster collaboration.

---

[12]The overview has been compiled from personal experience and discussions with peers. It also incorporates input from publications like [10–12].

In some organisations EA was set up as some group which was then working in the **ivory tower**. This refers to having a theoretical understanding of the business architecture without any practical experience ion operational processes—both, IT and business processes. In order to analyse architecture and conduct changes, an enterprise architect needs to understand relevant operational aspects of the organisation, like

* the reasons behind the current process design
* peculiarities of the business
* business rules and procedure

Enterprise architects also need to involve further staff from the company. But, instead of solving business relevant problems, architects often request their **participation** for EA purposes (e.g. collecting EA data, drawing maps, reducing the number of software applications).

Frameworks are the most prominent tools in EA. They are prominent in the literature but also with EA consultancies. Major frameworks (e.g. TOGAF) are influencing the EA organisation and its working mode. A framework provides a blueprint for EAM so that many companies just adopted them. We will have a look at frameworks in the following Chap. 6 and their potential for solving imminent problems. As in many cases, people should not just adapt a tool (i.e. a framework).[13] They should understand the problem to be solved first and then decide for an appropriate tool. Just adopting a framework will primarily result in having an EA organisation but necessarily solving problems if it was not fully understood before.

Producing a lot of **maps** (i.e. viewpoints) and **paperwork** (e.g. architecture guidelines and principles) is one of the pain point for business departments. We as enterprise architects set up methods that result in creating big posters (sometimes helpful posters). But very often this leads to a lot of paperwork with artefacts that are not required. Some artefacts focus on prescribing the future (e.g. to-be architecture). You might already imagine what happens when some disconnected enterprise architects in their silo define the future architecture of the organisation. This will lead to resistance and rejection by other departments. This is what happen frequently during the past years: Having the paperwork from the ivory tower, prescribing how the whole company should work in the future How can you substantiate such a decision without solid business knowledge?

Many of the standard maps (including the one prescribed by common frameworks) are **hard to understand** by business and IT people. Even when following a simple structure, they may grow large and present a lot of information. They get hard by people without EA experienced as they can get very abstract. If you have a team somewhere producing a lot of paperwork, posters that nobody understands, so how can you trust them that they know how to change the business?

There are a lot of initiatives that failed in the past, because EA did not result in any benefits for the company. They did not create any **tangible value**, except for

---

[13]*A fool with a tool is still a fool.*

collecting application data, creating paperwork, creating posters and running around with posters (pretending being the architect). Such an organisation can be perceived as costing money without providing any value. Having a successful EAM requires collecting a lot of information in order to improve business and IT. However, doing it properly will take a lot of time for data collection and establishing a method.

If you do it academically, disconnected from business, then you have a high risk that you are spending a lot of work without any result. A lot of EA initiatives started quite ambitious, but **failed**.[14]

Let us look on the right hand side of Fig. 5.17. There are a couple of publications available at the moment that want to drive towards a more **flexible**, **cooperative**, or **collaborative** approach for an EA organisation. An organisation that is implemented by and together with other stakeholders. An organisation that does not have a governance mechanism based on controls, but having a collaborative working mode. An organisation that focuses on **supporting** other departments, providing results and value. An organisation that is not caught in the ivory tower, but that is open for any kind of business needs, not just providing decisions from the silo, but understanding the other business stakeholders. This organisation is supposed to be involved in initiatives and activities throughout the organisation, and even participate in activities that are shared with all the stakeholders.

Some of these approaches also aim at adopting existing techniques that have been successful in various other disciplines. Some examples are ...

- ... adopting lean techniques from business process management
- ... agile methods from agile software development
- ... using principles from lean organisation design
- ... enable EAM tools with social media

They are basically aiming at developing a more flexible method with respect to EA, that does not only adapt a framework, but implements a methodology based on business needs. Such a methodology is not strictly aiming at long term objectives only, but that can be adjusted to changes in objectives easily. Such a methodology should not only print or create a lot of documents, but focus on those documents that are really needed by other departments. This should foster the provision of information and visualisation as needed by stakeholders.

The EA organisation should not start with collecting as much data as possible and then create fancy posters, but understand business needs first. It should then specifically get this kind of information, so that it can provide immediate benefit by delivering relevant (i.e. helpful) visualisation. This will require a clear value proposition based on business needs. The following sections provide an overview on some ideas how such an organisation could look like.

---

[14]I remember one of my bosses that hired me, because she wanted to set up EAM in an organisation. Only 7 months after I started my new position as business architect, she had to resign. She was only focusing on collecting data and creating maps, but did not manage to communicate the benefit towards corporate management.

Fig. 5.18 EA service centre: basic idea

5.3.1 *Enterprise Architecture Service Centre*

One idea of having an EA department being more cooperative is the idea of the EA service centre as depicted in Fig. 5.18. There are no corresponding publications available as this idea represents research in progress. The basic principle follows the concept of a sales organisation that is offering services on a market. Stakeholders in the company are treated like customers that can order and use EA services provided by the service centre. EA services are documented in a service catalogue that needs to be aligned with with business stakeholders (i.e. customers). Stakeholders still consist of corporate management, business departments as well as IT. Collaboration is supposed to be established by using services and adjusting services based on stakeholders' needs. Their needs can be fulfilled with services that are provided by an EA service centre, having a catalogue with a list of services that the EA service centre offers to all the stakeholders within the corporation.

The two drivers for such a kind of organisational form are **collaboration** and a clear **value proposition** (cf. Fig. 5.19). Collaboration can be established by being in a consulting role towards stakeholders. It can support projects within the company, interact with business departments and adapt to changes. If a service is not needed anymore, then it will be removed from the service catalogue. We can implement new services, so that we have services that are aimed at solving real problems in the corporation and not just provide an academic approach for a holistic view on the corporation.

And it is not only about collaborating with stakeholders, but also telling them what is the value of our service. This is the same as providing products and services on the market which need to have a value proposition. A customer only buys a service if it provides a value . We are aiming at transferring these concepts from marketing and sales to the EA service centre. The value proposition documents

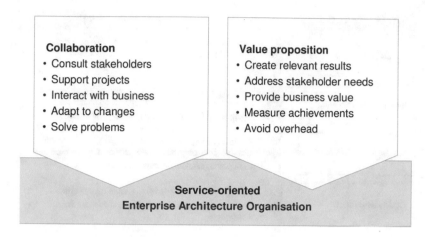

Fig. 5.19 EA service centre: drivers

the value as perceived by a corporate stakeholder (i.e. the customer of the service centre). The focus is on relevant results towards the customers.

The service catalogue needs to be established together with stakeholders. It should not reflect activities and artefacts as proposed by prominent EA frameworks. It should also not constructed by pushing obligations towards the stakeholders—for example requesting them to maintain EA information or changing their processes. The service catalogue needs to reflect a common understanding between the EA service centre and the stakeholders in order to provide relevant business value (value proposition). This also includes implementing measures for determining the business value. KPI are a well-established tool for measuring business performance and can also be defined for measuring service quality (similar to product KPI measuring a product's sale performance on the market). Relevance and value of a service can then be quantified by KPI which represent a mutually aligned service level agreement. Assessing the value of an EA service based on marketing tools will support changing the service catalogue based on value and demand.

In short: The vision for the EA service centre is having a service-oriented EA organisation providing value within the company.

How could a service catalogue for such a service centre look like? So far, we identified four different service types as shown in Fig. 5.20. There might be **consulting services**, services that can be acquired by other departments that help with understanding a problem, helping with finding a solution. If a department needs to have an integration software for integrating several systems, or even for having an API for doing e-business with external partners, EA can provide a consulting service telling them which integration solutions are available, what are the benefits, which one should we not adopt, and then helping them with making a good decision on which integration infrastructure they should use for their project.

Other services are supposed to be requested by corporate management. They need **information** about the business, about the EA, and also some kind of

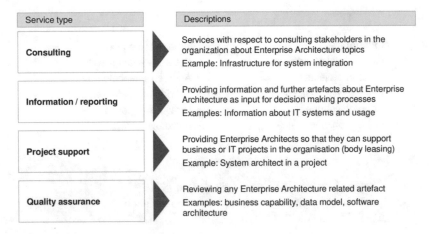

Fig. 5.20 EA service centre: types of services

reporting. CIOs, for example, need to have an overview on their IT systems. They also need to get an overview on who is using which IT systems. Consequently, one service provide the CIO with specific information. As you can already see here, for those services, it is not only about the EA service centre having the obligation for providing the service, but we also need to implement what is required from the users. If the CIO wants to have the information service, he also needs to make sure that the EA service centre is enabled for collecting all the data. He needs to instruct all his subordinates which kind of data each of them needs to be provided to EA so that they can consolidate the data for, then, performing the reporting and the information service.

Project support is one of the main activities of enterprise architects. Consequently, there should be a group of EA services for providing skilled staff for projects like ...

- **system architect**: a person being skilled in in software and EA, who can support projects with respect to defining software architecture
- **integration architect**: an architect specialised in integration technology that can support with using integration middleware
- **data architect**: supporting with respect to data modelling and adherinmg to corporate data standards
- **business architect**: providing knowledge on business capabilities and supporting with understanding business requirements

These resources provide EA services and are intended to become part of a project team. They can and help with implementing a new information system or changing an existing application. This refers to some kind of body leasing—i.e. providing resources which have EA skills and knowledge. Beside providing knowledge, they can also foster adherence to architectural standards and foster reuse across different projects.

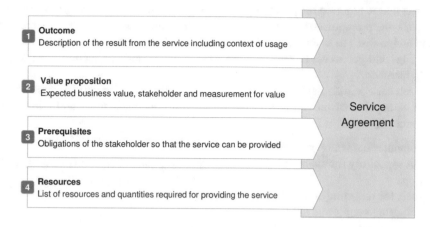

Fig. 5.21 EA service centre—service agreement

Quality assurance needs to be integral with other services but can also be offered as a service on its own. A dedicated service would consist of performing reviews and communicating improvement potential. Reviewing architecture and design documents of a software project would be one example. An architect can review the application architecture with respect to its fit to the overall EA. This check can also include identifying redundancies or overlaps with other business processes, projects or software applications. Having the big picture, architects can help finding reuse potential from other business areas doing similar implementations.[15]

Each EA service needs to be further specified by a **service agreement**. This is some kind of contract describing relevant properties of each service. It encompasses its output and also prerequisites for its execution as shown in Fig. 5.21. What is the result? Is it having a resource being available in a project? Or is it a document being created? Or is it a consultancy? Is it being some information or being involved in making a decision? These would be examples for the **outcome**.

Beside of that, we also need to describe the value provided to the stakeholders. It starts with determining the stakeholder as different stakeholders perceive a service's value differently. The value can then be specified in the the service agreement for each stakeholder as **value proposition**. Defining KPI will be part of the value proposition as we also need to specify expected target for the sercie's quality.

The service agreement does not only contain the obligations for the EA service centre, but there are also certain **prerequisites** that need to be fulfilled by the customer using the service. Example: If a stakeholder is asking for a consultancy service, the EA service centre is providing people and skills and documents. At the same time, the architect also need to have all the required information from the

---

[15]For example reusing a single software service for shipping label creation throughout the application landscape.

project that is required for providing the consultancy. If we are leasing resources to projects, the prerequisite is that the projects are not only just having the resource and then assign tasks to them. The architect also need to get involved in regular project meetings and get access to relevant documentation—equally to becoming a project team member.

Each service also have certain **resource** requirements. The service centre will only be capable of providing services if it has an adequate team and additional resources. This might be ...

- computer hardware or software
- EA repository for maintaining business capabilities and related software applications
- tools for reporting and graphical visualisations
- dedicated people and skills
- external consultant provided a specialist service

This is still ongoing research and categories for services might change over time. However, the overview provided by Figs. 5.20 and 5.21 is meant to illustrate the idea of the EA service centre and a service catalogue. The following sections each presents another approach for collaborative EA. Each of them is available as text book for further reading.

5.3.2   Chess and the Art of Enterprise Architecture

There is a nice book by Gerben Wierda, a Dutch guy, who is proposing that an enterprise architect should act like a chess player.[16] An overview on his criticism and basic ideas is given in Fig. 5.22. Based on a lot of examples from his experience as a consultant, he summarises typical issues with the way EA is done today. He mentions typical issues that we already discussed previously (starting from page 164): People are spending too much time on creating paperwork and artefacts which are not needed. EA does not provide any significant value for the organisation. His main concern is EA being focussed on the to-be architecture as presented in the context of managed evolution in Sect. 5.1.3. The to-be describes the target architecture we want to achieve (in perhaps like 10 years) and all planning will be tailored around this target state. However, Wierda clearly says that achieving a to-be in such a long period of time unrealistic. We don't know how the world will look like in the future. Why are we sticking so much to a to-be vision, to-be architecture, that will be part of the future? The business and its environment will change and EA needs to adapt to any of those changes.

What he is suggesting is to do architecture how a chess player is working. A chess player is not having the final position of all the figures in mind. A chess

---

[16]Wierda, G.: *Chess and the Art of Enterprise Architecture*, [10].

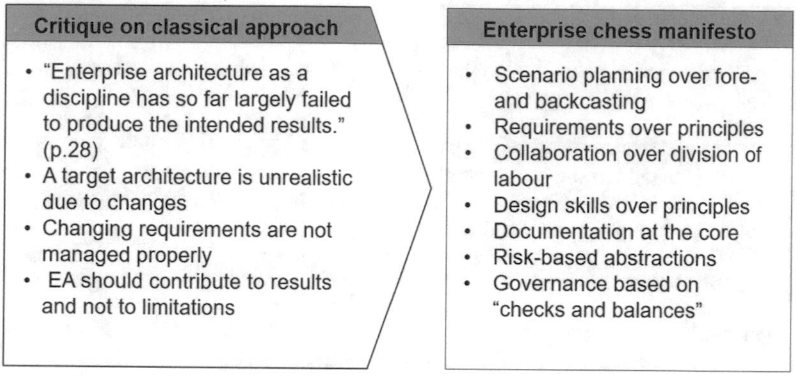

Critique on classical approach	Enterprise chess manifesto
• "Enterprise architecture as a discipline has so far largely failed to produce the intended results." (p.28) • A target architecture is unrealistic due to changes • Changing requirements are not managed properly • EA should contribute to results and not to limitations	• Scenario planning over fore- and backcasting • Requirements over principles • Collaboration over division of labour • Design skills over principles • Documentation at the core • Risk-based abstractions • Governance based on "checks and balances"

Fig. 5.22 Chess and the art of EA (overview)

player is looking at the current situation and then assesses various options for next moves—not only the immediate next move, but a series of potential moves. A chess player is also considering how the opponent might react. He will make step-by-step decisions; and also adjusting his or her strategy, depending on how the opponent is moving. he does not want to stigmatise business departments as opponents (or enemies). But Wierda wants to promote this working mode for the architect. An enterprise architect can support a change and then evaluate the resulting situation. He can evaluate the outcome and also consider reactions from other stakeholders. This will help with constantly adjusting plans and not being restricted by a— potentially unrealistic—target architecture.

The benefit of Wierda's approach is that you do not need a target architecture that might be misleading after a while. However, you will still need a vision for providing guidance for any EA activity. EAM should then support decisions making by guidelines on best practises. These will also support assessing each iteration and defining options for next steps. This rather resembles a dynamic planning approach. You can also try to anticipate a sequence of steps and different options for sequences (like the alternative strategies in chess).

Evaluating each iteration and evaluating subsequent steps involves understanding requirements from the business side (in order to not being disconnected from business. Listening to your business side, listening to your stakeholders will foster collaboration with people instead of telling people what to do. Architects will also have more freedom with respect to their choices as they are less restricted by a to-be architecture and principles. Because for each principle, there will be an exception. And it is also the art of architecture to analyse the situation and avoid principles if they are are not applicable.

The architect is not supposed to generate a lot of documents, but only providing those kind of documents that are really required by people. Also some risk awareness is a key skill. We should not document because of having documents, but only documenting things that will help us with managing risks. Also governance

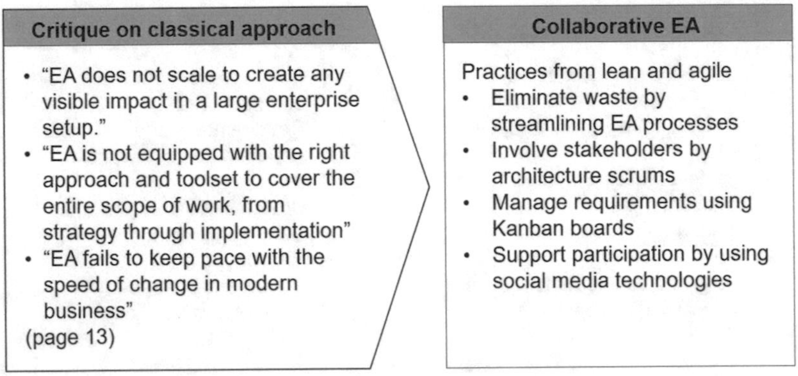

Critique on classical approach	Collaborative EA
• "EA does not scale to create any visible impact in a large enterprise setup." • "EA is not equipped with the right approach and toolset to cover the entire scope of work, from strategy through implementation" • "EA fails to keep pace with the speed of change in modern business" (page 13)	Practices from lean and agile • Eliminate waste by streamlining EA processes • Involve stakeholders by architecture scrums • Manage requirements using Kanban boards • Support participation by using social media technologies

Fig. 5.23 EAM 2.0—overview

mechanisms need to be reconsidered that they are not prohibitive but providing guidance.

I would like to recommend this book as some further reading. It doesn't take that much time for reading and it is not written in a scientific way. It is very hands-on, especially when motivating the issues he identified in EAM. Also his comments on the notion of the architect acting like a chess player is an interesting read.

5.3.3   EAM 2.0

There is another book that I would like to recommend. It is titled *Collaborative Enterprise Architecture* and describes an approach developed by three Tata consultants (cf. [11]). And in their book, they also refresh issues they recognised in existing EA organisations:

• EA hardly provides any visible impact or value
• common EA tools are not well suited for solving real world problems that companies are facing

They also see an issue in EA frameworks as there is no *one size fits all*. The biggest issue with those frameworks is that people want to define a framework for being applicable in any kind of company. But companies are so very different. Problems, they face are so different that there is no ultimate solution for all of them. And furthermore, applying a heavyweight frameworks only results in having a framework implemented that will control (or restrict) the business. But business changes frequently and at a very fast pace. The certainty about how we want to act next year will disappear during the next couple of months, as political aspects change, as the market will change, as customers change, as even there might be new innovators that we need to keep in mind.

What they are suggesting is an approach they call *EAM 2.0* in accordance with the buzzword *Web 2.0* (cf. Fig. 5.23). They propose to adopt existing methodologies from other disciplines. For example, adopting Lean methods from Lean business process management. Especially one of them: *eliminating waste* for making EA processes more efficient. They are explicitly not referring to set up processes as prescribed by the framework. They emphasise the customer focus from Lean in order to understand stakeholder requirements. You can then design your process around what is really needed by the stakeholder. Eliminating waste then refers to removing activities that are not adding any value. Value add can be recognised if a customer would directly pay for this activity or its outcome. In general, their processes should just create artefacts and results that provide a benefit to the stakeholder and eliminate any task that is not required.

Their second pillar consists of methods from Agile software development. The main motivation lies in making EAM more flexible by adapting Agile methods and principles. Agile software development is getting popular, because it is providing solutions in a similar context. 20 years ago, the criticism on software development methodologies was that they are heavyweight, document-centric, and do not achieve expected results. A lot of projects started, but failed because of a high risk and a lot of uncertainty. They were not able to flexibly react to changes as the whole project was based on extensive analysis and design documents. The story is very similar to what we currently see with EAM. In fact, they are trying to adopt Scrum into their EAM 2.0 approach for being more flexible. They also incorporate Kanban boards for planning and discussing changes.

Last but not least, they are borrowing technologies from Web 2.0—now yopu see where the name *EAM 2.0* comes from. The term Web 2.0 indicates the next wave of web applications providing more interaction (as being common in social networks and social media), instead of just static HTML pages. Web 2.0 foster the development of web applications that are interactive and that enable people to exchange information easily. Bente et al. are using those technologies for developing a novel EAM portal. This portal aims at collecting and maintaining information required for EAM by adopting similar user interfaces as we already know from social media. It feels like having Facebook for individual application or having the collaborative site for projects and change management.

This book as well as the book by Gerben Wierda, I think they are very influential because they show a problem and want to change it by proposing innovative solutions. Of course, each of them has its advantages and drawbacks. You cannot just buy the book and then have the blueprint for a perfect world. But both of them are inspirational in a way that they strive or provide a vision, how could EAM look like in the future, especially against the background that current implementations, that current EA organisations have their issues and we need to improve EAM for the future.

5.4 Further Reading

For terminating this section, there will be an overview on the most important further reading.

The first one is a paper published by two people. They did empirical research about what are critical success factors for EA initiatives: [8]. They were checking why did initiatives fail, what were the reasons, and they tried to cluster the reason. And they came up with a very interesting conclusion. They list a lot of issues. And some of them we also discussed already previously when talking about the criticism on existing EAM approaches. They covered some of them, but they have a common conclusion. They deducted everything back to the original reason is because we are not communicating properly and we are not collaborating properly. Whichever issue we can observe in EAM, we could solve it by just implementing proper communication mechanisms and collaboration platforms so that it is not about somebody doing something in a isolated way but doing things together. And doing things together requires collaboration and also communication. It is an interesting read and describes quite well the scenarios why so many initiatives failed in the past when setting up EAM on a corporate level.

The second one is the book published by Gerben Wierda: *Chess and the Art of Enterprise Architecture* [10]. You see from the subtitle that it is more about making the right moves to manage business IT complexity instead of having a vision and achieving it. Wierda has a strong background in in the ArchiMate EA modelling language but also a lot of experience from consulting. He, therefore, motivates his approach by referring to bad practices of applying EAM in today's enterprises.

And the last one is the book by the three consultants from *Tata Consultany* that aims at incorporating lean methodologies, agile techniques, and also enterprise or web 2.0 practises into EAM: [11]. It has been published in 2012 but the general general idea is still popular: Making EAM more flexible by learning from other disciplines.

5.5 Summary

That's it for this chapter on managing EA. Where are we on our EA roadmap? We started the journey with having a look at what is EA and EAM (cf. Fig. 5.24). We are looking at the promised benefits, why are we doing this. For then, having some understanding for the business architecture. Business capabilities and business objects are the central concepts for driving EAM and then using those concepts as an input for developing the application architecture. Developing application architecture as deriving it from our business capabilities, but also looking at which kinds of details are required on our applications, so that we can later on then analyse them with respect to improving our application architecture. The analysis of EA is based on certain maps, default maps, standard maps that are already available in tools and are described in many textbooks. And we had a closer look at one tool called the business support matrix.

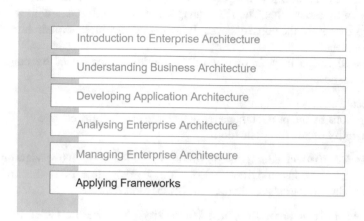

Fig. 5.24 Following next: applying frameworks

The result of the analysis, of course, is we need to change something if we want to improve our application landscape and how to manage those changes we discussed in this section called Managing Enterprise Architecture. We briefly had to look at the motivation, why do we need to manage changes. We did not discuss methodologies as this was already discussed in the governance part of this course. But we then had a brief look at typical activities during application portfolio management and also looking at typical activities performed by an enterprise architect, so that after understanding what an enterprise architect is supposed to do that we could discuss how to set up and EA as an organisational unit in the corporation. Having several options, having EAM within IT or even on a corporate level with pluses and deltas for each of them. There will never be the optimal decision for each and every company, hence, we sometimes need to decide for one organisation set up depending on the company and its context, but then we also had a discussion about existing frameworks and approaches are criticised heavily, because of experience of people in the literature based on empirical studies, or then looking at alternative approaches that offer more collaboration and also more service orientation towards the stakeholders.

This covers the whole story for EAM you might experience in the future. The nect chapter will summarise many of the topics discussed by looking at the notion of EA frameworks like TOGAF. They are still quite popular as they document best practices for EA and EAM.

5.6   Exercises

Exercise 5.1 (Managing Changes) You are supposed to replace an existing HR application by a new one. The HR manager feels uncomfortable with this change as he is unaware of the consequences. It is now up to you, to explain him properly what to expect.

Please, describe in your own words potential consequences by covering the following aspects:

1. expected effects of a change
2. obligations by the project manager in order to conduct the change
3. availability of an HR application

Exercise 5.2 (Project Management Tools) Please, provide an overview on project management methods and tools (max. 700 words). How does the application roadmap relate to them? Are there even similar tools?

Exercise 5.3 (Transformation in a University) You are the Chief Information Officer (CIO) of the Deakin University and are tasked to create a roadmap incorporating the following changes (max 2 applications to be changed at the same time):

1. *Payroll1* and *Payroll2* to be replaced by *PayrollNew*
2. Introduce new research method library application
3. Consolidate *PubMan1*, *PubMan2* and *PubMan3*
4. Shut down *Legacy1*, *Legacy2* and *Legacy3*
5. Migrate *Fin1* and *Fin2* into *Fin3*

Estimate realistic values for the planning. Draw the roadmap using the template and update the BSM.

References

1. P. Mooney, *The Transformation Roadmap, Accelerating Organisation Change* (Oak Tree Press, Oxford , 2012)
2. J. Kotter, *Leading Change* (Harvard Business Review Press, Brighton, 2012)
3. T.F. Cawsey, G. Deszca, C. Ingols, *Organizational Change, An Action-oriented Toolkit*, 3rd edn. (SAGE Publications, New York, 2016)
4. S. Murer, B. Bonati, *Managed Evolution, A Strategy for Very Large Information Systems* (Springer, Berlin, Heidelberg, 2011)
5. M. Dumas, M. La Rosa, J. Mendling, H.A. Reijers, *Fundamentals of Business Process Management*, 2nd edn. (Springer, Berlin, 2018)
6. G. Blokdyk, *Continuous Process Improvement, A Complete Guide*, 2019 edition (5STAR-Cooks, 2019)
7. M. Op't Land, E. Proper, M. Waage, J. Cloo, C. Steghuis, *Enterprise Architecture, Creating Value by Informed Governance*. The Enterprise Engineering Series (Springer, Berlin, London, 2009)

8. N. Banaeianjahromi, K. Smolander, Lack of communication and collabo-ration in enterprise architecture development. Inf. Syst. Front. **57**(1), 3 (2017)
9. C. Potts, *recrEAtion, Realizing the Extraordinary Contribution of Your Enterprise Architects* (Technics Publications, LLC, Denville, 2010)
10. G. Wierda, *Chess and the Art of Enterprise Architecture, Making the Right Moves to Manage Business-IT Complexity* (R & A, Utrecht, 2015)
11. S. Bente, U. Bombosch, S. Langade, *Collaborative Enterprise Architecture, Enriching EA with Lean, Agile, and Enterprise 2.0 Practices* (Elsevier/Morgan Kaufmann, Amsterdam, 2012)
12. S. Kotusev, Enterprise architecture: a reconceptualization is needed. Pacif. Asia J. Assoc. Inf. Syst. **10**, 1–36 (2018)

Chapter 6
Applying Frameworks

Where are we at the moment with our journey through EAM? We started with an introduction to EA and EAM in Chap. 1. We were talking about its purpose and some basic tools and visualisations.

Then, in Chap. 2 *Understanding Business Architecture* we rather focused on those concepts that are required for describing the business with processes, business capabilities, and also business objects.

Further on, we used the business capabilities as a starting point for developing the application architecture in Chap. 3. It was a simple methodology for just making a decision. How should the ideal landscape look like? But we already had a look at data that is required for analysing applications and also the whole application landscape.

The analysis part was continued in Chap. 4 by looking at visualisations that are used for analysing and improving the EA, like the business support matrix. This tool is aiming at describing and understanding the relationship between software applications and business-related concepts.

Afterwards, we are not that much focusing on describing architecture but looking at how we can manage EA in a corporation. Most of it is about managing changes. This requires an adequate organisation for also sustaining the work of the enterprise architect. At the end of Chap. 5, we looked at criticisms to classical approaches for EAM. We presented some modern approaches, which are suggesting new organisational aspects or new organisational setups for managing EA.

This Chap. 6 will now introduce the notion of *frameworks* which is commonly used within the EA community. A framework basically provides methods and tools that are required for setting up and implementing EA in a large-scale organisation.

© The Author(s), under exclusive license to Springer Nature Switzerland AG 2021   181
J. Jung, B. Fraunholz, *Masterclass Enterprise Architecture Management*,
https://doi.org/10.1007/978-3-030-78495-9_6

Learning Objectives

After completing this chapter, you will be able to . . .

- . . . summarise existing EA frameworks
- . . . explain elements of a framework
- . . . discuss TOGAF compared to concepts presented in this textbook
- . . . infer future EA projects

The learning objective for the current sections are as follows. After finishing the section, you should be capable of summarising a few existing EA frameworks. We will not discuss all of them but have a look at some of the popular ones in the subsequent Sect. 6.1. Section 6.3 provides an overview on TOGAF®, The Open Group Architecture Framework. It is an open standard, hence, documentation is widely available and TOGAF has been adopted in many organisations. After completing this section, you should be capable of explaining artefacts as well as methods and tools that are part of TOGAF.

Frameworks are based on best practices in the EA community and this also holds true for the textbook at hand. The book's purpose is not to publish a new framework but teach EA in a practical way. It also shares some commonalities with frameworks available today. These similarities are summarised in Sect. 6.4, showing how the contents of the book relates to existing frameworks. This will also serve as a summary of the previous sections. After completing this section, you should be capable of relating the contents to any framework—perhaps even develop a simple framework on your own.

6.1   Frameworks Overview

This section provides an overview on some frameworks and standards:

- *The Zachman Framework for Enterprise Architecture*™is supposed to be the origin for today's frameworks.
- The *Integrated Architecture Framework* provides more than two dimensions.
- *ArchiMate* is a modelling language specifically for EA.

The section will finish by providing a high-level overview on past and present frameworks.

Generic Classification Structure of Design Artifacts

	What	How	Where	Who	When	Why	
Planner							Scope
Owner							Concepts
Designer							Logic
Builder							Physics
Imple-menter							Technology
Operator		THE ENTERPRISE					Product
	Material	Process	Geometry	Instructions.	Timing	Objectives	

Fig. 6.1 *The Zachman Framework for Enterprise Architecture*™(Published with the permission of John A. Zachman and Zachman International®, Inc.—www.zachman.com)

6.1.1   Zachman Framework

When talking about frameworks, most people are starting with a very famous person called *John Zachman*. He is quite popular because he is supposed to be the first to develop an EA framework.[1] He first published his approach in the IBM Systems Journal in the 1980s. In this article, Zachman described his idea on a structure for providing various views on IT of a company[1]. *The Zachman Framework for Enterprise Architecture*™consists of several layers and views as shown in Fig. 6.1.

The top level of the framework suggests that we should understand the context of the company as well as its scope or markets (Fig. 6.1). We can then define something Zachman calls the enterprise model. It is a description of the company—including business processes and resources. A system model is then derived from the enterprise model. It is similar to what we introduced as application architecture in Sect. 3.1. It encompasses software applications and tools which are then further mapped to concepts in a technology model. Examples for those concepts networks, computer hardware or peripheral devices. The bottom layer refers to any details that are required for implementing information technology within the company.

---

[1]Zachman is still treated like a superstar when appearing at an EA conference.

This kind of model is not that different from what we already discussed so far. The business context and the enterprise model are quite similar to the business layer we already introduced in Chap. 2. In a similar way, the system model refers to the application layer and the technology model to the technology layer. The top four layers represent the view like the town planner, as it is introduced in Sect. 1.1.1.

Zachman suggests to focus on the top layers, providing the high level view on to the organisation. These layers are then further decomposed into a static view containing *data objects* on various levels of abstraction. You can have business objects in the scope layer (like market, competition, customer service). In the enterprise model, you can derive a data model for specific applications from the business objects. They can then be implemented in a specific technology (like a relational database).

A similar principle holds true for *functions*. We can start on a high level, similar to business capabilities on level 1. Functions on that level address how we want to establish our company on the market. They can then be decomposed into specific function (i.e. business capabilities) that are supposed to be implemented by the company. Functions are then implemented by functionality in software applications. Any application requires a certain technology. The implementation itself is then subject to the lowest level, which defines any details required for software development.

The same principle of various levels of abstraction is applied to each view of the Zachman framework. It starts with using high-level concepts the business context which will then be further specified in lower levels. Figure 6.1 shows examples for each remaining view: network, people, time motivation. The people view might start with strategic human resources which can then be further described by human resources, staff members, application users and roles, and then having detailed work description for each actor.

Even though Fig. 6.1 is showing some example concepts for filling in the framework, there is no extensive documentation of required modeling languages (cf. Fig. 6.2). Any of his publications, like the paper published in the IBM system journal

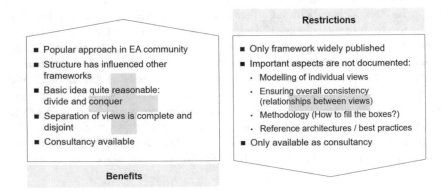

Fig. 6.2 Critical review of the Zachman framework

are basically describing the framework and its basic idea. Zachman is also owning a consultancy firm offering services for applying the framework in a client's company. You can hire a skilled consultant providing a specific solution for a company based on the framework. Nevertheless, Zachman is just the beginning. There are more frameworks available, including TOGAF. They can provide more specific concepts and tools relate to the cells defined by the Zachman framework.

6.1.2 Integrated Architecture Framework (IAF)

The Integrated Architecture Framework (short IAF) has been developed and published by Capgemini [2]. The IAF has its origins in preliminary work for defining a framework that can also support structuring large IT consultancy projects. An overview on the IAF is given in Fig. 6.3. It covers relevant views on an IT project together with its context (i.e. the motivation for the IT project). However, its shows several similarities with an EA framework.

It might not surprising that the IAF contains a building block labeled *Business*. It, in fact, refers to the business view on the IT project and uses similar concepts as the ones introduced with the business architecture in Chap. 2. It, furthermore, consists of building blocks for information systems (analog to the application layer) as well as a technology. The latter one covering technology components and networks.

The framework is complemented by a building block labeled *information*. It relates to any kind of data used within the company and managed by information systems. This is also nothing completely new for us. We already introduced the notion of *data architecture* in Sect. 3.4. In contrast to the IAF, we put it as an overarching layer across any of the other three layers representing business, applications and technology.

One of the obvious differences is that the IAF spans three dimensions. *Governance* and *security* represent relevant functions for managing compliance and risk

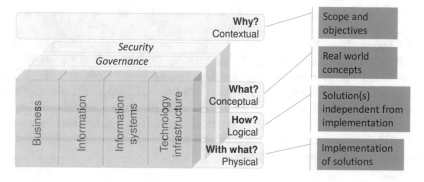

Fig. 6.3 Integrated architecture framework (based on a figure in [3, p. 67])

in an organisation. They are stretched across the previously discussed layers by providing controlling mechanisms. Governance ensures that an organisation follows existing laws, regulations and compliance rules for business and also IT. Security addresses any measure for protecting information and technology against theft and misuse.

The IAF is not the only framework adding dedicated layers for governance or security: *PEAF* (Pragmatic Enterprise Architecture Framework) includes a governance product [4], *FEAF* (Federal Enterprise Architecture Framework) a security reference model and security controls [5], *GERAM* (Generalised Enterprise Reference Architecture and Methodology) a governance reference model [6] or *E2AF* (Extended Enterprise Architecture Framework) includes both, governance and security viewpoints [7]. The last one provides it as cross-cutting views—similar to IAF. It is important having governance and security as overarching views instead of separate layers as they only work is corresponding processes and measures cannot be treated separately from business and application layer concepts.

Using the third dimension, IAF differentiates between three levels of abstraction together with the context (cf. Fig. 6.3). The top one (*Why?*) covers the context of an organisation or a project. It defines the scope and objectives, similar to the business motivation presented in Sect. 2.4. It does not specifically address architecture or solutions but rather the drivers for for the organisation.[2] It is further used for shaping the initiative by defining concrete boundaries (i.e. scoping) in order to have a focus for subsequent activities.

Each of the four contents layers—business, information, information systems and technology infrastructure—can be regarded on three levels of detail. The conceptual level (*What?*) covers concepts for documenting the application domain on a high level of abstraction. It rather refers to the perspective of the town planner as introduced in Sect. 1.1.1. It also does not comprise solutions but real world concepts that characterise the company or the project provided within the scope defined in the contextual layer. These concepts can be represent the business (i.e. business service), information (information object), information systems (information system service) and technology infrastructure (infrastructure service). Basically, this is the starting point for discussing corporate IT architecture with business stakeholders. We would also regard core concepts covered by this textbook (business capabilities, business objects and applications) on the conceptual layer.

The logical level (*How?*) serves as a blueprint for potential solutions implemented in the organisation. It is still independent from specific solutions—which can be found further down the line on the physical layer. Consequently, it does not contain deployable software solutions but logical components that represent the desired functionality. It also contains business processes, logical data objects (including information ownership) or types of technology infrastructure components. This kind of concepts can play the role of requirements that drive the implementation of information systems.

---

[2]Why are we doing business on the market? Why do we want to change our business?

Specific solutions and resources are then located on the physical level (*With what?*). We will match requirements with specific software products, databases and technology components. The logical level should be independent from those solutions so that we can evolve the organisation over time, without changing the conceptual or logical level. A similar principle is applied in database design. The conceptual data model captures real world concepts. They are then further detailed by a logical data model that can then be implemented by a specific database management system (DBMS). In case of changing the DBMS we can still use the same logical data model and implement it with a different DBMS product. the same leveling can be applied to business-related concepts (business capability $\rightarrow$ business process $\rightarrow$ automated workflow) or information systems (software service $\rightarrow$ software component $\rightarrow$ software implementation).

We did not discuss these kinds of levels in the course of our textbook. We rather provide a small amount of relevant concepts which can be the starting point for a more detailed architecture. However, real-world architectures will cover these or similar levels as the the view of the town planner needs to manifest in a live city. For further information on the IAF, we would like to refer to the references provided, especially [2].

6.1.3   ArchiMate

Technically, ArchiMate is not a framework, but a modeling language for EA. The name *ArchiMate* is short for *Architecture-Animate* and has its origins in a project funded by the Dutch government and executed by several Dutch research institutions [8]. It has been handed over to The Open Group which is maintaining it as a standard complementing TOGAF [9]. ArchiMate is a modeling language like the UML or BPMN and, thus, allows for describing specific architectures. It, therefore, provides typical elements like for example business functions, processes or software applications together with their relationships.

ArchiMate is using a similar layered approach as introduced in this text book. It distinguishes between business layer, the application layer, and technology layer (cf. Fig. 6.4). Each of them is further divided into views for the passive structure, behaviour, and an active structure. Can you imagine the concepts for each of them? Please, take some time and reflect what we have discussed so far with business and application architecture.

As you might have assumed, the passive structure contains static concepts like data or business objects. In contrast to this, the active structure encompasses concepts that can perform activities like for example software applications. The behavior part describes behavior that can be performed by elements from the active structure. Wierda describes the interplay of the by referring to the structure of a simple English sentence: subject, verb and object [10, p. 18]. An application (element from the active structure) performs an an operation (behavior) on a data object (passive structure).

	Passive Structure	Behavior	Active Structure
Business			
Application			
Technology			

Fig. 6.4 ArchiMate layers and views (based on a figure in [3, p. 69])

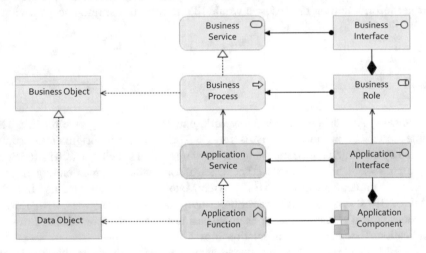

Fig. 6.5 ArchiMate language concepts (based on [10, p. 20])

The ArchiMate language structure follows a similar principle we already used for data architecture in Sect. 3.4. Elements of the static structure do not only relate to similar thing, but also provide views on different levels of detail. We can see this in Fig. 6.5 showing an example ArchiMate model consisting of business and application layer concepts. It contains the business object on the left hand side, which is *realised*[3] by a data object on the application layer (analog to Sect. 3.4). This data object might then be realised (i.e. implemented) by an artifact in a file or a database on the technology layer (not shown here).

---

[3]The meaning of the arrow (i.e. its semantics) between data object and business object is *realises*.

The same principle is also applied in the behaviour view and the activity structure using special relationships. A *business service* is is a service offering by an organisational unit. It is realised (i.e. performed) by a business process. A business process is *served* by an application service (service offering by an application) from the application layer which is, in turns, realised by an application function (i.e. functionality to be implemented in a software application). Please, note that application service and function do not refer to the actual application, but to the service or functionality that is expected to be provided by the application. They are part of the activity structure.

Some elements of the activity structure are shown on the right hand side of Fig. 6.5. They cover actors (i.e. business role) and software applications (application component). An application component realises an interface (i.e. a user interface) which can then be used by actors in a business process. There are no elements shown from the technology layer as we are focusing on the business and application layers within the text book at hand. However, you can imagine application components running on computers which are called *node* in ArchiMate.

There are also well defined relationships between the model elements. Realisation and service relationships have already been explained above. There are also relationships between the three views which allow for assigning active elements to behaviour and static objects. Actors are *assigned* to business processes and application components to application functions. In fact, an application function might be implemented by different applications. Behavioural elements *access* static elements shown be the arrows between business process and business object as well as application function and data object.

As already stated in the beginning, ArchiMate is a modelling language defined by syntax[4] and semantics.[5] It allows for a more detailed view on EA than the concepts provided in previous sections. It allows allows for combining EA models with other modeling languages, like BPMN[6] or the UML.[7] It also complements existing EA frameworks and has, thus, been adopted as an additional standard by the Open Group (see Sect. 6.3) [9].

---

[4]The syntax defines language elements and rules how to connect them properly (i.e. realisation relationship is allowed between a business object and a data object but not between two business objects).

[5]The meaning of elements of a modelling language is defined by its semantics.

[6]BPMN (Business Process Modelling and Notation) is a standardised modeling language for business processes.

[7]The UML (Unified Modelling Language) is defined for specifying software applications.

6.1.4   Historical Overview

It is quite impossible to introduce all EA frameworks as there are so many of them. The text book at hand rather aims at providing a practical introduction to relevant concepts for starting your EA journey. We only introduce some frameworks for highlighting how these concepts are applied in existing frameworks and also for showing the historical evolution of EA. Zachman has been chosen as it is often referred to as the very first framework providing an elaborate structure for managing large and complex information systems in a corporation. The IAF is one example for approaches having more than two dimensions and also incorporating typical IT responsibilities (i.e. governance and security). Many frameworks just cover the high-level perspective by providing a structure but do not go into detail. ArchiMate is one of the approaches that extends EA by providing a language for a more detailed description of an organisation ad its information systems.

An historical overview on prominent frameworks is shown in Fig. 6.6—and to be honest, it is only a small fraction of frameworks available. We find the Zachman framework starting in the '80s with the paper published in the IBM Systems Journal, then evolving into a more elaborate framework and still being used today by Zachman. Another representative of the early frameworks is the CIMOSA reference model. It provided a standard for describing information systems. The first version has been published in the 1980s and the latest version in the 1990s.

PERA (Purdue Enterprise Reference Architecture) has an academic background. It started in the 1980s and being available at its current version from 2001. DoDAF (Department of Defense Architecture Framework) is an example for frameworks being defined by an organisation for its own use. In fact, several large companies started to develop their own frameworks. the picture in Fig. 6.6 also contains some research initiatives. sebis (bottom right) is the Software Engineering and Business information Systems research group at the Technical University München, Germany. Members of this team do extensive research and provide best practices for EA including concepts for individual frameworks.

6.2   EA Frameworks

We started introducing the notion of an EA framework by just referring to some examples, providing an overview to existing frameworks. Let's try to cover it with some small definition.

Definition 6.1 (Enterprise Architecture Framework) An **Enterprise Architecture Framework** (or just framework) provides principles and tools for establishing and sustaining EAM in an organisation. It usually provides

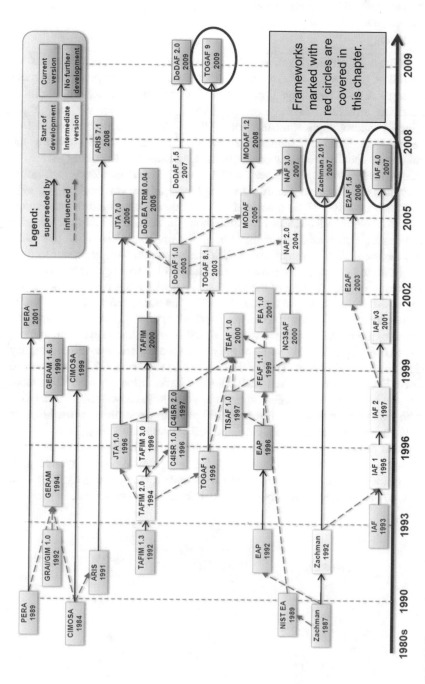

Fig. 6.6 EA frameworks overview (based on a figure in [11, p. 130])

- structure
- concepts (defined by a meta-model)
- visualisations
- methodology

The purpose of an EA framework is in providing some kind of toolbox—a toolbox full of principles, tools, methods—that we can use for implementing and maintaining EA in a company. Typically, an EA framework starts with defining an underlying structure, so the structure like the three layers we had in the beginning—business, application, technology layer—or some structure like the IAF we presented, or like the Zachman framework. And against this structure, the frameworks are usually providing concepts and also maps for describing EA.

Some of them address it in a very detailed way, others, like Zachman, rather on a very high level or even just by providing hints on how you could describe it. And they also usually define some kind of methods or some kind of procedures you need to implement for EAM, also some hints on skills required for enterprise architects, and a corresponding organisation in the organisation—in the company. This is the basic idea of a framework. And if we look at this one, with our lecture, we already started defining some kind of EA framework, so a framework which is not intended to be used outside of the university, but which has been developed for teaching EAM. It does not have a name. It will not be published. But we can see in the lecture, already, basic concepts that are required for an EA framework (Fig. 6.7).

When looking at existing frameworks, we will see they have even much more concepts to offer for EA work. Some of the aspects were already covered, like they provide some method or some kind of procedure that shows us, OK, if you want to implement EA in a company, then you should do it the following way. You should do the following steps in this order. Sometimes you need to have feedback and then start with some activities again. But they will provide some process that helps us with implementing EA and also making sure that we are maintaining EA over time.

They also provide, on a detailed or on an abstract level, information about the organisation that is required for executing the implementation and maintenance of EA. Beside of this, some frameworks also have a catalogue containing best practices, so best practices describing information or experiences made in previous

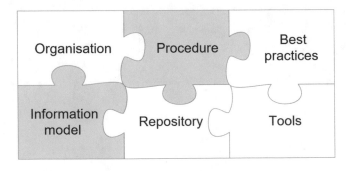

Fig. 6.7 Components of an EA framework

projects, that help people with making decisions within their own project, for setting up EA in their own company. The process and organisation in the best practise are usually accompanied by something they call an information model, which is often defined by something called a meta-model. The meta-model defines all concepts that are required for describing an EA. In our case, it would be defining that we need to collect information about business capabilities, applications, business objects, data objects. Any of the concepts we introduced would be subject to this kind of information model.

Beside of this, frameworks also offer some kind of tools. *Tool* can be a very broad term, here. It can refer to some document, some Excel spreadsheet, but even to a software tool that helps us with performing your EA work. And within this tool, very often you have a big repository with all the data. The data structures in this repository is defined by the meta-model. Remember that we already talked about the repository. In the beginning and also when talking about analysing EA, we had this working mode that bases on the fact we have a repository full of information for EA. It contains all our business capabilities and applications, which will then be used for generating views and maps for stakeholders. This is the same kind of repository in each and every EA framework.

6.3 TOGAF

The Open Group Architecture Framework (TOGAF®) is an open standard defined and published by *The Open Group*. The Open Group is a consortium of organisations including "customers, systems and solutions suppliers, tool vendors, integrators, academics, and consultants across multiple industries" (cf. [12]). They aim at defining and establishing various technology standards—including EA.

The TOGAF standard originated with its first version in 1995. It was based on an existing technical standard called *Technical Architecture Framework for Information Management (TAFIM)* (cf. [13][8]). The latest version 9.2 is available since 2018 and documented in [14]. The standard is also available for free as HTML after registration. Being a framework, TOGAF is providing a structure and concepts for describing EA in an organisation (cf. page 194). This supports structuring the architecture but also organising work around managing EA. Concepts establish a common terminology among people involved in EA. One of TOGAF's strengths is the method for describing and managing EA: Architecture Development Method (ADM). The ADM will be further described below (page 196). There are further aspects in TOGAF which are not covered by this textbook. The interested reader is referred to its specification in [14].

TOGAF is generic and is supposed to be applied in any kind of industry or organisation. Hence, we should have a clear understanding about its limitations how to apply it. Especially, TOGAF **is no**...

---

[8]This title is available in German only.

- ...*solution*: Introducing TOGAF in an organisation is not a solution. You need to understand your problem (i.e. motivation for introducing EAM) first. The adoption of TOGAF will not automatically solve all your problems.
- ...*cookbook*: reading the specification will help you understanding the concepts. However, it is not a step-by-step instruction for implementing EA in your organisation. People applying TOGAF still need a lot of experience.
- ...*toolbox*: TOGAF might look like a tool set for EA. However, it is rather a common framework for a toolbox. It needs to be complemented by software tools and specific methods (e.g. business process modelling).
- ...*organisational blueprint*: TOGAF does not specify how to establish an EA unit in your organisation.

In general, TOGAF is not *ready to use*. Adopting TOGAF still requires tailoring to an organisation's objective, organisation and processes.

6.3.1   Structure and Concepts

An overview on TOGAF's structure and concepts is shown in Fig. 6.8. It reflects similar layers as introduced starting from page 27 in Sect. 1.4. The middle part shows from left to right:

Business Architecture

The *Business Architecture* contains concepts for describing business-related aspects of an organisation. *Motivation* covers business drivers, objectives (goals) and measures (i.e. key performance indicators). These concepts correspond to those introduced as part of the *business motivation* in Sect. 2.4.

The *Organisation* part addresses the description of an organisation's structure consisting of organisational units, actors and roles. These (and some more) are covered by the *Business Execution* part in Sect. 2.4 in the textbook at hand.[9]

Behavior comprises any concept describing behavioural aspects of an organisation. *Business Services*, *Contracts* and *Service Qualities* specify the interaction with external partners via business services. Details on the usage of services are established via contracts and qualities attributes. *Processes*, *Events* and *Controls* are used for describing business processes anf the flow of control. They refer to classical business process models including business rules. Figure 6.8 lists some high-level behavioural concepts right beside the processes—including *Business Capabilities* as introduced in Sect. 2.2. Please note, that there is no concept corresponding to the notion of *business object* (cf. Sect. 2.3).

---

[9]The naming is slightly different but the purpose of the concepts is quite similar.

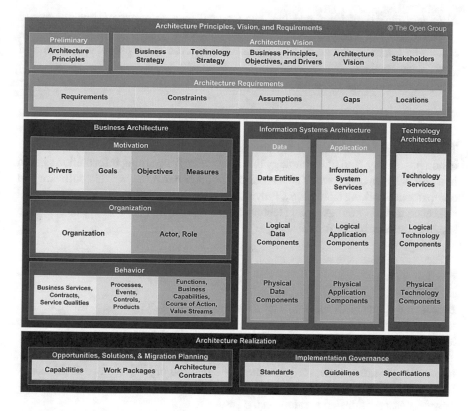

Fig. 6.8 Components of TOGAF (©The Open Group)

Information Systems Architecture

The *Information Systems Architecture* covers typical aspects of corporate information systems divided into *Application* and *Data*. It looks slightly different from ours as explained in Sect. 1.4 as the *Application Architecture* is only a part of it. The main difference is the data architecture which we introduced across the other layers, having concepts on business, application and technology level. TOGAF only locates it in the information systems part.[10]

The data architecture includes similar abstractions as provided by classical data modelling:

1. *conceptual data model* defined by entities (data entities) from the application domain and their relationships

---

[10]This statement is rather neutral as each approach has its positive and negative aspects. At this point, it is just mentioned as a difference.

2. *logical data model* representing data (logical data components) for a database
   paradigm (e.g. relational, object-oriented or XML)
3. *physical data model* being implementation-specific with respect to a dedicated
   database management system

Technology Architecture

The *Technology Architecture* is not discussed in detail within the textbook at hand. It
encompasses any kind of technology that is required for running information system
in a corporate environment. This includes computer hardware, system software and
computer networking technology. Previous versions of TOGAF provided a technical
reference model defining typical technology components.[11] It is now available as a
separate publication [16].

Further Views

Beside the three architectures for describing EA, TOGAF also provides two
views for managing EA. *Architecture Principles, Vision, and Requirements* cover
any aspect for guiding EA work. *Architecture Principles* define criteria for the
architecture of a given organisation. The *Architecture Vision* puts architecture work
into the organisation context. Corporate strategies and objectives need to drive how
EA is done in a company. *Architecture Requirements* can be derived from the as-is
or reflect assumptions/constraints on the future state.

Managing EA consists of planning, coordinating and executing many change
initiatives. This is covered by *Architecture Realisation* in Fig. 6.8.

6.3.2   *Method for Applying Enterprise Architecture*

One of the essential concepts is an elaborate method that explains basic activities
in order to manage EA. The TOGAF Architecture Development Method (ADM)
is a process model based on best practices and fits to the meta-model presented in
the previous Sect. 6.3.1. Figure 6.9 provides an overview on the ADM by showing
major phases and the control flow.

The *Preliminary* phase deals with defining the need for EAM in an organisation and setting up the corresponding capability. The capability consists of an
organisational model (e.g. dedicated EA team), tools (including an EA software
tool) and guidelines for architecture work. Afterwards, the *Architecture Vision* can
be established (see also Sect. 5.1.3 concerning the role of the vision in managed

---

[11]cf. Section 43 in [15].

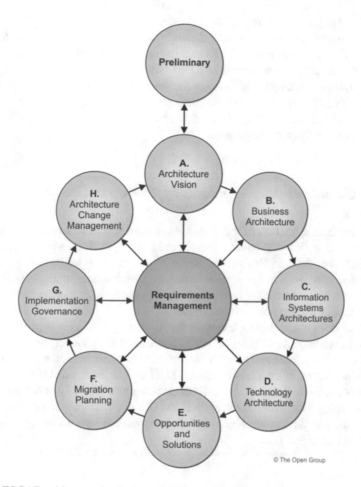

Fig. 6.9 TOGAF architecture development method (©The Open Group)

evolution). The subsequent phases *Business Architecture*, *Information Systems Architecture* and *Technology Architecture* then basically deal with documenting the three architectures as introduced in Sect. 6.3.1.

Phase E, *Opportunities and Solutions*, aims at identifying optimisation potential in the corporation. This can be done by tools like the analysis presented in Chap. 4 within this textbook. Architects need to identify opportunities (i. potential improvements) and define corresponding solutions (concrete improvements). Those solutions need to be implemented within initiatives that are planned in phase F *Migration Planning*. Tools like a roadmap (cf. Sect. 5.1.4) can be used here. The remaining phases *Implementation Governance* and *Architecture Change Management* will then enable steering the initiatives and guide their execution by a holistic change management (cf. Sect. 5.1).

The focal phase *Requirements Management* is needed for managing any architecture requirement. These are relevant throughout the other phases and even impact several initiatives. Furthermore, new architecture requirements may occur in any phase and even trigger a new cycle in ADM. The ADM is not meant to be executed once but rather iteratively. This allows for starting with small improvements and later on extend the use of EAM in the company. Especially if an organisation is new to EAM or resistance is to be expected, then EAM should not be implemented in the whole company in the beginning.

6.3.3   Complementary Standards by The Open Group

We only covered a fraction of the TOGAF standard so far. It also offers additional guidelines and techniques, typical visualisations (cf. Sect. 4.2) as well as a structure for the EA repository.[12] But still, TOGAF is generic as it addresses any kind of organisation and needs to be complemented by additional methods and tools. This includes standard methods for business process modelling (or management), change management or project portfolio management.

TOGAF does not include a language for modelling EA. This is provided by an additional standard, ArchiMate (cf. [9]). ArchiMate is a modelling language for describing architectures across all architectural layers. It implements most of the concepts presented in the meta-model of TOGAF (cf. Sect. 6.3.1). A preliminary standard is available focussing on business architecture (cf. [17]). The Open Group is also working on a standard for agile EAM (cf. citeTheOpenGroup.2019a). This standard aims at supporting the *Digital Transformation* by a more agile approach (compared to TOGAF).

6.4   The Framework Provided by This Book

Even though this textbook does not aim at defining a new framework, it covers concepts, tools and methods that are also common to an EA framework. This section reflects individual topics and relates them to elements of a framework. At the same time, it will also provide a summary of the textbook from a slightly different angle.

---

[12]The Open Group uses the term *Enterprise Continuum* for referring to any kind of documentation and knowledge that is relevant for managing EA. It covers architecture artefacts and solutions from any source. Sources include TOGAF but also industry standards or organisation-specific information.

Layer	Description	Examples
Business architecture	Depicts business-relevant concepts for aligning business needs with software applications in the application architecture.	process, strategy, goal
Application architecture	Depicts software systems (i.e. applications) required for supporting business processes as well as their interaction.	application, interface
Technology architecture	Depicts IT infrastructure required for running software systems in a corporate environment so that processes are supported in any location.	hardware, network, location

Fig. 6.10 Enterprise architecture layers

6.4.1 Structure

Each EA framework provides a basic structure. Such a structure usually defines certain layers or specific architectures. We introduced a very simple structure in Sect. 1.4.4. It divides EA into a business focused perspective (*Business Architecture*, the application landscape (*Application Architecture*) and the underlying technology (*Technology Architecture*) as depicted in Fig. 6.10. Each of them contains descriptive elements for each perspective and there can be relationships across the architectural layers.

EA frameworks usually come with their own layering scheme. IAF and TOGAF differ from the structure provided here (cf. Sects. 6.1 and 6.3). The structure of this book is the same as the one in ArchiMate (page 187). An overview on different frameworks and their layered structures is provided in [18].

6.4.2 Meta-model

Frameworks provide concepts for describing EA. These concepts are defined by an *information model*. This model is sometimes also referred to as *meta-model* as it emphasizes the fact that an EA is a model of the organisation. ArchiMate is a dedicated modelling language, therefore, requiring a meta-model for defining language concepts.

The meta-model describing the concepts used in this textbook is provided in in Fig. 6.11. I contains business architecture concepts introduced in Chap. 2 and application architecture concepts discussed in Chaps. 3 and 4. The technical architecture is indicated as a background but still empty as we did not cover it in this textbook.

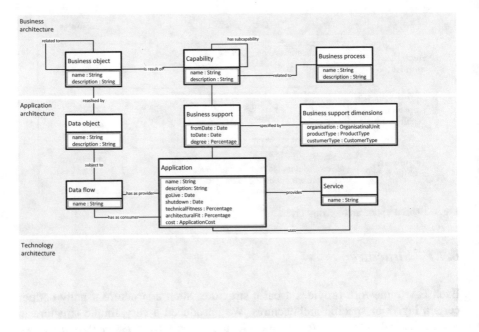

Fig. 6.11 Meta-model

The business architecture has business capabilities in its centre, because it is one of the focal elements in this book. A capability has a name and can be further described by text. It can be decomposed into sub-capabilities (relationship *has subcapability* in Fig. 6.11) and might have business objects as a result. Business objects can have relationships to each other. Business processes can provide further details on how capabilities are implemented in an organisation. Most of the business architecture concepts in Sect. 2.4 (e.g. *Strategy, Driver, Operating Model* or *Constraint*) are not listed in the meta-model. They are relevant for describing a business architecture but not discussed here in very detail. A more elaborate meta-model should include them.

Application architecture has a focus on software applications, their relationships (*Data flow* and *Service*) and their connection to the business architecture (*Business support*). Data flows relate to data objects being exchanged. A data object relates to business objects form the business architecture (cf. Sect. 3.4). A (software) service is provided by one application and can be used by others (pp. 90). Analysing and improving an application landscape require additional information (pp. 93). Such information can consist of an applications lifetime (provided by go-live date and sut-down) as well as quality attributes explained in Sect. 3.3.

Applications are linked to business capabilities by a concept called *business support* as explained in Sect. 4.3. Business support can have a temporal validity if an existing application is only used for a limited amount of time for a certain business capability. An Enterprise Architect can also estimate for a certain degree, if the capability is only partially supported. Further dimensions allow a more detailed view on application support for different product, organisational units or customer segments (pp. 127).

The meta-model used in this textbook is kept very small as the book aims at providing a practical journey through EA. more detailed view is given by, for example, ArchiMate's meta-model (cf. [8, 9]) or dedicated software tools for EA. An evaluation of existing tools is given in [19, 20].

6.4.3 Procedure

The textbook at hand is not explicitly defining an EA method like for example TOGAF's ADM (cf. pp. 196). However, the structure of the book indicates already a sequence of activities (Fig. 6.12).

1. There needs to be a clear understanding on why EA is introduced in an organisation. This is why the book started with a discussion on the purpose of EA in Chap. 1. This also relates to the *Preliminary* and *Architecture Vision* phases in TOGAF.
2. Describing EA start s with the business architecture as business drives IT. There are many concepts available, but is usually a good idea to only start with a minimal set (e.g. business capabilities and objects).
3. An optimal application landscape can be derived from the business capabilities. There are usually some factors that will drive detailed decisions for individual capabilities. A dedicated method for deriving an application landscape is presented in Sect. 3.2. Hence, it is recommended to describe the application architecture after having a solid view on business architecture. The same order of phases is specified in TOGAF and other frameworks.
4. EA analysis requires the availability of relevant information–expressed in business and application architecture (Chap. 4). This section correlates with the *Opportunities and Solutions* phase in TOGAF.
5. All changes implied by EA work need to be managed as described in Chap. 5. We discussed roadmaps and application portfolio management as related tools. TOGAF covers this aspect by phases *Migration Planning* and *Architecture Change Management*

However, the table of contents of this text books is not a method. Chapter 6 is out of sequence, as it summarises the whole topic by presenting frameworks. Also Chap. 5 does not represent the fifth step, as we need to consider organisational aspects already in the beginning of an EA initiative. We also skipped the Technology Architecture which needs to be incorporated for more elaborate analysis.

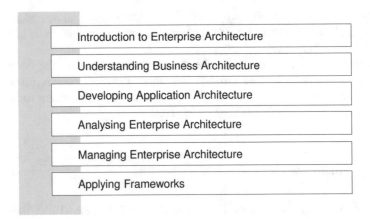

Fig. 6.12 Structure of this textbook

6.4.4 Organisation

Setting up an organisational unit for EAM is covered by Chap. 5. The chapter is not a detailed explanation on EA organisation, but provides an overview on relevant aspects. We covered

- Performing change management
- Typical activities of an Enterprise Architect
- How to set up an EA organisation
- Approaches for a collaborative EA

6.4.5 Tools

The term *tool* can be interpreted n a broad sense. It might be a software tool, a specific methodology or any artefact used in EAM. Using a software tool for maintaining EA information is crucial for any EA initiative. However, the purpose of the book is to teach the concepts. Software tools usually implement these concepts. This is why we did not use any software tool throughout the whole text book. Only Excel was mentioned as a pragmatic tool for generating and analysing the business support matrix (page 4.3.1). The interested reader can find a tool survey in [19, 20].

Beside of this, the following tools were used in the textbook:[13]

---

[13]The list is not complete and is only meant to provide an overview on some tools.

- **Capability map**: The capability map is a document (i.e. model, artefact or viewpoint) showing the business capabilities (cf. Sect. 2.2).
- **Viewpoints**: Viewpoints are artefacts, models or documents for visualising EA. Viewpoints are available in any EA software tool. Furthermore, TOGAF suggests a couple of common viewpoints [14, section 31].
- **Business Support Matrix**: The business support matrix is a tool for visualising relationships between business artefacts and IT systems. It can be used for identifying redundancies or gaps (cf. Sect. 4.3).
- **Deriving optimal application landscape**: The method for deriving an optimal application landscape from business capabilities is a also a tool. It provides some step-by-step instructions so that an Enterprise Architect can decide on which applications should exist under ideal circumstances.

6.4.6   Best Practices

The text book at hand also includes many examples showing best practices. They have been created based on experience and document how certain artefacts can look like. The example capability maps in Figs. 2.12 and 2.13 (pp. 53) are not reflecting real companies but show elements that can be seen in many maps. The same holds true for many examples and recommendations in this textbook.

This does not make it a best practices handbook (which never has been the intention). However, the examples can be reused and adjusted for similar companies or contexts.

6.5   Further Reading

We would like to close the sixth chapter of this book by also referring to some further readings, so books or papers that are recommended for having a look at for future purposes, but also, for the current activities we are about to have during the active seminars.

There is one paper which is quite old, but still is not irrelevant. It is a paper providing an overview on frameworks for EA [21]. A more up-to-date overview can be found in [22]. The authors categorise frameworks by four domains: military, company, government and manufacturing. They also draw links to historical standards that are usually not listed as typical EA approaches.

The second publication is The TOGAF Standard—the specification describing how TOGAF looks like [14]. It is published by The Open Group as a book, and you can buy it in the bookshop, but it is also available as a free resource in the internet. After registering at the home page of The Open Group, you can access the HTML version of TOGAF.

For those who are interested in having a closer look at ArchiMate, I would like to recommend a book which is some kind of textbook for teaching and learning ArchiMate published by Gerben Wierda, a name you might remember [10]. He is the same guy that also was talking about Chess and the Art of EAM. Instead of being the governance part, rather act like a chess player, adjusting decisions as the company evolves over time. He also published a good book on teaching ArchiMate.

6.6 Summary

That's almost the end of this textbook on *EAM*. Let us reconsider the topics we covered as shown in Fig. 6.13. After introducing the topic EA and EAM, we had a look at details for describing business perspectives and then describing applications and how they relate to the business perspective. We then learned some basic tools for analysing an EA, and then also talked about the skills of an enterprise architect and how should we set up an organisation for EAM in a company.

We were closing the book by a look at frameworks. There are many frameworks available and, at the end of the day, it is not important to know all frameworks or to choose the best framework you can find on the market. The most important thing is to understand basic concepts of EAM—which we did in the course of the first five chapters.

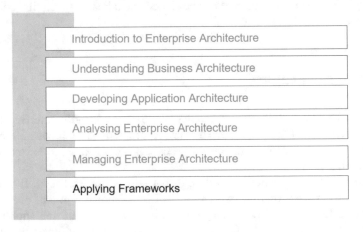

Fig. 6.13 That's all folks!

6.7   Exercises

Exercise 6.1 (TOGAF) You are the Chief Enterprise Architect of the Deakin University and the CEO asks you, whether the University should adopt TOGAF as framework for EAM. Your answer should cover the following aspects:

1. Overview on TOGAF and history
2. Explanation of methods and tools provided by TOGAF
3. Critical review on the effort required for adopting TOGAF

You should develop your answer based on the concepts provided in this textbook and the TOGAF specification.

Exercise 6.2 (PERA) The *Purdue Enterprise Reference Architecture* (PERA) is a reference model for EA developed at the Purdue University. You are the Chief Enterprise Architect of the Deakin University and the CEO asks you, whether the University should adopt PERA as a framework. Your now need to search relevant publications and evaluate PERA. Provide an evaluation by using the following categories:

1. Structure
2. Meta-model
3. Procedure
4. Organisation
5. Tools
6. Best practices

You should develop your answer based on the concepts provided in this textbook and the TOGAF specification.

References

1. J.A. Zachman, A framework for information systems architecture. IBM Syst. J. **26**(3), 276–292 (1987)
2. J. van't Wout, M. Waage, H. Hartman, M. Stahlecker, A. Hofman, *The Integrated Architecture Framework Explained, Why, What, How* (Springer, New York, 2010)
3. M. Op't Land, E. Proper, M. Waage, J. Cloo, C. Steghuis, *Enterprise Architecture, Creating Value by Informed Governance*. The Enterprise Engineering Series (Springer, Berlin, London, 2009)
4. K. Smith, *An Introduction to PEAF, Pragmatic Enterprise Architecture Framework* (Pragmatic EA, Limited, Great Notley, 2011)
5. Federal enterprise architecture framework, Version 2. Tech. Rep., Jan. 2013
6. P. Bernus, O. Norana, A. Molina, Enterprise architecture, Twenty years of the GERAM framework. Annu. Rev. Control **39**, 83–93 (2014)
7. J. Schekkerman, *Enterprise architecture: Good practices guide, how to manage the enterprise architecture practice.* (Trafford, Victoria, BC, 2008)

8. M.M. Lankhorst, H.A. Proper, H. Jonkers, The anatomy of the Archi-Mate language. Int. J. Inf. Syst. Model. Des. **1**(1), 1–32 (2010)

9. The Open Group (ed.), *ArchiMate 3.0 specification* (Van Haren Publishers, Zaltbommel, 2016)

10. G. Wierda, *Mastering ArchiMate: A serious introduction to the ArchiMate enterprise architecture modeling language, version 3.0.1*, Edition III (TC1, R&A, Utrecht, 2017)

11. A. Ernst, A pattern-based approach to enterprise architecture management. PhD Thesis, Technische Universität München, München, Germany, 2010

12. The Open Group, *The open group – who we are* (2021) [Online]. Available: https://www.opengroup.org/about-us/who-we-are

13. D. Matthes, Enterprise Architecture Kompendium, Über 50 Rahmenwerke für das IT-Management, German. ser. Xpert.press (Springer, New York, 2011)

14. The Open Group, *The TOGAF Standard, Version 9.2*, 11th edn. (Van Haren Publishing, Zaltbommel, 2018)

15. The Open Group, *TOGAF Version 9.1 (Togaf)*, 10th edn. (Van Haren Publishing, Zaltbommel, 2012)

16. The Open Group, The TOGAF Technical Reference Model (TRM), The Open Group. Tech. Rep., Sep. 21, 2017

17. The Open Group, Open Business Architecture (O BA), Preliminary standard, The Open Group. Tech. Rep., Jul. 1, 2016

18. R. Winter, R. Fischer, Essential layers, artifacts, and dependencies of enterprise architecture, in *2006 10th IEEE International Enterprise Distributed Object Computing Conference Workshops (EDOCW'06)* (IEEE, New York, 2006), p. 30

19. F. Matthes, S. Buckl, L. Jana, C. Schweda, Enterprise architecture management tool survey 2008. München: Techn. Univ. München, 2008

20. F. Matthes, M. Hauder, N. Katinszky, Enterprise architecture management tool survey 2014 update, München, 2014

21. H. Shah, M. El Kourdi, Frameworks for enterprise architecture. IT Professional **9**(5), 36–41 (2007)

22. Y. Gong, M. Janssen, The value of and myths about enterprise architecture. Int. J. Inf. Manage. **46**, 1–9 (2019)

Chapter 7
Summary and Outlook

7.1 Summary

We are about to reach the end of the textbook on EAM. Hopefully, it will not be the end but the beginning of your journey through Enterprise architecture. We did not cover the topic in its entirety but focused on central aspects in order to provide a kick-starter for your next steps.

Before diving into details about methods and tools, we addressed a central question: What do we want to achieve with Enterprise Architecture. Instead of applying a tool, EAM is still about providing value in an organisation. Consequently, we first need to understand its current situation, problems as well as the context. This will be the starting point for choosing appropriate tools serving a *purpose*.

Chapter 2 then provided concepts and visualisations for Business Architecture that helps with understanding the business (i.e. what an organisation is doing in order to provide value). It is always a good idea to reuse existing documents like business process models or similar documents. In case they are accepted and up to date, they provide a valuable reference for understanding the company. However, they are not available very often. We then can use proven concepts like *business capabilities* and *business objects* as simple but powerful tools. They cover a functional perspective on the business (business capabilities) together with a view on static objects (business objects). They can be complemented with further concepts for describing business motivation and business models.

A consistent business capability map can be used as a starting point for deriving an *application landscape* that fulfills a company's needs (as presented in Chap. 3). Software applications are the counterpart to business capabilities as they implement desired functionality. In the same way, business objects reflect a high-level picture on data objects maintained by business software. Applications and data objects are located in the Application Architecture, describing corporate information systems.

Business and Application Architecture are rather descriptive, providing transparency on information systems and their business context. They also provide

© The Author(s), under exclusive license to Springer Nature Switzerland AG 2021
J. Jung, B. Fraunholz, *Masterclass Enterprise Architecture Management*,
https://doi.org/10.1007/978-3-030-78495-9_7

the information required for analysing and improving the application landscape. Enterprise architects are using a plethora of visual tools for identifying optimisation potential as depicted in Chap. 4. We further elaborated on the *business support matrix* for identifying typical concerns in the application architecture—like gaps or redundancies.

EA is subject to frequent changes caused by architecture optimisation or driven by business needs. These changes need to be managed properly and require a respective organisation. Classical organisational forms follow a top-down approach—i.e. EAM is driven by the management. Recent experiences within classical organisations show that a more *collaborative EAM* approach is required. A prototypical example was presented in Chap. 5 together with an outlook on further research.

Even though we did not want to publish a textbook non *EA frameworks*, this topic is still relevant for any enterprise architect. An overview on classical frameworks is given in Chap. 6—with a detailed view on TOGAF. In fact, I would like to encourage any enterprise architect to get familiar with at least one framework. They provide best practice methods and tools for documenting and improving an EA. However, you always need to be capable to adjust these tools with respect to given concerns or needs within your organisation. This is why we started the textbook with benefits expected from EA and EAM in Chap. 1.

7.2 Topics for Future Research

We only covered the very tip of the iceberg so that you, as a reader, can familiarise yourself with basic concepts of EA and EAM. There are still many topics open for future research. This section will not provide a comprehensive overview, but rather list some topics which you might consider for your next research project.

In 2017, Gampfer et al. performed a text analysis in order to reveal past, present and future trends of EA [1]. As a result of this study, they identified the following topics as future trends with respect to EA:

1. Cloud computing
2. Adaptive or agile enterprise architecture
3. Sustainability
4. Smart machines
5. Internet of things
6. Big data
7. Entrepreneurship
8. Complexity theory

Cloud computing refers to technologies that help with overcoming limitations of classic hosting models. It allows for a faster acquisition of services (on-demand self-service) and a more flexible and automatic adoption to variations in resource needs (elasticity). Computing resources are shared by many customers (resource pooling) over a standard internet connection (broad network access). Customers only pay for the service level they actually used (measured services). Cloud computing might, therefore, shorten the time for performing changes in the application landscape. These changes may affect only only the underlying technology, but also allows for using software applications or even business processes as a cloud service (cf. [2, p. 14]). A discussion on related aspects (e.g. security and privacy) can be found in [1] and [3].

Agile software development is already established in professional institutions since the beginning of 2000s (cf. [4, 5]). Corresponding methods like *Scrum* or *eXtreme Programming* improve software projects by reducing risks and faster availability of results. However, it seems that short development cycles in software development do not match with methods addressing a long-term perspective. This may result in a conflict between EAM (long-term perspective) and flexible adaption to customers' needs in agile development. Some publications refer to this aspect of IT with two different modes of speed as *bimodal* IT (e.g. [6]). Furthermore, some authors aim at making EAM more agile. Examples for those approaches are *Architectural Thinking* [7, 8], *The Open Group Agile Architecture Standard* [9] opr the approaches presented in Sect. 5.3.

Sustainability with respect to the protection of our environment is one of the current big endeavors [1]. EAM can be regarded as a methodology not only considering the organisation but also its context (cf. Sect. 1.3.1). It therefore also incorporates the impact of a companies business on the environment and might, therefore, support ecological aspects. However, the term *sustainability* does not only have an ecological connotation but also refers to the impact of decisions in general.

The term *smart machine* refers to autonomous machines that are capable of adapting to their environment (cf. [10]). Similar to *Internet of Things* (IoT), they impose a new concept on the technology layer and its impact onto the business. In contrast to classical computer systems and network, they are mobile and adaptive. Consequently, people are proposing new ways of managing such IT devices as part of the EA (e.g. [11, 12]). These approaches need to cope with a large number of mobile devices which may frequently adopt their behaviour as required by their context.

Big data technologies are widely used today and allow for managing and analysing large amounts of (unstructured) data (cf. [13]). Its relevance for EA has two aspects: EA can help with setting up Big Data technologies based on data architecture. Big data may also provide solutions that help with managing data about EA. The classical manual way for maintaining data on EA requires a lot of manual data maintenance. Big data might help here with collecting data from various repositories and documents automatically. A similar approach is for example presented in [14]. A similar distinction will hold true for *Artificial Intelligence* (AI) in general. AI has the potential for significantly changing the business by improving efficiency or changing the way how business is done (e.g. new business models, products or markets). AI technology is also already evaluated with respect to changing EAM (cf. [15]).

Principles of *agile* and *lean* are nowadays also applied to organisations (*Entrepreneurship*). Management structures need to ba flat so that a company can easily adjust to changes [16]. Especially small and medium-sized companies as well as start-ups do not have resources for an elaborate EA organisation. Hence, further research is required on how to set up a minimal EA for small and potentially agile companies. This also involves ideas already presented in Sect. 5.3. An EA organisation should aim at providing value in the company as well as following a collaborative working mode.

The topics above are, obviously, not disjoint. There is an overlap between entrepreneurship and agile organisations. Big data is also often involved when implementing IoT solutions. All of them share an inherent *complexity* with respect to EA and its development over time. There are further studies identifying similar research topics (e.g. [3]). They mainly address EA organisation, methodology and tool support.

Further research is also conducted on benefits of EAM in an organisation. Even though it seems to be obvious on a hight level (cf. Sect. 1.2), EA teams still lack of presenting immediate benefits [17]. Consequently, academic research tries to understand tangible benefits from EAM (e.g. [18–21]) as well as why EA initiatives failed in the past (e.g. [22, 23]).

Also traditional methods and tools are still subject to academic research. One of the drawbacks is the plethora of EA visualisations as well as their complexity. people try to reduce the amount of maps (e.g. [24, 25]) or new ways for EA visualisation. Abandoning the two-dimensional sheet of paper may enable multi-dimensional and interactive views. Some example projects develop and evaluate prototypes using game engines (e.g. [26]) or augmented reality [27].

Research on the notion of *EA debts* adopts the concept of technical debts and applies them to EA (cf. [28]). In a similar way as technical debts, an EA debt represents an ad-hoc artefact (like a workaround or a low quality process or inadequate IT system) that hampers implementing an optimal solution. The research objective of this project is in developing a method for detecting and managing existing EA debts in an organisation.

7.3 Digital Transformation

Digital transformation refers to a radical change in society and companies through the adoption of digital technologies [29, 30]. It is motivated by by recent improvements in technologies and corresponding products and services. Many see it as an enabler for innovations in corporations as well as new business models. It has the potential for driving significant improvements in operational performance. Digital transformation is often presented as a technological topic.

The acronym *SMACIT* (Social, Mobile, Analytics, Cloud, Internet of Things) is used for referring to (so called disruptive) technologies enabling digital transformation [31]. According to Ross et al., there are even more technologies like for example artificial intelligence and blockchain [32]. The acronym is pronounced *smack it* in order to underline their impact on digitisation of a company. However, it also may have a negative connotation as the affected change can have a negative impact on an organisation. Technology as a means on its own never solves a real-world problem. Only applying it appropriately does. Hence, organisational capabilities are required as well [33]. In fact, short-term successes for digital transformation can even be achieved by using conventional technology [34].

However, digital transformation is not (only) about technology, but about people, skills and strategy [35]. Tabrizi et al., therefore, highlight relevant aspects when planning for a digital transformation [36]: Digital transformation needs to be guided by a corresponding business strategy. It requires clear guidance and commitment to radical changes. The change also needs to be developed from within the organisation by existing staff. This further requires a change of skills and mindset. Changes need to be driven by customer experience from the outside in. It starts with an innovative product or business model for gaining new markets. This will then define the requirements on the technical solution.

Digital transformation and EAM share some commonalities. In fact, definitions seem to be similar to *enterprise ecological adaption* as presented in Sect. 1.3.1. They both need to be driven by the business and follow clear objectives (*purpose* in Sect. 1.2). They start with understanding the business based on strategy, capabilities and changes (Chap. 2 and Sect. 5.1). This will be the baseline for determining relevant software applications and technologies (Chap. 3). Changes need to be visualised, planned and monitored (Sects. 4.2, 1.4 and 5.1). It seems that both, Digital Transformation and EAM, might be two sides of the same coin ...

References

1. F. Gampfer, A. Jürgens, M. Müller, R. Buchkremer, Past, current and future trends in enterprise architecture. A view beyond the horizon. Comput. Ind. **100**, 70–84 (2018)
2. N. Ruparelia, *Cloud Computing* (MIT Press, Cambridge, 2016)
3. S. Kaisler, F. Armour, 15 years of enterprise architecting at hicss: revisiting the critical problems, in *Proceedings of the 50th Hawaii International Conference on System Sciences*, January 4, 2017
4. A. Scheerer, *Coordination in Large-Scale Agile Software Development, Integrating Conditions and Configurations in Multiteam Systems* (Springer International Publishing, Berlin/Heidelberg, 2017)
5. P. Kruchten, S. Fraser, F. Coallier (eds.), *Agile Processes in Software Engineering and Extreme Programming*. Lecture Notes in Business Information Processing, vol. 355 (Springer International Publishing, New York, 2019)
6. B. Horlach, P. Drews, I. Schirmer, Bimodal it, Business-it alignment in the age of digital transformation, in *Multikonferenz Wirtschaftsinformatik (MKWI) 2016*, ed. by V. Nissen, D. Stelzer, S. Straßburger, D. Fischer (Universitätsverlag Ilmenau, Ilmenau, 2016), pp. 1417–1428
7. W. Goebl, Foundations of the architectural thinking framework, Aug. 9, 2018 [Online]. Available: https://architectural-thinking.com/wp-content/uploads/2018/09/Foundations-of-Architectural-Thinking.pdf (visited on 03/12/2021)
8. R. Winter, Architectural thinking. Bus. Inf. Syst. Eng. **6**(6), 361–364 (2014)

9. The Open Group, The open group open agile architecture standard, The Open Group. Tech. Rep., Jul. 23, 2019
10. T. Davenport, J. Kirby, Just how smart are smart machines? *MITSloan Management Review* (Spring 2016)
11. A. Zimmermann, R. Schmidt, K. Sandkuhl, D. Jugel, M. Möhring, M. Wißotzki, Enterprise architecture management for the internet of things, in *Digital Enterprise Computing (DEC 2015)*, ed. by A. Zimmermann, A. Rossmann (eds.) (Gesellschaft für Informatik e.V., Bonn, 2015), pp. 139–150
12. J. Kaidalova, K. Sandkuhl, U. Seigerroth, How digital transformation affects enterprise architecture management – a case study. Int. J. Inf. Syst. Project Manage. **6**(3), 5–18 (2018)
13. J. Moorthy, R. Lahiri, N. Biswas, D. Sanyal, J. Ranjan, K. Nanath, P. Ghosh, Big data: prospects and challenges. Vikalpa **40**(1), 74–96 (2015)
14. P. Drews, I. Schirmer, B. Horlach, C. Tekaat, Bimodal enterprise architecture management: the emergence of a new eam function for a bizdevops-based fast it, in *2017 IEEE 21st International Enterprise Distributed Object Computing Workshop (EDOCW)* (IEEE, New York, 2017), pp. 57–64
15. R. Schmidt, M. Wißotzki, D. Jugel, M. Möhring, K. Sandkuhl, A. Zimmermann, Towards a framework for enterprise architecture analytics, in *2014 IEEE 18th International Enterprise Distributed Object Computing Conference Workshops and Demonstrations*, 2014, pp. 266–275
16. J. Humble, J. Molesky, B. O'Reilly, *Lean Enterprise, How High Performance Organisations Innovate at Scale*, The Lean Series (O'Reilly, Sebastopol, 2015)
17. J. Jung, Purpose of enterprise architecture management: investigating tangible benefits in the german logistics industry, in *2019 IEEE 23rd International Enterprise Distributed Object Computing Workshop (EDOCW)*, Oct. 2019, pp. 25–31
18. R. Foorthuis, M. van Steenbergen, S. Brinkkemper, W. Bruls, A theory building study of enterprise architecture practices and benefits. Inf. Syst. Front. **18**(3), 541–564 (2016) (visited on 02/09/2021)
19. B. Scholtz, A. Calitz, A. Connolley, An analysis of the adoption and Usage of Enterprise Architecture, in *Proceedings of the First International Conference on Enterprise Systems: ES 2013* (IEEE, Cape Town, 2013), pp. 1–9
20. B. van der Raadt, M. Bonnet, S. Schouten, H. van Vliet, The relation between EA effectiveness and stakeholder satisfaction. J. Syst. Softw. **83**(10), 1954–1969 (2010) (visited on 02/09/2021)
21. M. Pulkkinen, Systemic management of architectural decisions in enterprise architecture planning. Four dimensions and three abstraction levels, in *Proceedings of the 39th Annual Hawaii International Conference on System Sciences (HICSS'06)* (IEEE, Kauia, HI, 2006), p. 179a
22. M. Lange, J. Mendling, J. Recker, An empirical analysis of the factors and measures of enterprise architecture management success. Eur. J. Inf. Syst. **6**, 411–431 (2015)
23. M. Lange, J. Mendling, An experts' perspective on enterprise architecture goals, framework adoption and benefit assessment, Oct. 2011, pp. 304–313
24. S. Kotusev, *The Practice of Enterprise Architecture: A Modern Approach to Business and IT Alignment* (SK Publishing, Carlton, VIC, 2018)
25. S. Kotusev, Enterprise architecture: a reconceptualization is needed. Pacif. Asia J. Assoc. Inf. Syst. **10**, 1–36 (2018)
26. K. Rehring, T. Brée, J. Gulden, L. Bredenfeld, Conceptualizing EA cities: towards visualizing enterprise architectures as cities, in *Proceedings of the 27th European Conference on Information Systems (ECIS)*, June 2019
27. K. Rehring, F. Ahlemann, Evaluating the user experience of an augmented reality prototype for enterprise architecture, in *15th International Conference on Wirtschaftsinformatik*, March 2020, pp. 909–924
28. P. Alexander, S. Hacks, J. Jung, H. Lichter, U. Steffens, Ö. Uludağ, A framework for managing enterprise architecture debts – outline and research directions, in *Proceedings of the 10th International Workshop on Enterprise Modeling and Information Systems Architectures*. Lecture Notes in Informatics (LNI), ed. by A. Koschmider, J. Michael, B. Thalheim (2020)

29. G. Vial, Understanding digital transformation: a review and a research agenda. J. Strat. Inf. Syst. **28**(2), 118–144 (2019)
30. I. Mergel, N. Edelmann, N. Haug, Defining digital transformation: Results from expert interviews. Govern. Inf. Quart. **36**(4), 101–385 (2019)
31. I.M. Sebastian, K.G. Moloney, J.W. Ross, N.O. Fonstad, C. Beath, M. Mocker, How big old companies navigate digital transformation. MIS Quart. Execut. **16**(3), 197–213 (2017)
32. J.W. Ross, C.M. Beath, M. Mocker, *Designed for Digital, How to Architect Your Business for Sustained Success* (MIT Press, Cambridge, 2019)
33. C. Riera, J. Iijima, The role of IT and organizational capabilities on digital business value. Pacif. Asia J. Assoc. Inf. Syst. **11**(2), 67–95 (2019)
34. S.J. Andriole, Five myths about digital transformation. *MIT Sloan Management Review* (Harvard Business Publishing, Brighton, Spring 2017)
35. B. Frankiewicz, T. Chamorro-Premuzic, Digital transformation is about talent, not technology. *Harvard Business Review*, May 2020
36. B. Tabrizi, E. Lam, K. Girard, V. Irvin, Digital transformation is not about technology, *Harvard Business Review*, March 2019

Index

© The Author(s), under exclusive license to Springer Nature Switzerland AG 2021
J. Jung, B. Fraunholz, *Masterclass Enterprise Architecture Management*,
https://doi.org/10.1007/978-3-030-78495-9

Printed in the United States
by Baker & Taylor Publisher Services